Pierre Chareau

建築家ピエール・シャローとガラスの家

Pierre Chareau, architect of the House of Glass :
A Modernist in the time of Art Deco

ポンピドゥー・センター、パリ国立近代美術館＋パナソニック 汐留ミュージアム＝編

鹿島出版会

展覧会データ

建築家ピエール・シャローとガラスの家
Pierre Chareau, architect of the House of Glass :
A Modernist in the time of Art Deco

パナソニック 汐留ミュージアム
2014年7月26日(土) − 10月13日(月・祝)
Panasonic Shiodome Museum
26 July – 13 October, 2014

主 催

パナソニック 汐留ミュージアム、東京新聞
ポンピドゥ・センター、パリ国立近代美術館

協 力

エールフランス航空

後 援

一般社団法人日本建築学会
公益社団法人日本建築家協会
在日フランス大使館／アンスティチュ・フランセ日本
公益財団法人日仏会館
日仏会館フランス事務所
日仏工業技術会、港区教育委員会

Pierre Chareau – architecte de la Maison de verre,
un moderne au temps de l'Art déco

This exhibition is organized by
the Panasonic Shiodome Museum,
THE TOKYO SHIMBUN and
the CENTRE POMPIDOU, Paris.

Centre Pompidou

Cooperation

Air France

Support

Architectural Institution of Japan
The Japan Institute of Architects
Embassy of France (Institut français du Japon)
La Maison Franco Japonaise, French bureau
Société Franco-Japonaise des Techniques et Industries
Minato Ward Board of Education

ごあいさつ

　このたびパナソニック汐留ミュージアムと東京新聞は、パリのポンピドゥー・センターの全面的な協力を得て「建築家ピエール・シャローとガラスの家」展を開催いたします。ポンピドゥー・センターのパリ国立近代美術館・産業創造センター（MNAM-CCI）は、世界有数の近現代美術のコレクションを有しており、1992年に加わった建築とデザインの部門もその充実した内容で高く評価されています。本展ではその収集と研究のハイライトのひとつ、1920-1930年代のパリを背景に、家具、インテリア・デザイン、建築の3つの分野で比類のない造形を生み出したピエール・シャロー（1883-1950）の制作活動と代表的な作品を展観します。

　ピエール・シャローは、フランスの装飾美術の伝統と20世紀都市文化の新しい視覚芸術の融合であるアール・デコが一世を風靡した時代に、家具およびインテリアのデザイナーとして名声を獲得し、その優雅な作風は、裕福なクライアントたちを魅了しました。そしてシャローは、同時代のル・コルビュジエが牽引した新しい建築の方向性を自らも探求し、デザインの新たな地平を切り拓いていきました。

　シャローの代表作であり、日本で広く知られている「ガラスの家」は、セーヌ左岸の一角に、今も当時のまま保存されています。ダルザス医師夫妻の依頼で建てられたこの家は、既存のアパルトマンの低層部をくり抜き、そこにガラスと鉄を駆使してつくられた、いまの言葉で言うところの「リノベーション物件」で、当時としては革新的な住宅作品でした。この「ガラスの家」の創造の謎も、彼の活動全体のなかに位置づけることで解き明かされることでしょう。

　本展は、代表作「ガラスの家」を中心に、先鋭的なデザインによる家具や照明器具、デザイン画、建築模型、当時の出版物といった貴重な資料をパリ国立近代美術館と東京国立近代美術館の所蔵品の中から展示し、近代という時代に対する思いを創作と活動の変遷にこめたシャローの稀有な才能の全貌を、我が国で初めて本格的に紹介する意義深い展覧会です。

　最後になりましたが、共に企画にあたったポンピドゥー・センター、大切な作品をご出品いただいた所蔵館、ご協力いただいたエール・フランスに深い謝意を表します。また本展を日仏文化協力90周年事業のひとつとして位置づけご後援下さった、在日フランス大使館／アンスティチュ・フランセ日本、および各機関、関係各位、ご尽力を賜りました日仏関係者に厚く御礼申し上げます。

パナソニック 汐留ミュージアム
東京新聞

Message

Panasonic Shiodome Museum and The Tokyo Shimbun have the honor of presenting the exhibition "Pierre Chareau, architect of the House of Glass" with the full cooperation of Centre Pompidou (MNAM/CCI), home to one of the world's largest collections of contemporary art. The center's architectural and design wings created in 1992 have also established strong reputations, and the exhibition will be highlighting their research and accumulation of works by Pierre Chareau (1883 – 1950) — an artist who produced unparalleled works of furniture, interior design, and architecture in Paris during the 1920s and 30s.

Chareau's fame as a furniture and interior designer came at a time when the world was enamored with the fusion of traditional French decorative art and 20th century urban culture that was art deco. Even as his bold works caught the attention of wealthy clients, Chareau explored the new architectural movement being led by his compatriot Le Corbusier and helped open up new possibilities in the field of design.

Chareau's masterpiece, the House of Glass, is well known in Japan. Commissioned by Dr. Jean Dalsace and his wife, it was constructed by hollowing out the lower levels of a Parisian apartment building and remaking it with glass and steel — what we would today call a renovation project. Considered hugely innovative at the time, the House of Glass remains to this day, preserved in its entirety. However, only by placing it in the context of Chareau's artistic career does it begin to truly reveal itself. While the focus of the exhibition will be on this work, there will also be displays of innovatively designed furniture and light devices, architectural drawings and models, and publications from Chareau's time. Together, these valuable materials on loan from the MNAM/CCI and The National Museum of Modern Art, Tokyo will paint a complete picture of the exceptional talent that Chareau employed to express his views of the contemporary era he lived in. This will be the first ever Japanese exhibition to explore Chareau so thoroughly.

We would like to finish by offering our deepest gratitude to Centre Pompidou for their invaluable assistance, the museums that have generously loaned us their valuable works for the occasion, and Air France for their cooperation. We would also like to thank the Embassy of France / Institut français du Japon for helping to promote this exhibition as a key event in the celebration of 90 years of cultural partnership between Japan and France, and all other organizations and individuals involved in relations between the two countries.

Panasonic Shiodome Museum
The Tokyo Shimbun

序

　ピエール・シャロー展の開催は、私たちにとって大いなる楽しみにほかなりません。控えめでありながら輝きに満ち、機能的でありながら繊細さも兼ね備えた見事な世界をご紹介できるからです。代表作「ガラスの家」は、現代建築史の道標として颯爽と登場しました。そこは個人住宅という性格ゆえにプライバシーが守られてきたにもかかわらず、完成直後から神秘の場所となり、後進の建築家や学生たちを引き寄せてきました。かつて、レンゾ・ピアノとリチャード・ロジャース率いる若き建築家グループが、ポンピドゥー・センターの設計競技で勝利を収めてパリに拠点を築いたとき、彼らはうやうやしくガラスの家を訪れたのでした。のちにピアノが手がけた銀座メゾン・エルメスは、当人が明言しているようにこの家からアイデアを借りていました。

　しかし、ガラスの家がいかに特異で魅惑的であっても、シャローの傑作は決してそれだけに留まりません。シャローそれ以前から、各種の家具やインテリアデザインを手がけるなかで、因習から脱却して近代性（モデルニテ）を確立していました。その個性的なスタイルには、同時代の建築家たちには真似のできない才気がほとばしっていました。彼はアール・デコ全盛の真っただ中で、「木と金属」の家具、躍動する空間設計、半透明のファサードなどを通じて既成概念を打ち壊しました。シャロー展を訪れる人々が感動せずにはいられないのはこの点なのです。

　このたびは、パナソニック汐留ミュージアムから日本初のシャロー展をご提案いただき光栄に存じます。パリ国立近代美術館の豊かなコレクションが当プロジェクトに十分に応えられるのは、ヴェレ・ダルザス家をはじめとする寄贈者の方々のご理解のおかげです。この場を借りて、あらためて謝意を表したいと存じます。思い起こせば、私たちが1993年に大規模なシャロー回顧展にこぎつけたのは、当時の総裁ドミニク・ボゾーの努力の賜物でした。折しも彼は、建築・デザインのコレクションを創設したばかりでしたが、残念なことに回顧展が始まる前に他界してしまったために、自らのビジョンの正しさを確認できませんでした。それは、まだ知名度の低かったシャローという天才クリエイターに光を当てるなら、必ずや大方の熱狂を生むに違いないという信念だったのです。国外初となるシャローコレクションの紹介は、私たちがボゾー亡き後に辿ってきた道筋を評価する好機ともなるはずです。末尾になりましたが、素晴らしい展覧会をご企画くださったパナソニック汐留ミュージアムと東京新聞に対して心より御礼申し上げる次第です。

パリ国立近代美術館・産業創造センター館長　　ポンピドゥー・センター総裁
ベルナール・ブリステーヌ　　　　　　　　　　アラン・スバン

Preface

Exhibiting the work of Pierre Chareau is always a pleasure: that of allowing a public to discover a world that is both discreet and luminous, functional and delicate. The Maison de Verre, his masterpiece, emerged from the outset as a milestone in the history of modern architecture. Hidden out of sight of Parisian passers-by and protected by its status as private property, it has nonetheless become a mythical site since its creation, attracting successive generations of architects and students. When the young winners of the Pompidou Centre competition led by Renzo Piano and Richard Rogers settled in Paris, a ritual visit was mandatory. When, at the turn of the century, Renzo Piano designed the Hermès building in Tokyo, he explicitly referred to the Maison de Verre, affirming the citation and inspiration he drew from it.

But just as unique and magical as it is, the work of Chareau cannot be reduced to this sole edifice. In his day, it was through furniture then interior design that Chareau's creativity was to first liberate itself from tradition and assert itself as resolutely modern. With a brilliance that distinguishes it from his contemporaries, his design is truly in a class of its own. Visitors to the exhibition will assuredly be sensitive to this particularity: how Chareau was able to revolutionise codes, during a period when Art Deco dominated, whether it was with his so-called "wood-metal" furniture, his work on spaces to set them in motion, or his translucent façade.

We are honoured that the Shiodome Museum has invited us to produce this exhibition, the first in Japan dedicated to the work of Pierre Chareau. If the collections of the Pompidou Center's National Museum of Modern Art are able to respond to this invitation through their rich diversity, it is thanks to the generosity of our donors, foremost among whom are the Vellay-Dalsace family, whose support we would like to gratefully acknowledge once again. Dominique Bozo, President of the Pompidou Center, was responsible for having made the major retrospective of Pierre Chareau's work possible in 1993, when he had only just initiated the creation of the architecture and design collections within our museum. He passed away several months prior to the inauguration and was thus never able to verify the appropriateness of his vision: showcasing this little-known designer in his own country and taking a gamble on the public's enthusiasm. The presentation of these works from our collection for the first time abroad thus provides the occasion to appreciate how far we have come since then. For having extended this invitation, we express our deepest gratitude to our partners from the Shiodome Museum and The Tokyo Shimbun.

BERNARD BLISTENE	ALAIN SEBAN
Director of the National Museum of Modern Art	President of the Pompidou Center

謝 辞

本展の開催にあたり、
下記の関係機関に多大な協力を賜りました。
記して深く感謝の意を表します。

ポンピドゥー・センター、パリ国立近代美術館
東京国立近代美術館
建築・文化財・都市 フランス国立博物館

Remerciements

Nos remerciements s'adressent tout d'abord à Rieko Omura et Frédéric Migayrou, à qui revient l'initiative de cette exposition. Celle-ci a été rendue possible grâce à l'ensemble d'œuvres que conserve la collection du Musée national d'art moderne – Centre de création industrielle du Centre Pompidou. Nous ne pouvons que renouveler nos plus vifs remerciements à ceux qui, par leur générosité, l'ont enrichi au fil des années: Monsieur et Madame Vellay; la Fondation Louis Moret; la Scaler Foundation; Madame Julia Ullmann; la famille d'André Dalbet; Madame Denise Salomon. Ces dons ont souvent été aidés par l'entremise de personnes à qui va notre gratitude: Marc Vellay; Bruno Vocat et Olivier Vocat, Christian Leprette, Jean-Paul Felley et Olivier Kaeser; Jacques Boissonnas; Francis Lamond; Françoise Dalbet et Pierre Vetter; Natacha Salomon.

Par leurs prêts, la Cité de l'Architecture et du Patrimoine et le musée national d'art moderne de Tokyo, nous ont apporté leur concours: qu'ils en soient ici remerciés. Que le soient également ceux qui nous ont aidés: Corinne Bélier, Bernard Bauchet, Richard Copans, Jacques Repiquet ainsi que Robert Rubin pour sa bienveillance.

Nos remerciements s'adressent également à nos collègues des équipes du Centre Pompidou: Véronique Borgeaud, Jean-Claude Boulet, Sylvia Bozan, Franck Buisson, Christophe Chomet, Nathalie Cissé, Clotilde Cooper, Anne Delebarre, Bruno Descout, Laurence Gueye-Parmentier, Xavier Isaia, Valérie Leconte, Eric L'hospitalier, Olga Makhroff, Georges Meguerditchian, Philippe Migeat, Valérie Millot, Fatima Oussi, Maria Pasvantis, Cloé Pitiot, Bertrand Prévost, Isabelle Prieur, Perrine Renaud, Stéphanie Rivoire, Ludivine Rousseaux, Jerome Tillaud, Catherine Tiraby, Matthieu Vahanian, Brigitte Vincens.

凡 例

・本カタログはパナソニック汐留ミュージアムの「建築家ピエール・シャローとガラスの家」の展覧会の内容に基づいて構成されている。

・テキストおよび作品データはポンピドゥー・センター、パリ国立近代美術館より提供された仏文(うち解説執筆オリヴィエ・サンカルブル)を、阿部順子と小川隆久が翻訳を行い、千代章一郎が監修・監訳した。英文は仏文から訳している。

・作品データは出品資料番号、作家名、作品名、制作年を記した。写真資料の場合は撮影年および撮影者を、出版物の場合は出版社と出版年を併せて記した。なお、とくに作家名の記載がない場合は、ピエール・シャローの作品である。

・カタログの作品は会場展示に対応しており、各資料に付した番号は出品資料番号と一致する。なお、各資料に付した番号のうち、ref.(参考)としてあるものは、カタログのみに掲載した参考図版である。

・出品資料の詳細情報については、巻末の「出品資料リスト」に記載した。

・外国語の固有名詞を日本語で表記する際は、原則として原音に近いカタカナで記したが、一般的なものに関してはこの限りではない。

・出品資料番号は展覧会場での陳列番号と一致するが、陳列の構成と順序とは必ずしも一致しない。

・本文中の図番号は、出品資料番号を示している。

口 絵

p.2
146 門を入ったところの中庭に面した玄関側ファサード｜撮影：ジョルジュ・メゲルディトシアン

p.4
176 夜の玄関側ファサード｜撮影：ジョルジュ・メゲルディトシアン

p.7
156 2階サロン｜撮影：ジョルジュ・メゲルディトシアン

目 次

8 ごあいさつ

10 序
ベルナール・ブリステン、アラン・スパン

第Ⅰ部

45 出発——家具デザインからの始動

57 確立——作風と名声の形成

63 飛躍——インテリアから建築へ

71 モデルニテ——建築の探求

第Ⅱ部

83 ガラスの家——装飾・家具・建築の統合

第Ⅲ部

121 苦難の時代——不況下の模索と支援

131 新天地を求めて——新たな展開

論 考

17 ピエール・シャロー：近代的な、どこまでも近代的な
オリヴィエ・サンカルブル

35 1920年代：ピエール・シャロー、装飾芸術家の中で
エリーズ・クーリング

113 1930年代：ピエール・シャローとUAMの10年
ジャン＝フランソワ・アルキエリ

資 料

104 サン＝ギヨーム通りの住宅
ポール・ネルソン

106 訪問観察記
ジュリアン・ルパージュ

109 ガラスの家
ピエール・シャロー

110 『家具』序文
ピエール・シャロー

166 略歴

168 参考文献

170 出品資料リスト

Contents

9 Message

11 Preface
Bernard Blistène, Alain Seban

PART I

45 The Early Years

57 The Consecration

63 The Apogee

71 Modernity

PART II

83 The House of Glass

PART III

121 The Difficulties

131 In Exile

Articles

136 Pierre Chareau: Modern, Resolutely Modern
Olivier Cinqualbre

141 The 1920s: Pierre Chareau, among Artist Decorators
Elise Koering

145 The 1930s: Pierre Chareau, a decade of the UAM
Jean-François Archieri

Documents from the 1930s

148 The House in rue St-Guillaume
Paul Nelson

149 A Visitor's Observations
Julien Lepage

150 La Maison de Verre
Pierre Chareau

151 **Notices**

167 Biography

168 Selected Bibliography

170 List of Works

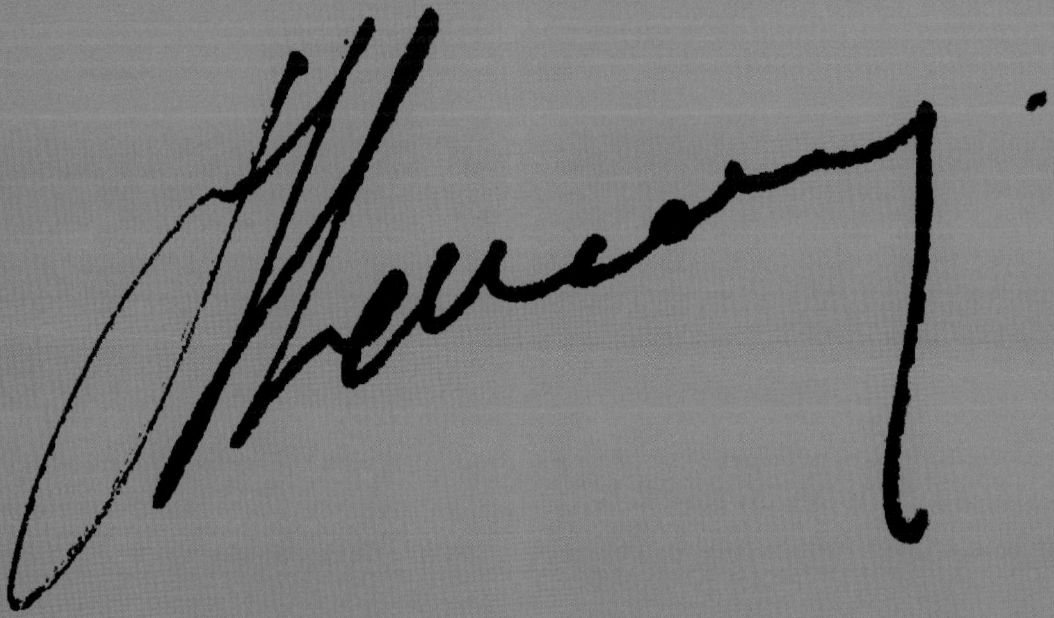

001 ピエール・シャローの肖像｜1925年撮影｜撮影：ロール・アルバン＝ギョ

論考　ピエール・シャロー：近代的な、どこまでも近代的な
オリヴィエ・サンカルブル

　かなり以前から、そして現在でも、『ル・プチ・ラルース・イリュストレ』というフランスの学生が使う標準的な事典には、ピエール・シャローの項がある。この項では、とても簡潔にシャローがパリの「ガラスの家」の作者であることを示しているが、ル・アーヴル生まれであるとする伝記的な誤りも犯している。シャローは、実際にはボルドー生まれである。他にも、父親は本当はワインブローカーであるが、船主となっている。確かに取るに足らないことであるが、たとえ作品が有名だとしても、シャローの人生についてはよく知られていないことは確かである。19世紀末にはじまった67年間の人生は、5年間の兵役で第一次世界大戦を経験し、第二次世界大戦後に幕を閉じる。1920年代に展開するまばゆいようなキャリアは、世界恐慌によっていきなり中絶される。そして、そのキャリアはフランスでも亡命先のニューヨークでも、真に復活することはなかった。かくして、同時代の批評家によって高く評価された作品は、作者が消えたとき、ほぼ忘れ去られたのである。しかし、20世紀末になって突然、その時代の建築家や学生によって丹念に観察されたある建物と、コレクターを絶えず熱くする家具のデザインを通じて、突然日の目をみる。

　真の伝記はいまだ書かれていない。本論で明らかにしていくのは、作品の発展過程、あるスタイルの確立、形態の創造性、そしてシャローの探求の道のりである。それは家具からインテリアデザインへとごく自然に発展し、異例ともいえる、建築への探求へといたる。

　役所への届けによれば、シャローは1883年8月4日ボルドーの生まれである。1893年頃、家族はパリに居を構える（つまり、シャローは出世のためにパリにやってきた田舎の若者ではない）。1904年7月11日、イギリス人の小学校教師ルイザ・ダイト、通称ドリーとの結婚をパリ17区の区役所に届け出る。1914年に砲兵隊に入隊し、1919年に除隊する[*1]。

　職業的な教育はおそらく学校で受けたものではない。「16歳の時にピエール・シャローは絵画、音楽、建築のいずれに進むか迷っていました。建築を選択したピエールは、ボザールのとある教授の指導のもと、一年間勉強しました」[*2]。シャローが亡くなった時、妻はこう証言している。1900年に2回、国立美術学校の建築学部を受験するも合格とはならなかった。というわけで、ピエール・シャローはいわゆる、建築学部を出て政府に公認された免許のある建築家ではない。

　シャローはイギリスの企業ワリング・アンド・ギローという家具会社のパリ支店に勤めながら修業を積んだ。1903年に製図工として入社し、1914年に辞職した際の肩書きはチーフドラフトマンであった。ワリング・アンド・ギロー社のカタログには、ホテル、劇場、大型客船のインテリアなど、規模の大きな案

件を見ることができる。この会社は、クラシックなものから今日的なものまで、幅広い様式の家具を生産しており、会社の出身国であるイギリス風のデザインが特徴である。

はじまり

ピエール・シャローにとって、すべては第一次世界大戦後になって本格的に始まることになる。この恐怖の数年間がすぎれば、何事も以前のようではいられない。それはシャローが自分の名で独立して開始した、創造のための新しい人生である。

1919年、シャローはサロン・ドートンヌで展示した最初の注文の作品によって世に知られるようになる。それは、サン＝ジェルマン大通りにあるアパルトマンの改修で、納品前にサロンに出品するために選んだ作品は、若い医師の診察室と寝室である。それについて何も触れない批評家は、シャローの運命が動き出しているとは思ってもみていない。顧客はある若い夫婦で、ピエールとドリーのシャロー夫妻が最良の関係を維持することになる医師のジャン・ダルザスとその妻のアニー・ベルンハイムである。ドリーはアニーの幼い頃の英語の家庭教師であった。多くの将来の注文を確実にすることになる友情と大きな家族の輪のなかに招き入れるのは、彼らダルザス夫妻である。エドモンとエミール・ベルンハイム、エレーヌ・ベルンハイム、エドモン・フレッグ、テプランスキー家、レヴィ家、ドレフュス家、グリュムバッハ家といった面々がジャンとアニーのダルザス夫妻を介して紹介される。ガラスの家の施主になるのもダルザス夫妻で、作家シャローのパトロンと思われるほど永続的な支援を続けることになる。

シャローはサロン（展覧会）への最初の出品の後も参加を続け、毎年、サロン・ドートンヌと芸術家装飾家サロン（SAD）に最新作を出品する。これは、顧客から託された家具とインテリアデザインを引き渡し前に一般公開する機会となり、すぐに恒例のことになった。寝室、浴室、ダイニング、書斎、子供部屋、若者の寝室など、シャローは住宅内のあらゆる所要室に取り組み、形態と使い方の刷新を探求し、新しい材料を研究し、新しい装置を提案する。シャローにとって非常によい時期で、想像力も豊かである。批評家たちは誤ることなく、シャローの仕事を注視するようになり、それを支持するにしても黙殺するにしても、敬意は払うようになる。

「ピエール・シャローは珍しいフォルムやオリジナリティよりもアイディアの実現を追求する。今日的な問題の解決のために試行錯誤を繰り返し、建築のなかで抱いたアイディアを追求する。建設に配慮しているために、センチメンタルな一貫性の欠如に陥ることは免れている。シャローは高価な材料を好み、それらの材料の装飾的、建設的可能性に関して適切で洗練された感覚で、それらを使いこなす。マホガニー、紫檀、黒檀、トネリコ、カエデ。シャローはそれらの材料の実用的メリットと同じくらい心理的メリットを熟知している。魅力的な調和も不協和音もそれらから引き出す。大胆さは論理性のなさとは限らない。ピエール・シャローは建設者でありつづける。家具では、ヴォリュームと平面の巧妙な組み合わせが全体の輪郭をつくる。この年、シャローが発表したある邸宅のための3つの寝室に置かれた家具は、私たちの心をあまり魅惑しない。大きなコル

ref.001　玄関ホール　ダルザス家のアパルトマン、サン＝ジェルマン大通り｜『フランスのインテリア』誌よりpl.5、ジャン・バドヴィッチ編集、1925年、アルベール・モランセ出版、パリ

008　飾り棚｜撮影年・撮影者不詳　　　　　　　　009　伸長式のテーブル｜撮影年不詳　撮影：アンリ・ガルニエ

ベイユ・ベッドと肘掛け椅子は、まるで写真の歪みを見ているようなカーブを描いている。しかしそれでも、これらは、おそらく私にはエスプリの自制という点でとても特徴的に見える。それは常に私たちをひきつけ、注意深い考察をうながすものである」[*3]

「彼の建設への心配り……ピエール・シャローは建設者(コンストラクトゥール)であり続けている。……」

この筆者と同様に、他の批評家の文章にもその表現は再び現れる。

「シャローはアイディアをもっているし、しばしば見事な実作がある。すばらしい建設というはっきりした方針をもっている」[*4]。

建設者(コンストラクトゥール)、この表現は重要である。というのも、批評家はシャローを装飾家(デコラトゥール)たちと区別しているからである。もちろん、住宅の一室をものにするとき、シャローは天井と床の材の色を選び、壁紙と壁布（彼はモチーフをデザインする）を用い、創意ある空間に家具を備え付け、友人の芸術家の作品を展示し、部屋の表面すべてに介入する。とはいえ、家具のデッサンは、それらの配置のデッサンと同様に、無駄なものや余計なものはない。スタイルは洗練され、家具の構造体は明確にされ、ラインはシンプルで、使用する材料が強調される。木材の種類は貴重で凝ったものであるし、非常に上質な高級家具製品である。主流のアール・デコの限界に挑むそれらの家具は、やはり独特なものであり続けている。

この非常に活動的な時期には、他にも重要な要素がシャローに影響を及ぼすことになる。まずひとつめの要素は、創作の世界のなかに身をいきなり委ねたことで、シャローはフランシス・ジュールダンやロベール・マレ=ステヴァンスのような大立者と出会い、以降、同じサークルに所属したことである。その機会に恵まれるやいなや、シャローは自分が彼らの側にいることに気づく。アイリーン・グレイやエレーヌ・アンリといった女性作家たちと自身のプレゼンテーションで協働し、ジャック・リプシッツやジャン・リュルサといった芸術家と仕事をする。家具は、そのオリジナリティによって、マルセル・レルビエ監督の映画「人でなしの女」（1924年）のセットのような活動の場を広げている。

ふたつめの要素はおそらく、1922年のパリの芸術的な金物職人ルイ・ダルベとの重要な出会いである。エミール・ロベールのアトリエ（ジャン・プルーヴェも後にここで修業することになる）で修業したダルベは、ピ

19

エール・シャローと急速に密接なかかわりをもつようになる。シャローは、例えば、しっかりと確立されたノウハウがある場合にのみ実現することができるしなやかさに満ちたラインをもつフロアスタンド《修道女》のように、自分のインスピレーションを金属で形態に翻案することのできる人物をダルベに見出した。シャローはまた、自分が作家をフォローする能力のある企業家でもある、ということを発見する。テーブルランプであれ、ウォールランプであれ、ペンダントランプであれ、ダルベの工房が照明器具のすべての要素を念入りにつくり上げ、照明器具を備え付ける現場で、シェードの代わりになるアラバスターのプレートを裁断する(特別あつらえの切り抜き機が使用された)。

この時期にはまた、シャローはサン＝ジェルマン地区のシェルシュ＝ミディ通り3番に店舗「ラ・ブティック」を開店して、宣伝のための「手段」をもつようになる。シャローはそのときから、自分の創作物を潜在的な顧客に向けて展示したり、完成した作品の写真集を見せたりした。そして、ジャン・ブルクハルトといった自分より若い人の作品集を編集したり、すぐ後にちょうど隣でギャラリーを開いたジャンヌ・ビュシェと共同で芸術家の展覧会の企画も可能になった。

始まったばかりのシャローの名声は出版物の中にも感じられる。賞賛であれ、懐疑的なものであれ、サロンの報告に過ぎなかったものが、今度はシャローそのものに捧げられた記事の掲載が始まる。『家具と室内装飾』誌の1922年末に発刊された第1号と、『芸術と装飾』誌の1923年5月号の中で、ガストン・ヴァレンヌが「ピエール・シャローの現代的な精神」という記事を署名入りで書いている。1924年の『芸術と芸術家』誌では、作家マキシミリアン・ゴチエの寄稿で「装飾芸術——ピエール・シャロー」という記事が掲載されている。建築家のジャン・バドヴィチが編集する『住宅の芸術』誌上で繰り返し取り上げられることは別としても、多くの出版物に登場している。シャローが受けた大きな注文が雑誌に掲載されたのは1926年のことで、扇状の可動間仕切りを取り入れた空間をつくることに初めて取り組んだラニック家のアパルトマンの改修である。1925年に博覧会が開催されているために、掲載と1924年の竣工引き渡しとの間には少し時差がある。

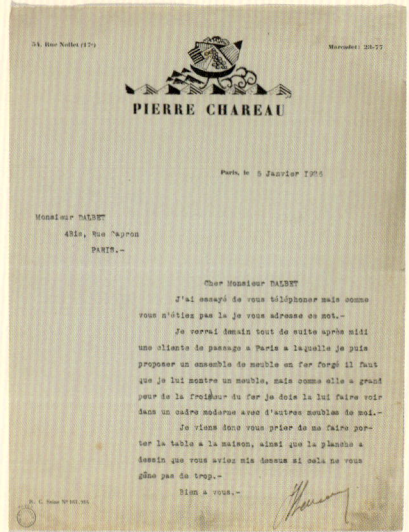

030

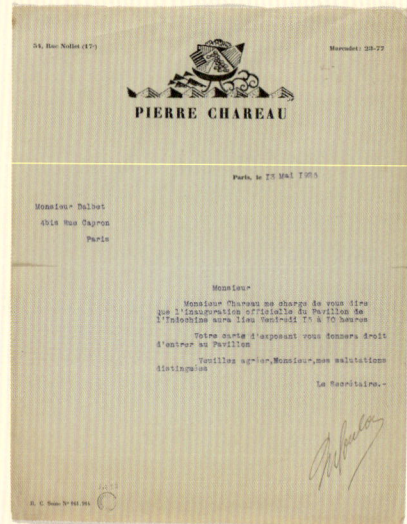

031

028　工房でハンマーを振り上げる鍛冶職人｜撮影者不詳

20

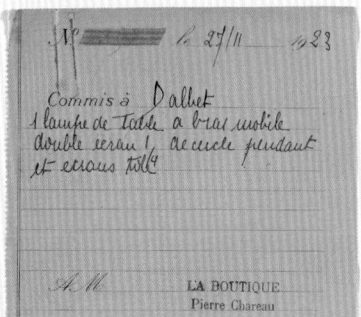
032a

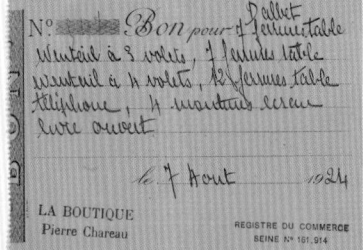
032b

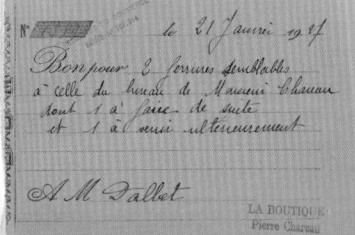
032c

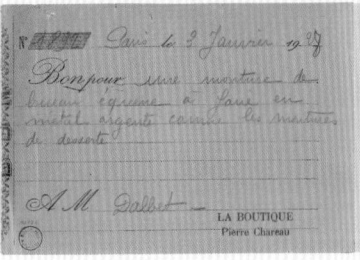
032d

シャローからダルベに宛てた手紙と注文書

030
パリ、1926年1月5日／パリ、キャプロン通り4bis／ダルベ様／さきほど電話で伝えようとしたのですが、あなたが不在だったので手紙を出すことにしました。私は明日、パリに滞在中の女性客に午後一番に会って、錬鉄製の家具セットを勧めることができると思います。そこで実際に家具を一つ相手に見せる必要があるのですが、なにしろこの女性は鉄の冷たい感じがひどくぞっとするというので、違うタイプの私の家具と一緒にモダンな雰囲気の中で見せなくてはいけません。というわけで、もしもよかったら例のテーブルと、あなたが以前その上に置いていた製図板の両方を、家まで届けてくれるように手配をお願いします。ではよろしく。シャローより

031
パリ、1925年5月13日／パリ、キャプロン通り4bis／ダルベ様／拝啓、インドシナ・パヴィリオンの除幕式が15日金曜日の午前10時から始まる旨、あなた様にお知らせするようにシャロー氏から言い付かりました。当日は、あなた様の出品者証をお持ちいただければパヴィリオンに入ることができます。それではよろしくお願い申し上げます。敬具　秘書より

032a
第252号／1923年11月27日／ダルベへ以下発注　複数の腕付きテーブルランプ1基、四分円の吊り下げダブルスクリーン／ラ・ブティック　ピエール・シャロー

032b
ダルベへ／第547号／以下発注　3つのパーツからなる扇状テーブルの金具7ケ、4つのパーツからなる扇状テーブルの金具7ケ、電話機用テーブルの金具12ケ、4つの本を開いたときの形状のような蝶番状金具／1924年8月7日／ラ・ブティック　ピエール・シャロー／商業登記　セーヌ第161.914号

032c
第1389号／1927年1月21日／商業登記　セーヌ第161.914号／以下発注　シャローの仕事机のものと同類の金具2ケ。うち1つはすぐに製作し、もう1つは後日着のこと。／ダルベ氏へ／ラ・ブティック　ピエール・シャロー

032d
第1892号／パリ、1927年1月3日／以下発注　直角定規状の机に付ける金具1ケ（配膳用食器台の金具と同様な銀張り金属製）。／ダルベ氏へ／ラ・ブティック　ピエール・シャロー

029　作業机に向かう金物職人ルイ・ダルベ｜撮影者不詳

189　シェルシュ＝ミディ通り「ラ・ブティック」正面 『商店のショウウィンドー』より、
L. P. セズィーユによる序論と監修、1927年、アルベール・レヴィ出版

名声

パリ現代産業装飾芸術国際博覧会（通称アール・デコ博、1925年博）において、シャローの社会的な評価が確立したことは間違いない。この博覧会を伝統や古典主義と闘う場としたモダニストの中で、シャローは3つの貢献を通じてその存在感を示している。SADの「フランスの大使の館」と題されたパヴィリオンに、主室となる「書架のある執務室」を実現し、さらにフランシス・ジュールダンによる体操室の延長部分にある小さい優美な休憩室を手掛けている。そして、インドシナ・パヴィリオンでは、食堂も手掛けている。シャローはこれらの参画によって、レジョン・ドヌール勲章（訳注：ナポレオンが制定した国家への功労者に与えられる最高勲章）を受け、書架のある執務室の家具一式は装飾芸術美術館に買い取られている。フランスの公的なコレクションに加えられたシャローの最初の家具である。翌年には、肘掛け椅子もコレクションに入る。展覧会はブリュッセルのエレーラ夫人やアーマン・モスといった顧客をシャローにもたらすことになる。シャローは数多くのインタビューを受ける。ポール・フォロ、ジャック＝エミール・ルルマン、ジャロ、アンドレ・グルルトといった著名な装飾家たちの例にならって、ジョルジュ・ルフェーヴルとのインタビューに同意する。

「もしいつの日か装飾芸術の会議に中心的な人物を招集したならば、ピエール・シャローはおそらく後ろから2列目の最も左の席を占めるだろう。常に興味深く計算された大胆さ、それに加えられた妥協のない原則が、この芸術家を"大臣候補"と廊下で人々が囁きあうほどのリーダーにしている。肩幅こそ広いが、あまり体格がよいとはいえない人物である。瞳は澄んで青い。こめかみから後ろに髪を流しているグレーがかった髪、常に沸き立つ思考で休むことを知らず、口調は歯切れがよい。シャローは自らの教義をこう定める――装飾と家具の関係性。テーブル、肘掛け椅子、タンスの制作にかかわる人間は、まず建築家(アルシテクト)でなければならない。常に人の心をひきつけるものは全体の調和なのである。使われるのが白い木であれ、マカッサル産黒檀であれ、ルールは同じであるべきである。私は大使の館で、ある種の私的な書架のある執務室といった部屋のデザインを任された。人々が私に期待したものに反して、真の"道楽"を実現することに私を駆り立てる、ある種の創造的熱狂に身を任せて、どこにもないよ

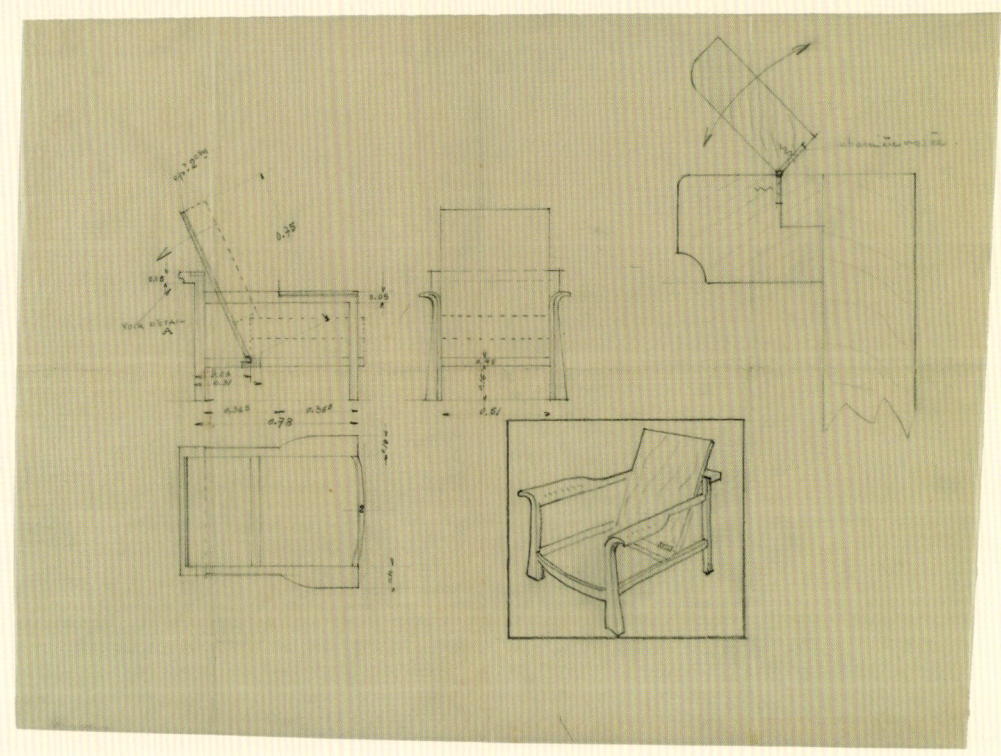

006 リクライニング式の椅子　平面図、立面図、詳細図、透視図 ｜ 1923年

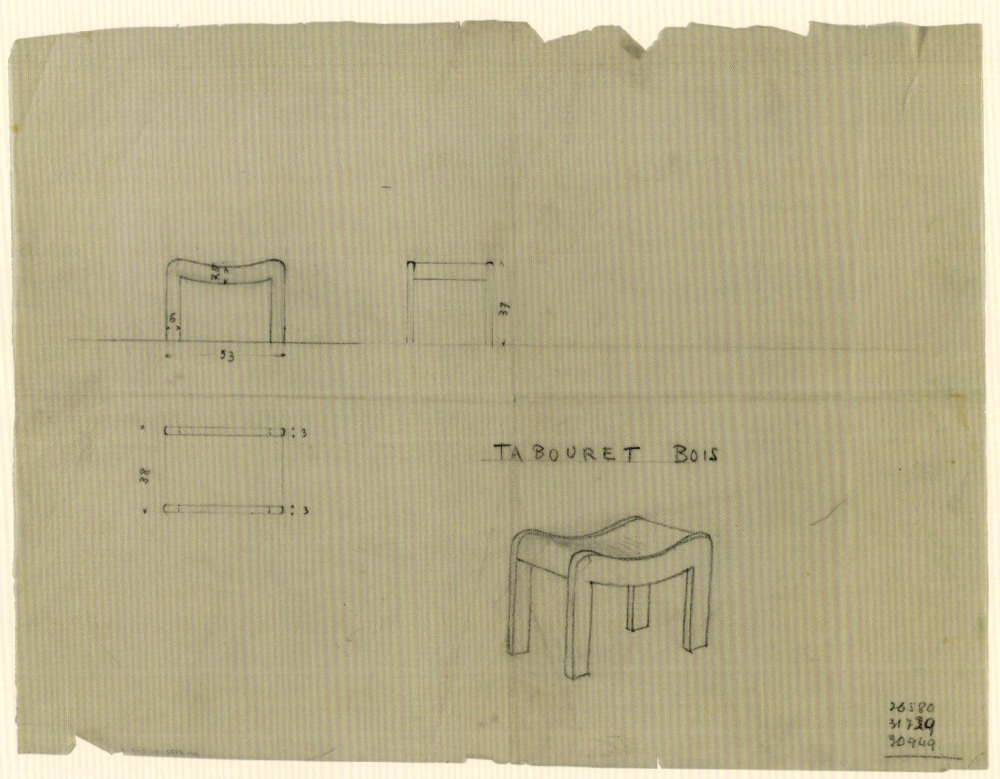

007 木製スツール　立面図、平面図、透視図

うな非常に珍しい木材を使用した。たしかに貧乏人にはその同じ白い木が高価過ぎると思われるかもしれないが……一回くらい派手に羽目を外してもよいのではないか」*5

批評家によって建設者(コンストラクトゥール)として認められたのち、今、シャローが主張するのは建築家(アルシテクト)としての地位である。「明日の住まい」についてのギョーム・ジャノのアンケートに回答して、シャローはこう明言している。

「現実の建物の平面計画というものは職業上の問題である。それは建築家(アルシテクト)の役割である。興味をそそられるのは、全体にかかる構想を示すことである。そもそも、応用は自由でなければならない。主導権は施工者に委ねなければならない。言ってみれば、建築家(アルシテクト)の務めは、実行者に責任を委ねながら、その計算を実行する決められたプログラムの代数の解の提供に留めることではなかったか。そこにあるのは、一見中世の方法論である。実務家の創意を尊敬し、刺激しなければならない。家具と同様に建設においても、ひとりの職人は作家が想像しなかったような、思いがけない発見をする。協働のこのやり方に立ち戻る必要がある。建築家(アルシテクト)は職業人ではない。建築家(アルシテクト)は数学者であり、哲学者なのだ——造形的な組み合わせを考察するものであり、石工ではない。時代の近い我々の先輩たちは、ふたつの活動を混同し、芸術を職業的器用さの下にみなしたがった。芸術はエスプリであり、何物もそれを埋め合わせることはないのである」*6

飛躍

1925年博が終わり、シャローの活動はさらに拡大する。人々に求められたのは装飾家(デコラトゥール)であり、室内の改修の仕事の数を増やす。家具作家としても自分が人に知られた存在であると自覚し、革新していく。シャローは建築家(アルシテクト)とも見なされ、建物を建てる機会が与えられる。

シャローが受けたインテリアの注文の中で、ふたつの作品がとりわけ注意をひく。最初の作品は、パリ16区の建築家の名を冠した通りにある、ロベール・マレ゠ステヴァンスによって設計されたレファンベール夫人の邸宅のワンフロアすべてのインテ

093　『現代趣味目録』1928–1929年、アルベール・レヴィ出版、パリ

24

リアデザインである。シャローが実現したのは、邸宅の女主人の寝室と応接室である。各階の他の部屋は、何人もの装飾家たち（男性も女性も）に託される。シャローがそれまでにかかわる機会があったパリのアパルトマンと違い、この建物は近代的なものである。ヴォリュームや動線を再発見する必要も、足りない同時代性をパーティションやさまざまな仕掛けを使ってそこに吹き込むことも不要である。ここでは空間のヴォリュームを決定する必要はあまりないのである。応接室の入口を規定するために、シャローは天井を下げる。他にも、アラバスターの小さな板でできた「リュッシュ」（蜂の巣箱）という、横長の傾斜した照明器具を埋め込むために、天井を彫り込む。レファンベール夫人の寝室では、天井から吊られた湾曲したカーテンレールによって、小サロンの空間と（就寝の）空間の境界を規定し、音楽学者である顧客の楽譜を収納する家具の価値を高めるために、ギャラリーの天井と壁を木材で覆っている。

ふたつめは、ベルンハイム家から発注されたもので、グラン・オテル・ド・トゥールのエントランスロビーの改修である。これはシャローにとって、まず規模において、そして公共的性格という点で初めての実施作で、それまでの家庭的な雰囲気と規模の作品とは全く異なっている。空間のデザインの内容によって、シャローは用途を規定し区別する。シャローは部屋の中に、機能に従って照明器具と家具をすばらしい階調で配置する。まさにシャローの作品のカタログである。ふさわしい家具がなければ、シャローはその場に合わせてつくる。バーのスツールとテーブル、手紙を書くための部屋の文具箱も同様である。したがって、モデルとなるデザインは独特で、飾り気のない黒っぽい色の鋼管（スチールパイプ）でできた脚部に特徴がある（図067, 068参照）。シャローが金属をこの形で使用するのはこれが初めてで、それ以降もずっとダルベによって制作される。しかし、シャローは危ない橋は渡らない。シャローの鋼管はモダニストたちが仕立てあげたアイコンとは異なっている。

それにもかかわらず、金属の使い方では家具の考え方を改革し、徹底的に自身の美学を一新し、ときに批評家たちを唖然とさせる。

127　ガラスの家｜1932年｜撮影者不詳

045　シャロー自邸のサロン、ノレ通り｜1927年頃

「シャローは機械をつくるときに用いる荒っぽい材料を好む。創意に富んだ家具の配置を創造するだけに飽き足らず、飾り棚や図書室でも役に立つ休息兼談話用のコーナーの大きな寝椅子のように、もしくは先端が扇状に展開する一式の板になっている半円形の化粧台のように、鉄と鋼で木材を補強することを好む。全くもって粗野な鉄の脚部が、利用者の右側に心地よく直角に延長され、机に付属する板を支えている。鋼製のある種の箱がふたつ、交互に組み合わされ、昔からの引き出しの代わりに置かれている。私たちが向かうのはここなのだろうか？　明日の家具の特徴とは、これなのだろうか？」[※7]

シャローの家具における金属の使い方は、そのように非難され、鉄の厳格さと幾何学的なラインの厳密さは糾弾される。シャローの過去の作品との決別は筋の通ったものである。以前の家具は、無駄な装飾要素のないもので、ドグマにうちたてられた機能性を目指し、建築家(アルシテクト)のにおいをただよわせるものと認識されうるものであった。しかしながら、これらの家具は、製法の問題が趣味にいたるシャローの進化であり、家具というジャンルにとどまりつづけるものである。

「木と金属」シリーズをもってして、シャローは今日アール・デコとみなされる同時代の作品と完全に決別した。しかし同様に、モダニストの作品とも異なる。それほどシャローの発案は個性的でオリジナルなものである。概して、事務机、化粧台、収納棚がそれにあてはまるのだが、モダニズムの世界にそれらを押しやっているのは、ライン、コンポジション、デザインなのである。というのも、それらの実物は伝統的な技術の上に成り立っているからである。シャローの家具の固有の美を強め、家具に力強さを与えているのは、厳密に言えば、このギャップがあ

るからこそ、なのである。一方で、設計図は絶対的なミニマリズムに行きついている。つまり、垂直方向であれ水平方向であれ、効果を増大させているのは、組み合わされる面がすべてである。このことは建物の立面図のような厳密なエレベーションを大きく掲げられた準備段階のデッサンのなかに完璧に読みとれる。もう一方で、比類のない特異性とポエジーは材料相互の対比から生まれている。ハンマーの打撃痕から継ぎ目まで加工の跡がよくみえる金属の薄板の飾り気のなさや硬さは、品質のよくわかるシンプルな板の、材料としてのエレガンスとは対照をなしている。建築のパラダイムを家具にも適用していることは明らかである。家具の幅いっぱいに床から立ち上がっている薄い板を、専門家は脚部というよりは構造というだろう。

建 築

同じ頃、シャローは建築の分野に力を注いでいる。そこでも再び、シャローの顧客はベルンハイム家である。注文、計画、引き渡しの間の時間的な流れはさまざまな事情によって変わりやすい。シャローの実作を、ひとつひとつの竣工年を考慮に入れながら考察すると、シャローの場合、仕事が乗りに乗っているのは、複数の仕事が同時進行したり、研究が入り組みあったり、大切にしている問題解決手法が変化したりするような時期である。

コートダジュールのサン＝ラファエルとサン＝トロペの間に、1927年シャローはボーヴァロンのホテルのゴルフ場クラブハウスを計画し、実現する。これが最初の建築のプロジェクトではないにしても、実際に建設された最初の建物である。確かに規模こそささやかなもので、バー、広間、テラス、クロークといった用途としては大変特殊なものであるが、それでもやはり最初の作品である。鉄筋コンクリート造、これ見よがしの柱、滑らかなファサード、帯状の開口部。これがシャローが自分のものにしたモダニストの美学である。シャローはすぐ近隣にも、同じモデルを採用した家族のための大邸宅をつくっている。これらのデビュー作には、ある種のぎこちなさが刻み付けられている。プロポーションの釣り合いはあまり巧みではなく、ピロティは貧弱で、配置はもっとシンプルにできたはずである。それでもやはり、これらの建物はある種の格調があり、モダニストの建築家の作品の中にあっても決して価値を損なわないということに変わりはない。建築は研究の新しい土壌となるが、シャローはどこであっても易きに流れない。この不器用さは建築作品の設計者としてのシャローの資質に関する本稿の説明と

037　パブロ・ピカソ｜シャルロット菓子のある静物画｜1924年

矛盾するかもしれない。オランダでヨハネス・ダイカー（1890-1935）と協働するオランダ人建築家ベルナルト・ベイフォトがシャローのもとで働いている。しかし、経歴を考えるとき、シャローとの蜜月がそこには見られない反面、ベイフォトを実施のための建築家とみなすのは間違っている。おそらく本当の意味での協働があり、ベイフォトは独学者の発明の才能の前にして、建築学校で学んだことを意識的に引っ込めていたという仮説を立てることができよう。

1925年博の後、多忙になってもシャローはサロンと展覧会から離れない。むしろ、参加を増やしている。トゥールのホテルの改修はかくして、1926年と1927年のサロン・ドートンヌに出品される。シャローは定期的にパリのギャラリーで展覧会を行い、それ以降は国外でも、1927年にはニューヨークとライプチヒで展示をした。同年、シャローは「扇子構造の折りたたみ椅子」で特許を登録する。その家具はふたつの映画、「めまい」（マルセル・レルビエ監督、1926年）と「モンテカルロの終末」（ポール・ブジ監督、1927年）で意味ありげに登場する。そして1929年には、詩人で劇作家のエドモン・フレッグ（彼の友人であり顧客でもある）の、コメディ＝フランセーズで上演される3幕のコメディ「パリの商人」の舞台セットを手掛ける。しかし、それ以降、シャローの関心をひいたのは建築のみ。自分が手掛ける建築、自分の周囲で手掛けられる建築なのである。

マレ＝ステヴァンスと親しくしていたシャローは、ル・コルビュジエとも近しくなる。シャローはシュツットガルトのヴァイセンホーフを1927年に訪れ、アヴァンギャルドの建築家が手掛けた住宅地の中で、ル・コルビュジエとピエール・ジャンヌレの署名のある2軒の住宅を高く評価した。1928年に彼らはジョルジュ・ベルネーム・ギャラリーでの展覧会に一緒に参加し、その6月、スイスのラ・サラ城のCIAM（近代建築国際会議）の第一回総会で再会する。もしシャローが設立者の一人になるとすれば、それは明らかにメンバーを選んだル・コルビュジエの誘いがあってのことで、当時ル・コルビュジエはフランス人のライバル（マレ＝ステヴァンス）を遠ざけ、もう一人の有力建築家（アンドレ・リュルサ）とは対立状態にあった。この新会員の指名は、ル・コルビュジエがシャローに抱いていた好意的な評価を確証する。たとえシャローが、「ガラスの家」という名前を与えられることになる、重要な作品をまだ自慢することができなかったとしても、同等ではないにしろ、まず競争相手になったり干渉したりすることのない人物と、ル・コルビュジエはみなしている。

ガラスの家の工事許可がダルザス氏に実際に与えられるのは8月21日のことである。コンセプトを練り上げた期間は長く（おそらく3年近く）、工事期間もまたそのくらいになる。ル・コルビュジエが工事現場を訪れたこと、ガラスブロックのファサードにとりわけ興味をもったこと、同時期にパリの大学都市のスイス学生会館でより小規模にそれを実験したことが知られている。工事期間中は、特にガラスの専門誌でいくつかの記事がガラスの家について報告しているだけだが、竣工後はフランス国内でも国外でも建築専門誌でも装飾専門誌でも記事はたくさん出ている。どちらの領域でも同じ方向の批評が見出せる。実際、ガラスの家はトータルな作品である。外観においても、構成においても、ヴォリュームの質においても、快適性のための設備においても、プログラムが要求するものに最大限に応えるために、顧客の支援という強みを生かして、ピエール・シャローはひとつのインテリアデザインの依頼を建築的創造に変える。そしてこの建築作品こそが、この作家（クレアトゥール）に新しい身分を与える。翌年にはクラブハウスの方が早く竣工しているのにもかかわらず、それよりも早く、1933年の『今日の建築』誌に最初に掲載される。シャローが機会あるごとに人に見せていたのはガラスの家の人目を引く模型と写真である。シャローはそれ以降、完全に建築家（アルシテクト）であり、同業者たちによってそれと認められるひとりの近代建築家となるのである。

後退

この建築家（アルシテクト）がガラスの家を完成させた頃、装飾家（デコラトゥール）としてのシャローは同様に世論の高い評価を受けるふたつのインテリアデザインを世に送り出している[*8]。ふたつともパリのアパルトマンで、批評家にはおなじみの、絶頂期にあったシャローの作風を代表するガラスの家のヴォリュームとは共通点を持たず、各空間はここでは、必要に応じて自由に組み合わせできるような、軽い、ガラスがはめられた可動の間仕

049 ジャック・リプシッツ｜静物｜1918–1929年

038 ジャック・リプシッツ｜横たわる女｜1921年

切りによって区切られ、ひと続きに切り分けられている。ガラスの家と同時代のこれらのふたつの実施作は、依頼に恵まれた時期の終わりを示している。アメリカで端を発した世界恐慌はヨーロッパに到達し、どちらの現象も互いの結果のようにみえた。つづく数年間はシャローにとって厳しいものとなった。建築の設計競技に呼ばれることも、公共工事の依頼を受けることも、この縮小の時期において不可能なことであった。というのも、建築家として頭角を現してきたとはいえ、公的な資格がなく、「旧守派」がのしていくなかで、シャローはモダニストだからである。シャローは設立後に合流したUAM（近代芸術家連合）と、支援委員会のメンバーである『ラルシテクチュール・ドージュルデュイ［今日の建築］』誌のさまざまな行事に参加している。そして、学校家具や大型客船の家具から鉄骨構造の建物までをテーマとした設計競技や展覧会を毎年主催しているOTUA（鉄利用のための技術局）の行事にも参加する。若いスイス人、ルイ・モレとともにスイスのヴァレー地方でのクライアント探しを試みるが、一時しのぎの手段でしかなかった。これらの年月、シャローはひとりの女友達ジェメル・アニクのためのささやかな田舎の別荘（1937年）しか建てていない。シャローは急場しのぎの借金生活を送り、行政の援助を願い出て、ガラスの家の模型を政府に買い取ってもらう。そんな状態にもかかわらず、政府の役人と同業者たちからは信認されている。1935年、ブリュッセルの万博で、彼はフランス館における建築部門を委嘱される。しかし、先の見通しと金銭的な援助を再び与えるのは1937年のパリ万博である。シャローはそこで、家具グループの報告者に任命され、UAMのパヴィリオンで家具を展示し、政府とパリ市に買い取ってもらい、ル・コルビュジエとピエール・ジャンヌレの新時代館で模型を1点発表する。シャローはレジョン・ドヌール・オフィシエ章の叙勲を受ける。国立美術館の作品購入委員会のメンバーにもなる。1938年、シャローは芸術家の支持を得て、外務省のある局長室の改修のための家具一式の依頼を受ける。そして、フランシス・ジュールダン、ルイ・ソニョ、ジャック・アドネとともにフランス学士院の事務長の応接室と執務室の改修に参加する。1939年には、ドリーとピエール・シャロー夫妻がルイ・モレと続けていた文通のなかに危機感の高まりが感じ取れる。そして1940年7月、シャローはフランスを去り、モロッコとポルトガルを経由してアメリカに向かうのである。

ニューヨークでは、戦時中、「自由フランス週間」作戦、「永遠のフランス」展（1942年）、「自由フランス」の職員食堂ラ・マルセイエーズのインテリアデザイン、「永遠のフランス」によるド・ゴール将軍の歓迎会の企画（1944年）といった、愛国的な行事のすべてに参加しているシャローの姿を見ることになる。戦争が終わっても、シャローはニューヨークにとどまり、フランスの芸術に捧げられた展覧会の企画を続ける。しかし、活動は大変限られたものである。これらの厳しい年月の中から、ふたつの建築の実施作が浮かび上がる。ひとつは1947年の画家のロバート・マザウェルのためのもので、もうひとつは1950年の音楽家ジェルメーヌ・モントゥと作家のナンシー・ローリンのための小さな建物であるが、この年の8月24日、シャローは逝去する。マザウェルの住宅兼アトリエは、この作家の白鳥の歌のように響く。経済的なこだわりから、軍の工業製品の建築物を手に入れ、それを仕事と生活にふさわしい空間へ変貌させ、シャローはいま一度、その発明の才を発揮したのである。発明の才、それはおそらくシャローの作品を定義する中心的な言葉である。1954年にルネ・エルブストによって出版されたUAMの友人たちによって捧げられたオマージュ、的確に題された『ひとりの発明家、建築家ピエール・シャロー』がそれを証明するように。

*1
ボルドー市公文書館およびパリ市公文書館
*2
ドリー・シャロー『ラルシテクチュール・ドージュルデュイ』誌、31号、1950年9月
*3
「ピエール・シャロー」『家具と室内装飾』誌、no.1、1922年11–12月号、p.27
*4
ガストン・ヴァレンヌ「家具と装飾芸術」『アール・エ・デコラシオン［芸術と装飾］』誌、1921年12月、p.182
*5
ジョルジュ・ルフェーヴル「アール・デコ博において――何人かの装飾家の宣言」『アール・ヴィヴァン［生きている芸術］』誌、no.12、1925年6月15日、p.28
*6
ギヨーム・ジャノー「新しい形態と新しいプログラム」パリ、1925年
*7
ルネ・シャヴァンス「五人組」『家具と装飾』1928年7月、p.50
*8
それらは、ドレフュス家とファリ家のアパルトマンである。

PART

第 I 部

出発──家具デザインからの始動
THE EARLY YEARS

確立──作風と名声の形成
THE CONSECRATION

飛躍──インテリアから建築へ
THE APOGEE

モデルニテ──建築の探求
MODERNITY

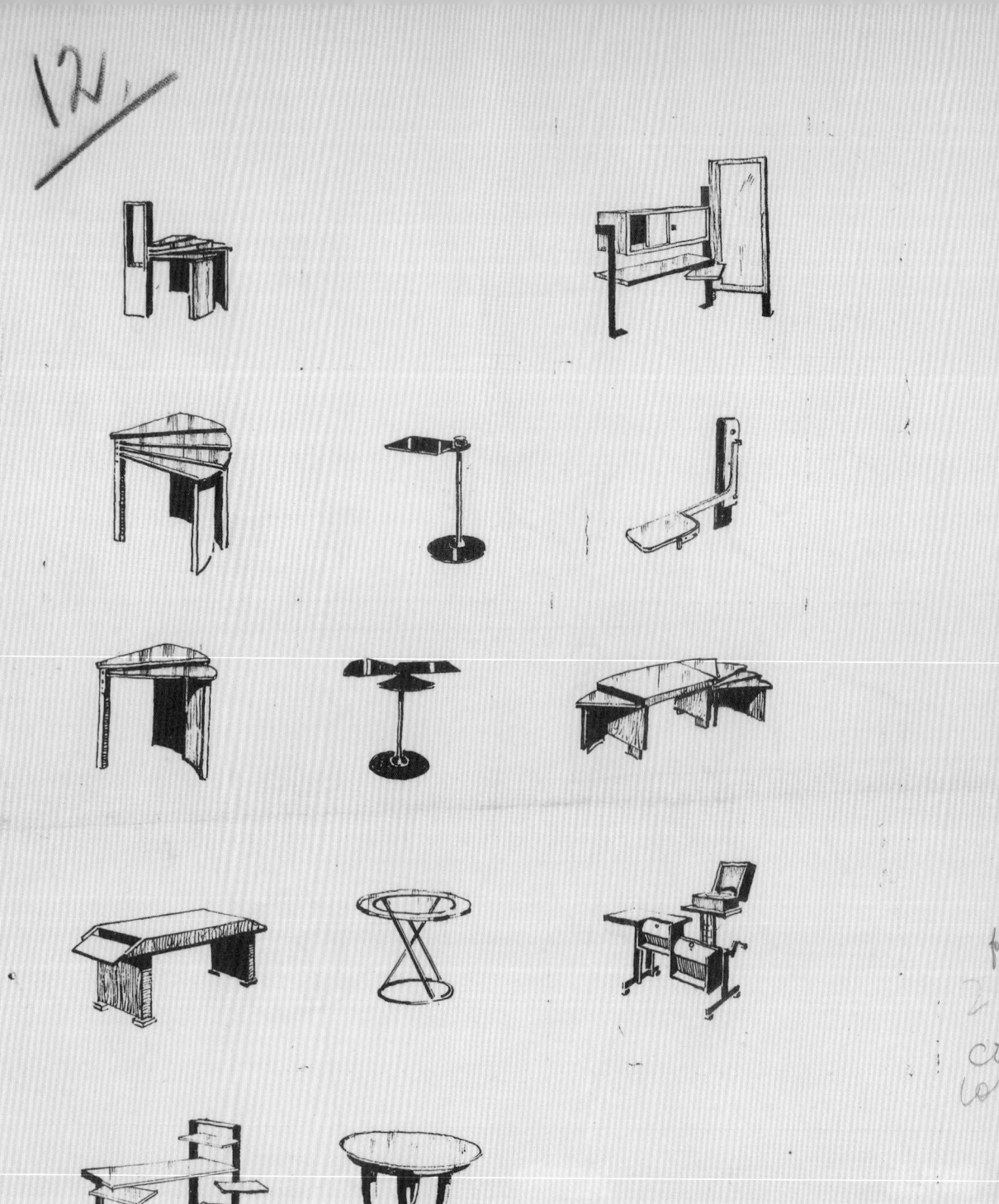

004　家具各種スケッチ

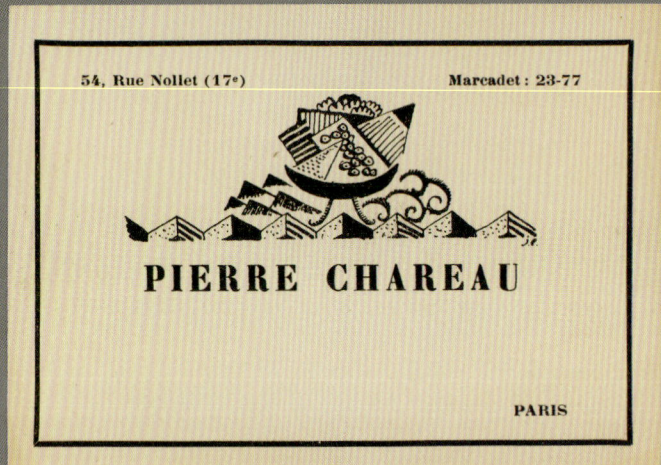

論考　1920年代：ピエール・シャロー、装飾芸術家の中で
エリーズ・クーリング

「ピエール・シャローは偉大な芸術家(アルティスト)と偉大な技術者(テクニシャン)の長所を併せもっている」*1

1919年のサロン・ドートンヌへの最初の出展から5年もたたず、「すべての装飾芸術の展覧会の室内装飾家たち(アンサンブリエ)」のなかでシャローを「随一」という人もいた*2。シャローは高い評価を享受しつつ、斬新な装飾言語が開花するのを見たいという同時代人の望みを具現化する。「ルイ15世様式やルイ16世様式、その他の堕落した様式とは完全に無関係な新路線」が、「木や弓形のテーブルの脚に彫られた玉飾りや花綱装飾のあるありきたりのモダン」を棄却して、「20世紀のフランス様式」の誕生を望む人たちに代案を、とりわけその場を具体化するのである。
　年齢的なこと——フランシス・ジュールダン、ロベール・マレ=ステヴァンス、ル・コルビュジエ、アイリーン・グレイの先輩格にあたる——と、イギリスの家具会社で働いたという型破りな経験は、パリの作家(クレアトゥール)のシーンへの遅い登場、独特な作風と相まって、シャローにパリの装飾芸術の状況の中で特別な地位を授ける。1923-1924年には、シャローはモダニストの新しい世代の代表者のひとりとみなされており、先駆者であり、原動力とさえ思われていた。シャローの影響力を、批評家たちは賞賛する。その頃には批評家はもはやためらうことなくシャローを一派の長、たとえばモーリス・デュフレーヌもしくはポール・フォロのような人物とみている。シャローは果たして、1925年、『ラール・ヴィヴァン[生きている芸術]』*3 誌上で自分の考えを表明し得た唯一のモダニストであった。「リーダー」の責任を負う彼は、ジョルジュ・ルフェーヴルの的確な表現によれば、「信奉者、模倣者、あるいは盗作者さえも携えている」。
　1925年の博覧会の際に、ガリエラ美術館学芸員のアンリ・クルゾと歴史的建造物視察官のギョーム・ジャノーはフランスの装飾芸術の現状報告書を作成し、その起源について近視眼的な分析を試みる。このふたりにとって、この時期に発表された作品にはふたつの傾向が明らかであった。
　1910年代のはじめに登場した最初のグループは、ジャック=エミール・ルルマン、スー&マル、アンドレ・グルルトたちのグループである。彼らは、「新伝統主義(ネオ・トラディショナリスム)」*4 と呼ばれ、アール・ヌーヴォーと縁を切ることを望み、過去のものと自由に関係づける創作を提案する。つまり、「よき伝統を変革しつつも継承する」*5 という一派である。
　第二のグループは、社会の激変と近代世界をしっかりと捉えた成果であった。クルゾが言うところの「1919年の完全なるモダニズム」もしくは「1919年の未来主義者」、ジャノーに倣うところの「モダニスト・グループ」もしくは「1919年派」であり、1919

020　化粧台、スツールと炉辺椅子｜制作年・撮影者不詳

年になるまで明らかではなかった傾向である。「旧来のすべてのスタイルから解放し、新しい家庭生活や経済の状況から生まれる前代未聞の形態のみ認める」*6 という以上、このグループは「新伝統主義」の反動である。ジャノーによれば、このグループは、近代世界とその「心理的興奮」*7 を装飾にも持ちこんだものである。

1919年、シャローはアパルトマンのインテリアデザインの最初の依頼を受け、サロン・ドートンヌに初めて展示する。同じく1919年、グレイはジュリエット・レヴィのために一軒のアパルトマンの装飾の最初の工事を完成し、1913年以来初めてフランスで展示する*8。また同じく1919年、ルグランは既に本の装丁の分野を革新していた。一年後にはサロンに初めて出品し、ジャンヌ・タシャールの屋敷の空間の改装準備にとりかかっている。

シャロー、グレイ、ピエール・ルグランは、フランスの伝統と切り離された新しい言語を認めさせつつあった。ジャノーとクルゾにとって、彼らは完全なるモダニズム、この独創的な「1919年派」を構成している。彼らによれば、この言語は簡素なライン、シンプルな幾何学的形態、的確なプロポーションを重視している。そして、装飾的な次元よりも建設面を重んじ、それ自体で完結した実用的かつ合理的で基本的なオブジェという考え方で建設する。それは近代的な生活によって生み出された「新しいニーズ」から考えられている。

この3人の作家は同様に、探求心の強さ、発明の才、創造的なオリジナリティ（クレアトゥール）の面でも異彩を放っている。希少な材料の達人である彼らは、新機軸の組み合わせ、コントラストの作用、しばしば強烈な印象を与える素材の効果を積極的に試していく。彼らの美学はフランスの様式とはかけ離れている。グ

36

ref.004　『住宅芸術』誌（現代装飾を代表する傑作選集）
1923–1926年（1924年冬号）、アルベール・モランセ出版

レイとシャローにはイギリス経験があるし、3人の作家(クレアトゥール)がアヴァンギャルド芸術だけではなく、東洋美術やプリミティブ・アートにも関心を示したとしても不思議ではない。グレイとルグランの作品はとりわけ、遠く離れた、もしくは想像上の場所や過ぎ去った時代をテーマに盛り込んでいる。

この3人はしばしば詩的また夢幻的な雰囲気をつくり出すことに卓越している。グレイはジュリエット・レヴィ邸を「詩のように美しい一式」[9]で構成する。シャローはトゥール市のグラン・オテルの宴会場を「海緑色の広大なひろがり……その中で、夜、橋の下を流れるセーヌ川の光に似た、曖昧な光が映し出される広大なひろがり」[10]に変化させる。

彼らが示してみせる創意工夫の才能はかくして、過去から解放された創造、とりわけ近代生活の新しいリアリティに合わせた解決手段を備えた創造に役立っている。人々のニーズ、それと同様に「人々の嗜好や習慣」[11]は、伝統主義と急進的な機能主義者にときに対向する繊細な創作をするシャロー、グレイ、ルグランの主要な関心事であり続ける[12]。しかし、だからといって、このまぎれもない精神性とこだわりある探究心の共同体、それをジャノーが下くくったようにひとつの「流派」とまで、主張してもよいのだろうか？

「1919年派」に着目すると、複数の独立した装飾家(デコラトゥール)をまとめて語り、リーダーとなる大物が指揮する明確なグルーピングをしようというジャノーの意図が露呈される。このリーダーとはシャローである[13]。1928年、シャローはそれ以降「建築家」(アルシテクト)のレッテルを貼られ、一派のリーダーとしての地位にあり続けたのみならず、それ以降自分の名前がその一派に冠せられることを誇ることさえできた。「ピエール・シャロー派」は、シャローの「かなり思いがけない装飾的、絵画的な秩序に対する関心」から生まれていて、ジャノーによれば、「最初の有資格者」で、「かくも美しき才能をもつ」ルグランとグレイが含まれている。シャロー派の「関心」に反して建築家になる術を心得、「美学ではなく、詩学の信奉者」であるシャローに対し、ルグランとグレイは、同じ地位を主張することはできなかった。ルグランとグレイは「装飾家、そしてただの装飾家」(デコラトゥール)にとどまっていたと見なすことによって、批評家ジャノーは単純化させすぎた分類作業に新しい段階をもたらすことができた。

実際のところ、それぞれの作品と過程を分析すれば明らかなことであるが、グループの形成や装飾スタイルの共有ばかりでなく、シャローの一派のリーダーとしての役割についても否定せざるをえない。

他の何人かはそれを理解していたのだが[14]、シャロー、ルグラン、グレイの各自の作品は徹底的に個性的で、それぞれの特徴によって輝いている。さらに、ジャノーがしたように、「建築家」(アルシテクト)のカテゴリーからグレイを締め出すことは、シャローとルグランと同様、家具と空間を同時に考え、生きている人間の身体のためにダイナミックな空間を創り出したグレイの作品に対する無理解を表明している。さらなる意外なことに、理解の欠如は、その当時、グレイもシャローのように南フランスで建てていたことからもわかる[15]。

したがって、シャローは名を冠した派閥の長というよりは、いわゆるモダニストの傾向をもつ芸術家(アルシテクト)=装飾家の世代の最先端の人物であり、とりわけ「大胆な推進者」[16]とみなされるべきである。

装飾家(デコラトゥール)はモダニズムの強い方針のもとに単発的に何回も集められた、ゆるやかな芸術家集団のなかでオーガナイザーもしくはプロモーターの役割を果たした。作家(クレアトゥール)たちは、みな近代的な人間と調和した世界をつくりたいという同じ願望をもつとしても、作品の特有のオリジナリティやアイデンティティによって識別されるものである。

当時のジャーナリズムによれば、「近代的なアパルトマンの応接と安らぎ」という展示をつくるために、シャローが「そこそこ大物の」10人ほどの芸術家を装飾家芸術家サロン(SAD)に集めたのは、1924年のことである。これらの「第一級の男女のメンバー」によって展示されたインテリアは、各自の際立って個人的な美学とこだわりの成果を明らかにしており、彼らの作風が一緒くたにされうるものではない、ということは明らかである。

表向きは批評家たちの大半を魅了し、ル・コルビュジエの興味を引いた装飾芸術再編の元締めであるにもかかわらず[17]、シャローは自らの影響と才能によってしかありえない芸術上の出来事を牽引するのではなく、もっぱら提唱者としてとりまとめ役に徹していたといわざるを得ない。「偉大なる伝統」であるリュルマンの作品がグレイの抽象芸術のような作品の共存し、力強い創造的な特異性と多様性が生み出され、批評家たちを驚かせたのである。シャローのすることは実際のところ、同じ頃に、サロ

38

005　肘掛け椅子のスケッチ

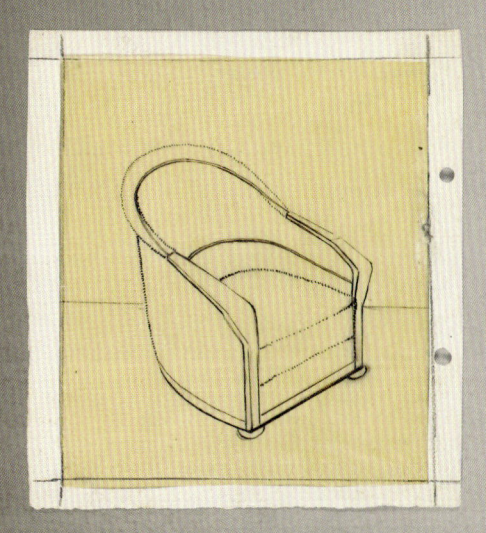

ref.006　六角形の肘掛け椅子｜撮影年不詳｜撮影：フォトグラフ・リラストリュシオン

082　テーブル付き長椅子｜撮影年・撮影者不詳

に数多くの展示者を集めようと誘ったマレ=ステヴァンスのような人物とはかけ離れている。

　イエール（コート・ダジュール）で、この建築家はヴィラ・ノアイユの構想に没頭していた。「ウィーン工房」のような職人と芸術家の協力を賛美し、協働の現場を愛した、正真正銘のチームリーダーであるマレ=ステヴァンスは、近代的でトータルなひとつの芸術作品を生むために、友人との協働者をはたらきかけた*18。ここでは、最も革新的な建築家=装飾家たちが部屋を提案し、インテリアデザイン一式を考案していた。ジュールダンはミニマリストの大時計を壁に備え付け、テオ・ファン・ドゥースブルフが「花の部屋」に色をつけ、ヴァン・ラブステイン（ファン・ラーフュスタイン）はゲストルームを考え、ジョ・ブルジョワはダイニングルームを完成させ、ガブリエル・ゲヴレキアンは「キュビスト」の庭園をつくった。シャローはノアイユ子爵の寝室を担当した。シャローはそこで、金属製のゴンドラのように吊られたベッドと、大きなガラス引戸によってオープンエアにもなる空間という、驚くべき考案をみせる。

　シャローはしばしばマレ=ステヴァンスのそばで、1920年代に開催された装飾芸術の大イベントに姿を見せるが、そのなかにはモダンなものと、あまりモダンではないものと両方があった。シャローの参加は1925年の博覧会の中でも内容の充実したものであった。マレ=ステヴァンスの観光館のための照明器具の制作者として、シャローはSADの「フランスの大使の館」の中の、とりわけマレ=ステヴァンスとジュールダンの隣で展示を行った。マレ=ステヴァンスがホールの設計をする一方で、ジュールダンは「家具を置かない」という原則に則ってスモークングラウンジとシャローの休憩室に接続している体操室を考案する。

　シャローとマレ=ステヴァンスは統率力があったのだが、奇しくもグレイのようなモダニストが不参加の理由はまだ解明されていない。かなりエリート向けの伝統主義者の傾向をもった現代の装飾芸術にのみ割り当てられた大イベントのなかで、モダニストの数はごくわずかで、彼らの失望感は大きかった。社会全体のための芸術の擁護者であるジュールダンは、博覧会を「効果なし」「意義もなし」と判断し、糾弾する*19。1924年のサロンのときと似たような気分で、ドミニク工房、ピエール・ルグラン、ジャン・ピュイフォルカ、レイモン・タンプリエとシャローは、ガリエラ美術館で一緒に展示を行うことを決心する。何のプログラムもなく、一派の長もなく、「五人組」のメンバーは個々に自分の近代的

な創造物を展示した。ジョルジュ・バスタール、ル・コルビュジエとピエール・ジャンヌレが後に加わり、「五人組」は1929年まで共同展示を続ける。その年は装飾芸術とSADによりフランスの近代性の歴史のなかで決定的な年となる。

サロン・ドートンヌの都市芸術部門のように、サロンに集められた展示物のなかに、もしくは1910–20年代の芸術家たちの協働を可能にしたイベントに、1920年代末にモダニストの芸術家の結集の前提と原因をみなければならない。

1928年のSADでは、ジョ・ブルジョワ、ルネ・エルブスト、シャルロット・ペリアン[20]が彼らのインテリアデザイン一式をとりまとめる。それは1924年にシャローとその仲間によって実現された行動のくりかえしであるが、総合という原則へ署名するようなものではなかった[21]。

シャローやマレ＝ステヴァンス、彼らの仲間と協働した現場や展覧会に慣れていたので、ジョ・ブルジョワはジュールダンの原則を自分のものにして、とりわけ限定された空間のインテリアデザインで有

079　書架机

026　肘掛け椅子と暖炉用品の空間展示｜1926年のSAD会場にて

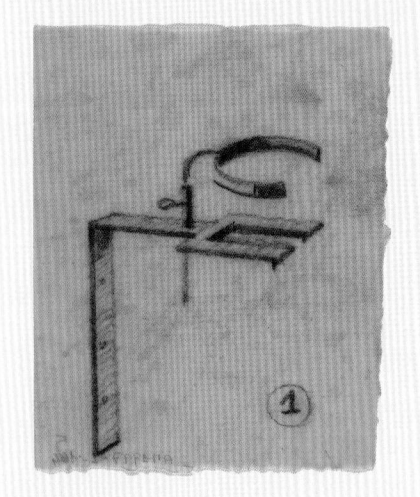

027　植木鉢入れ　透視図

025　暖炉のスクリーン｜1924年頃

024　暖炉用品　スコップと薪挟み｜1924年頃

名になる。同じ仲間で、「道の風景」に魅了されていたエルブストは、家具における工業素材の採用についてフランス的な探求を始める。新顔のシャルロット・ペリアンは、現代装飾芸術の感興のなかで仕事をした後、1927年末にル・コルビュジエとジャンヌレのところで家具を担当するため彼らの協力者になった。

　この新しい世代は、彼らの先輩の世代によって主導された探求の中に自分たちの研究を組み入れ、新しい住まい方についての考察に身を投じる。

　2年間のSADの活動に不満を示した後、シャローは仲間とともに愛着のある合同展示という形式に戻ることを望む。20名ほどの作家のなかから、最終的にはマレ=ステヴァンスに監修が任されることになる共同の展示スペースをシャローは要求した*22。しかし、SADは未来の出展者たちにはおそらく満足がいかないようなスペースを提案してきた。そこで、彼らは出展を断念し、大多数はサロンも脱退し、自分たちの団体、近代芸術家連合（UAM）をつくることになる。

　一般的に言われていることとは反対に、UAMの誕生にシャローの役割は不可欠のものであった。シャローはエルブストとマレ=ステヴァンスの近くにいて、SADでの合同展示ブースの計画の責任者であり、推進者であった。そして、出展の拒否とサロンとの分裂を導くことになる人間のひとりでもあり、その結果として、UAM設立の発起人でもあった。したがってシャローは、新しい芸術家の結集の基礎を固めた、本質的なムーヴメントの張本人のひとりなのである。

　UAMの設立メンバーでありながら、シャローは委員会メンバーにもならず、活動もせず、1929年の総会にもおそらく足を運んでいない。1930年のUAMの初めての展覧会に、シャローは参加するものの、招待会員という資格であった。シャローの芸術的な意図、組織をつくることを好む性格、社会にコミットした過去と相容れない不可解な身分と不在ぶりである。

　ところが、シャローの一通の手書きの手紙がこの不可解な空白状態の真実を明らかにする。1929年5月3日、UAMが設立の途上にあるとき、「沈思黙考し、重要な建設工事を完成するためにすべての活動から手を引くことが絶対に必要」*23 とシャローは伝えている。十分に参加することができないことを自覚し、シャローは「しばらくの間、どんなムーヴメントにも所属しない」*24 ことを選んだ。隠棲はそれゆえ、一時的なものであり、決断であった。変節を意味するどころではなく、反対に、信念の強さと重みを示している。「ご存じのように、私は何事も軽々しくはできないし、受動的に適当にかかわることを私は甘受できないだろう」とこの手紙に書いている*25。

　1931年、シャローは自分の友人たちが本当は決して離れていなかったことに気付く*26。シャローは、メンバーとして当然の地位を受け入れ*27、マレ=ステヴァンスのもとでできた、新しい執行委員会に加わった。関わり方は変わらない。この団体がその存在理由を見つけるのに苦労しているとき、明確な「目的」を定めるように仲間を仕向け、腹が立つような質問をすることもためらわず、「UAMは利益を共有するための集団なのか？ それとも思想を共にする集団なのか？」*28 と問いただした。とりわけ、1924年の展示の企画者は、より戦闘的で集団的なひとつの精神に向かってUAMを成長させようと試みた。2回目の展覧会の後、シャローはSADに失望した芸術家たちのグループの精神にふさわしい共同展示*29 を考えに入れた。やめたこともなければ、やめることもない「大胆な推進者」の役割を、再び引き受けるのである。

*1
ワルデマール・ジョルジュ「ピエール・シャローのインテリア」『芸術の愛』誌、1923年3月、pp.483–488

*2
『ラルルカン』誌、1923年6月

*3
ジョルジュ・ルフェーヴル「アール・デコ博において——何人かの装飾家の宣言」『ラール・ヴィヴァン』誌、no.12、1925年6月15日、pp.27–28

*4
アンリ・クルゾ「家具のアンサンブル」『フランスの芸術の再生と贅沢品の産業』誌、1925年8月、pp.349–362
ギヨーム・ジャノー「アール・デコ博に関する序論　近代精神についての考察」『アール・エ・デコラシオン[芸術と装飾]』誌、1925年5月、p.136

*5
レイモン・シューブ「序文」(アンリ・クルゾの中)「近代的な鉄工芸」新シリーズ、エディション・ダール、シャルル・モロー出版、パリ、出版年なし、頁番号なし

*6
アンリ・クルゾ「近代的なフランスの家具」前掲書

*7
ギヨーム・ジャノー「アール・デコ博に関する序論　近代精神についての考察」前掲書

*8
アイリーン・グレイは《夜》という題のついたてをSADにて展示している。エリーズ・クーリング「アイリーン・グレイと装飾芸術：もうひとつのまなざし」『ファブリカ』誌、no.4、2010年12月、p.114–143 参照。

*9
エリザベート・ド・グラモン「ミス・アイリーン・グレイの漆」『芸術の一頁』誌、1922年2月

*10
イヴァノエ・ランボソン「トゥールのグラン・オテル」『アール・エ・デコラシオン』誌、1928年2月、pp.33–39。ジャン・バドヴィチ「アイリーン・グレイの芸術」『ウェンディンゲン』誌、no.6、1924年、pp.12–15。ガストン・ヴァレンス「ピエール・ルグランのいくつかのアンサンブル」『ラムール・ド・ラール[芸術の愛]』誌、1924年、pp.401–408

*11
ガストン・ヴァレンス「ピエール・シャローの近代的精神」前掲書

*12
ベルナルト・ベイフォットがピエール・シャローについて語った「人が生活する環境の創造における、『人間』というものの根本的な重要性を彼は深く理解していた」という言葉は、ルネ・エルブストによって『ひとりの発明家、建築家ピエール・シャロー』(サロン・デ・ザール・メナジェ—UAM出版、パリ、1954年、p.12) の中で引用された。

*13
一部の人々にとってシャローは、彼ひとりでひとつの方向性なのである。ワルデマール・ジョルジュ「ピエール・シャローのインテリア」前掲書

*14
アルベルト・ブケン、「サロン・ドートンヌ1923年」翻訳文書、アイリーン・グレイ・アーカイヴ、ヴィクトリア＆アルバート博物館、ロンドン。クリスチャン・ゼルヴォス「現代芸術の今日的傾向 I. 家具：昨日と今日」『芸術雑誌』誌、1925年1月、pp.68–75

*15
ジャン・バドヴィチとの協働。ヴィラ「E1027」、ロクブリュヌ＝カップ＝マルタン

*16
リュシアン・サンティーニ「芸術家装飾家協会サロン」『近代建設』誌、1924年7月27日、p.505

*17
ル・コルビュジエはこの「アンサンブルは重要で興味深い」と判断している。しかし、作家たちの「装飾家」過ぎるエスプリについては批判的なままである——「魅力のある、知的な椅子、しかしおそらく冗漫である。肘掛け椅子も同様である。椅子と肘掛け椅子はピカソ、レジェ、ドゥラン、ユトリロ、リプシッツを意気消沈させるとしても、椅子と肘掛け椅子はやはり型破りで大胆なものである」。ポール・ブラール (＝ル・コルビュジエ)「グラン・パレの装飾芸術のサロン」『レスプリ・ヌーヴォー』誌、no.24、1924年7月、頁番号なし

*18
ガラス工芸作家ルイ・バリレ、彫刻家ロランスとリプシッツ、金銀細工師クロディウス・リノシエ等

*19
フランシス・ジュールダン『芸術的生活年報』1925年、pp.494–495

*20
ジャン・フケ、ジェラール・サンド、レイモン・ビュイフォルカ、ジャン・リュスとヴァン・ニコラ社と協働した。

*21
彼らのアパルトマンは、実際のところ、個人の展示を並べ置いたものである。

*22
「病気によって、彼はこのアンサンブルを監修することを断念する」。セシル・タジャン「1929年　SADとUAMの分裂」美術史修士論文、ソルボンヌ・パリ第4大学、2005年、p.9

*23
ピエール・シャローはその当時、ガラスの家の建設に没頭しているのである。

*24
1929年5月3日付のピエール・シャローの手紙、個人的書類「ピエール・シャロー」、UAMアーカイヴ、装飾芸術美術館図書館

*25
シャローは「私はあなた方と連帯したままである。そして、私はあなた方と同様、ひどく失敗したとみなしている、SADから脱退するという確約をあなた方に繰り返す。心の底からあなた方とともに」と付け加えている (前掲資料)。反面、シャローは五人組の「解散」を容認している。

*26
1930年3月3日の会合にシャローは出席している。総会議事録、UAMアーカイヴ、装飾芸術美術館図書館

*27
1930年12月 (前掲資料)

*28
「シャローにはそれがひとつの思想的結集のように思えている。というのも、その結集には、自分達より経済的にも知名度的にも優れている芸術家装飾家 (協会) との分裂という目的がありそうだからだ」委員会会合、1931年7月2日 (前掲資料)

*29
委員会会合、1931年7月2日、同年7月11日、同年10月14日 (前掲資料)

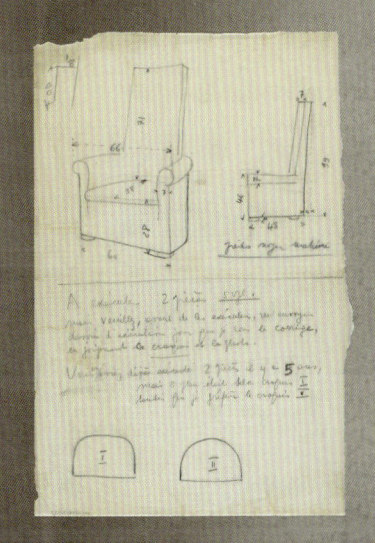

018

018　ハイバックの肘掛け椅子
透視図、立面図｜1924–1927年

019　炉辺椅子｜1930年｜撮影者不詳

019

出 発 ── 家具デザインからの始動
THE EARLY YEARS ｜ LES DEBUTS

シャローは英国の家具会社ワリング・アンド・ギローのパリ支店で働き、第一次世界大戦後に独立する。1919年のサロン・ドートンヌに発表した診察室のインテリアデザインが実質的なデビュー作である。依頼主は、のちにパトロン的存在となる医師のダルザス夫妻。洗練されたスタイル、吟味された素材とシンプルで明確なラインといった作風は、すでに顕著である。シャローはデザインだけではなく新しい材料の研究、空間の使い方の提案などに取り組む一貫した姿勢によって、「装飾家(デコラトゥール)」としてではなく「建設者(コンストラクトゥール)」として当初より認識されている。なかでも、前衛芸術家たちとの交流、そして優れた職人との出会いが、シャローを新しいデザイン言語の創造へと導く。

LES DEBUTS

シャローとリュルサの協働作品

長椅子（1921年）と
肘掛け椅子（1924-1927年）

長椅子（1921年）とハイバックの肘掛け椅子（1924年）はタピストリー作家ジャン・リュルサとピエール・シャローの協働を象徴する2作である。共通の知人である医師ジャン・ダルザスを介して始まったふたりの関係は、シャロー本人のキャリアの非常に早い時期に始まったが、その後も途絶えることなく続いて息の長い友情が育まれた。この協働作品は批評家たちから歓迎され、シャローが初めて雑誌で紹介されるきっかけとなった[*]。

肘掛け椅子のデザインにはさまざまな準拠が混在している。すなわちプロポーションの点では中世風であり、肘掛けについては19世紀調であり、背もたれの高さはマッキントッシュばりである。しかし、たとえそうであっても、このふたつの家具には「純化された形状」という共通の特徴があり、椅子のシルエットと張地の色彩表現のコントラストが際立っている。

ふたりの共作ではない場合、パリ郊外のヴィルフリクスのベルンハイム邸、ガラスの家、ドレフュス家のアパルトマンなどでは、シャローの家具類はリュルサが手がけた壁画やついたての前でくっきり映えている。この長椅子と肘掛け椅子以外でも、リュルサのタピストリー（つづれ織り）がシャローの椅子の座面と背もたれやスツールの丸座を覆うようになっている。またリュルサは1930年代終わりごろ、ハイバックの肘掛け椅子の制作用に、タピストリーのカルトン（原寸大の下絵）を再び提供する機会を得ることとなる[**]。

[*]
ミシェル・デュフェ著「二人の近代的装飾家、シャローとリュルサ」、『現代文学美術選集 フイエ・ダール』第1号、1921年10-11月、pp.39-46

[**]
とりわけインテリアデザイナーのルイ・モレがスイスで行った複数の制作のため（ルイ・モレ財団史料館）

022　ミシェル・デュフェ著、ジャン・リュルサによる挿図「二人の近代的装飾家、シャローとリュルサ」『現代文学美術選集　フイエ・ダール』誌1921年10-11月、第10号より、ルシアン・フォーゲル出版、パリ

022

022

017

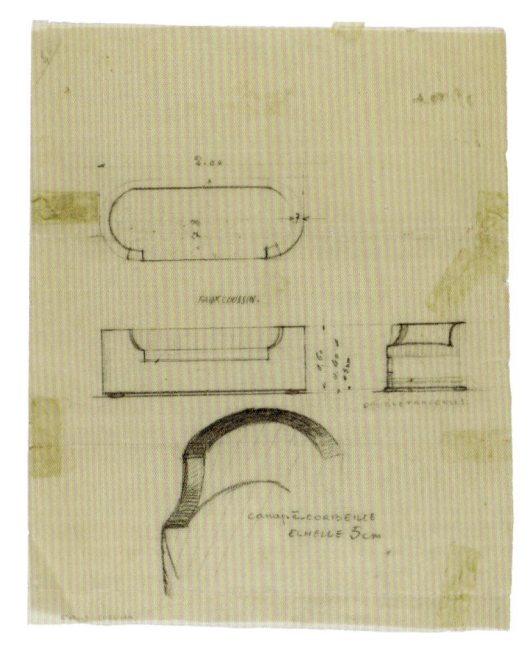

016

017　ジャン・リュルサ｜タピストリー下図

016　アンティーク調ソファー　平面図、立面図

021　柳製の家具のある子供部屋、第15回
芸術家装飾家サロン（SAD）出品作｜1923年｜撮影者不詳

021

第Ⅰ部　　出発──家具デザインからの始動
PART I　　THE EARLY YEARS

LES DEBUTS

アラバスター製
三角プレートの照明器具

修道女（1923年）

フロアスタンド、テーブルランプ、およびベッドサイドランプの3タイプからなる照明器具の《修道女》シリーズの頭部には、アラバスター製（雪花石膏）三角プレートの2枚もしくは4枚が組み合わさる形で載っている。1923年に制作された《修道女》モデルは大きさも3種あり、支柱の材質としては金属または木材が使われている。

木材タイプでは主にキューバ産マホガニーを使用しているが、テーブルランプ用にはカエデを使用している。どちらも大きさに幾つかのバリエーションがあるものの、最小のモデルを別とすれば、やはり材を曲げてつくった襞のある円錐形のデザインになっている。すなわち、金属タイプではもっと自然に表現されるデザインと同一である。

金属タイプのほうも、選択した彫刻方法や技術手順の成果によってやはり複数のバリエーションがある。金属タイプの《修道女》はピエール・シャローの創造力と、ダルベの工房の製作力との間で実現した協働考案の一例である。この点は、アンドレ・ダルベが説明している。

「ピエール・シャローから依頼される作業の中には、かなりの機転と創意を発揮しないと成し遂げられないものがありました。湾曲した金属板で円錐の脚部がつくられている《修道女》と呼ばれる照明器具の場合がまさにそうでした。例えば、しっかりとした円錐のベースとなるようなカットラインを見出すために、水桶の中に脚部を入れてやりました。ランプにふさわしい高さが水面の位置になるように工夫したのです。そうして円錐の水面の濡れ跡で脚部のカットラインを決めたのです」*

なお、《修道女》シリーズの中には羊皮紙や布地のシェードになっているものも存在する。前者の例としては1923年に制作されたテーブルランプがあり、後者の例としては、1927年に制作されたフロアスタンド（グラン・オテル・ド・トゥール内）がある。

*
ベルナール・ボシェが1990年12月28日に行った、ルイ・ダルベの子息アンドレ・ダルベ氏との対談

036 壺（フロアスタンド《修道女》と同じ形状による）｜1923年頃
035 フロアスタンド《修道女》｜1923年

036

035

48

LES DEBUTS

アラバスター製
四分円形プレートの照明器具

テーブルランプ（1923年）

　四分円（クオーターサークル）というよくある単純な幾何学形が、シャローの探求と金物職人ルイ・ダルベの制作の出発点になった。その際、ダルベは台と枠をつくっただけでなく、アラバスターの大きさを決め、調整も行っている*。

　四分円形プレートの一番簡単な使い方は、その1枚を電球の前に扇にするウォールランプモデルや、2枚を重ね合わせたモデルで示されている。そして、バリエーションの拡大作業の次段階としては、2枚をつなぎ合わせて角度をつけたペアにして、あたかも蝶の2枚羽に見立てるやり方である。このペア方式はシンプルタイプや重層タイプを含めて、いろいろなウォールランプモデルを生むだけでなく、ひいては3枚のプレートの間にもうひとつのペアを3つ入り込んだシャンデリアにも通じることにもなる（このシャンデリアモデルは1923年のサロン・ドートンヌに出品された）。

　このペアの上下を逆にすると、テーブルランプの2つのバージョンや腕木付きウォールランプにも使える。この場合、シェード部分の形状は可動性の導入に見合ったものになっている。すなわち腕木に沿った移動、本体部分の回転、及び折り曲げた三角金属薄板からなる脚部の支柱回転などの可動である。

　当該のテーブルランプモデルには2つのバージョンがある。1つは1923年のサロン・ドートンヌに出品されたランプシェードで、もう1つは縦管とバランス棒からなる支柱付きモデルである。さらに後者には、1924年に制作された子供部屋用の木製タイプや、散光部分だけでなく金属反射体も備えたタイプがある。

*
パリ国立近代美術館（産業創造センター）、カンディンスキー図書館、ルイ・ダルベ・アーカイブ

039　テーブルランプ｜1923年

040　照明器具のシェードのために切り出した
アラバスターのプレート｜1923年頃

LES DEBUTS

アラバスター製プレートの
照明器具「鞘翅」・「庇ブロック」

アラバスター部品（1923年）

シャローは、ランプ類を創作する際に通常のシェードの使用をやめて、ランプの光にアラバスター製プレートを用いるようになる。1923–1932年にかけて制作されたすべての照明器具は、アラバスター製プレートの形状の違いによって大きく4つのグループに分かれる。

四分円（クォーターサークル）と三角形に加えて、長方形もシャローがよく使った単純な幾何学形である。この長方形プレートを複数並置して、「リュッシュ（蜂の巣箱）」（1924年作）と称するウォールランプの照明装置ができ上がる。その大きさは用途によって異なり、普通はまっすぐの横長になっているがアーチ形になることもある。壁の非常に高い位置にこれを設置して、モールディングの代わりとする場合も少なくない。また、天井に付けられると、まるで天井の窪みに嵌め込まれているかのように見える。

他方、シャローはこうした最も単純な使い方とは反対に、構成を工夫して多面のプレートから光の回折現象を生じさせるようにもしている。例えば、8枚のアラバスター製プレートからなるシーリングライト（天井灯）や、昆虫の「鞘翅」のウォールランプである。3枚のプレートからできている「鞘翅」モデルは、プレートの向きが反対の2バージョンがある。

上記の各照明装置で、単純な幾何学形プレートを複雑に組み合わせて散光させるようになっているが、それらとは異なり、「庇ブロック」モデルの場合はアラバスターの鉱物特性を一層生かしている。すなわち、発光体の電球を覆うブロックが基本になっている。このブロックは切り出しだけではつくれないので、複数のプレートを継ぎ合わせて構成されており、やはり厳密な幾何学構造ではあるが、見た目は三角プリズムに似た単純な立体になっている。

041 照明器具のために「庇ブロック」の形に切り出したアラバスターのプレート｜1923年頃

042 照明器具のためにL字形に切り出したアラバスターのプレート｜1923年頃

042

041

043 「庇ブロック」モデルの照明器具がとりつけられたサロン　ロベール・ダルザスのアパルトマン｜1926年

LES DEBUTS

「扇」の形態

書斎机とローテーブル（1923–1924年）

046

046　電話機用の扇状ローテーブル｜撮影年・撮影者不詳
047　書斎机、椅子
044　扇状テーブル　平面図、立面図、アクソメ図｜1923年

047

シャローは、デザイナーとしての全キャリアを通じて扇の形状に愛着を抱いていた。しかし、彼が個々の作品に採用した扇の着想は、自らつくった家具類に由来するものなのか、それともインテリアデザインに由来するものなのかははっきりしない。シャローは1923年のサロン・ドートンヌに婦人用の小サロン（ブドワール）のパネルを出品した際に、初めて扇の配置を取り入れている。一方、当時の複数の出版物を見る限り、この形を取り入れたテーブルは数年後（1924年と1926年）になってようやくアパルトマンに設えられるようになっている。

このテーブルは2–4枚の折りたたみ式のパーツを含むことがある。曲面の縦材と三角形の天板からできている各パーツは大きさが少しずつ異なっていて、それぞれが入れ子式に嵌め込まれており、結合部を金具で留めている。この金具はダルベの工房で製造されたものであるおかげで、その製造年月日を正確に特定することができる。なお、「電話機用の扇状ローテーブル」の場合は、脚部の代わりに直方体の支柱が付いている点が特徴になっている。この直方体の支柱には、電話帳を置くことができるように長方形の空洞が空けられている。そして、支柱の一番高い面に電話機が置けるようになっている。

シャローの扇の使用に関連して次のコメントがある。

「シャローは玄関をうまく活用することに秀でており、扇状の扉で隔離した隅を必ず設けるようにしていた。そのドアの内側には化粧台や書棚や便利箪笥などがある。（中略）シャローの手による複数の台を持つ小テーブルは、我々の祖母世代の入れ子式テーブルに比肩するもので、それはちょうど、ダンスの"チャールストン"が昔のダンスの"ボストン"に比肩するのと同様である［訳注］。したがって、人の距離を縮めてくれるが神経もすり減らす電話機がそこに載っているかどうかはともかく、数多くの玄関でこういう小テーブルに出会いたいと皆思うことだろう」*

ピエール・シャローはその後も一度ならず扇の原理を取り入れるようになるが、以前とは異なり、金属を素材とする「プロペラ」風テーブルにおいてそれを具体化させていくことになる。

*
アーネスト・ティスランド、『ラール・ヴィヴァン［生きている芸術］』、1926年2月15日、p.148

［訳注］
「チャールストン」は、1920年代にヨーロッパで流行したアメリカの黒人文化のなかから生まれたダンスでテンポが速い。「ボストン」は1882年に遡るダンスでゆっくりしたワルツのテンポで踊る。

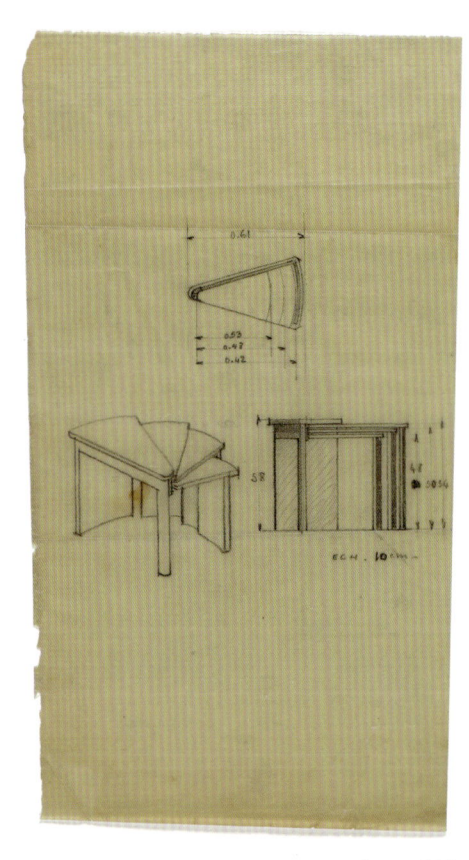

LES DEBUTS

ラニック家のアパルトマン

パリ、アンリ・マルタン通り
72番地（1923–1924年）

ref. 002

ref. 003

048　小サロン　ラニック家のアパルトマン｜『住宅芸術』誌より、春夏号、1926年、アルベール・モランセ出版、パリ

ref. 002, 003　ブリッジゲームのためのテーブル、通称「ハンカチ」（002 閉じたところ／003 開いたところ）｜撮影：アトリエ・シャロー

048

ここではインテリアデザイナーで建築家のフランシス・ジュールダンが食堂の装飾を任される一方で、シャローはアパルトマンのその他の部分を取り仕切るように依頼された[*]。このアパルトマンの改修の仕事は、シャローの経歴においては格別に重要である。その理由としては、第一にルイ・ダルベとの協働が初めて本格的に発揮されたからであり、第二に可動性に関するシャローの研究成果である配置方法を試す場にもなったからである。

この仕事では、ダルベの金物製作の技術は本来の家具にはまだ採用されていないが、照明器具としては、ランプ「リュッシュ（蜂の巣箱）」、吊りランプ「フラワー」、ウォールランプ「庇ブロック」、付属品類としてはフラワースタンド「三脚」、壁掛け棚、壁につくりつけた回転プレート（ベッドサイドテーブルの代わりになる）、暖房ラジエーターカバー、及びカーテンロッドなどには常に役立っていた。しかも、ダルベの技術は小サロンの可動部分をつくる際にもひと役買っていたようだ。

ここの小サロンはまさに本格的な創作品であった。そのユニークな空間をうまく処理することによって、気品さえ漂わせる部屋に仕上げられているからである。しかも、そこからそれぞれの部屋に通じる大事な中継ポイントとしての機能もきちんと維持している。シャローはそのために、壁の曲面の制約を上手に利用して、むしろカーブを部屋全体にまで広げて完璧な円筒にした。円形の天井には複数の梁が中心部からスポーク状に広がり、その中心部は、小サロンへの入口として扇状に開く間仕切りの回転軸にもなっている[**]。

ここには、折りたたみ式の通称「ハンカチ」という名の遊戯テーブルが、空間に抑揚をつけるシンボルとして無理なく収まっている。

---

[*]
シャローは作業を進めるに際して友人の彫刻家ジャック・リプシッツと組み、リプシッツの複数の作品、彫刻類、及び付属品類を全体的に配置している。

[**]
シャローは、1923年のサロン・ドートンヌで発表した婦人用の小サロン（ブドワール）用に工夫したやり方をここでも踏襲している。

LES DEBUTS

モチーフ：楽器の「リラ」

長椅子MP215と肘掛け椅子SN37
（1923年頃）

1923年頃のシャローは、スツール、安楽椅子、各種肘掛け椅子、および長椅子を含めてさまざまな椅子のモデルを制作している。そのいずれにおいても前脚部が楽器のリラ（竪琴）の形に刳ってある点からすると、これらの椅子は同一の家具グループに属しているとまでは言えないまでも、少なくとも同一の家具の製作時期に属していた。すなわち1925年に、「フランスの大使の館」の「書架のある執務室」で展示されることになる時期である。

初期の肘掛け椅子の中には、前脚部がリラの形でありながら刳り形のないタイプがあった。しかし、ほどなくしてどの椅子に対しても、刳り形によって洗練されたタッチが加えられるようになっていく。執務用肘掛け椅子や安楽椅子は「ゴンドラ」の形をしていたが、背もたれがまっすぐになっている別タイプの椅子もある。この違いは肘掛けの形状や構成にも関連している。椅子の素材として最もよく使われた樹木種はブラジル紫檀材やクルミ材である（ただし骨組み部分はブナ材）。椅子の張地としては皮革やビロードが用いられ、テキスタイル・デザイナーのエレーヌ・アンリが描いた模様入りの布地が使用される場合もあった。

また、二つの角度に背もたれを動かせるリクライニング式のユニークな肘掛け椅子もある。その仕組みは非常に単純である。すなわち、リクライニングヒンジが背後にあって、背もたれの高さを調節できるようになっている。これらのモデルによって、シャローの椅子類は、初期の作品にはなかったような軽快さと優雅さを獲得するようになる。シャローの初期の肘掛け椅子はどこか重々しくて、あまりにも古風な規準を採用していたのだった。

050　肘掛け椅子《SN37》｜1923年頃

051 長椅子と肘掛け椅子
平面図、立面図、透視図 | 1923年頃

052 光沢仕上げの梨材とキルティング・サテンを
用いた肘掛け椅子と長椅子　平面図、立面図

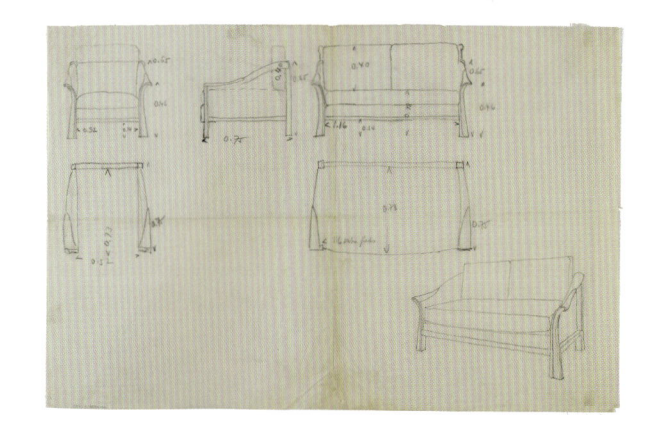

051

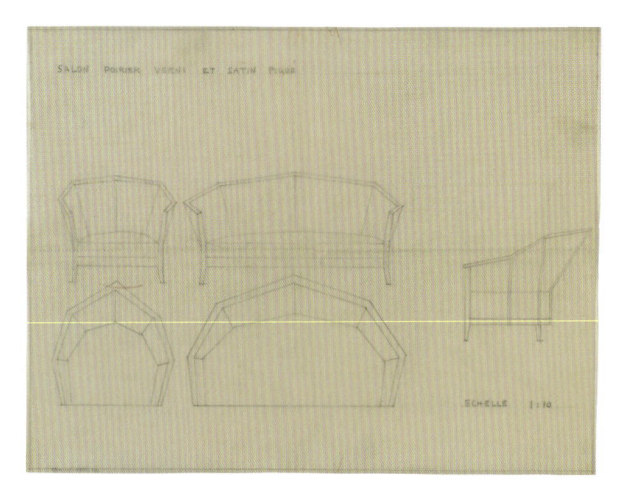

052

ref.005　長椅子《MP215》 | 1923年頃

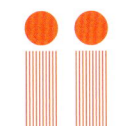

確 立 —— 作風と名声の形成
THE CONSECRATION | LA CONSECRATION

1925年のパリ現代産業装飾芸術国際博覧会（アールデコ博）において、シャローの社会的評価は確立される。博覧会の目玉であり、SADが主催する「フランスの大使の館」において大使の執務室を担当する。前年のSADでは、モダニストの作家たちのグループが展示を実現させていた。しかし、アールデコ博はフランスの伝統に基づいた装飾芸術を喧伝する一大祝祭であったため、主要なモダニストたちが不参加となった。そのなかでもシャローは、プレスや新しい顧客の注目を集めることに成功する。こうしてシャローは徐々にアールデコ様式を脱し、家具と空間全体との調和を考えていくなかで建築的な思考を深めていく。

054　カタログ『フランスの大使の館：芸術家装飾家サロン』より、パリ現代産業装飾芸術国際博覧会、1925年、シャルル・モロー出版、パリ

LA CONSECRATION

書架のある執務室

パリ現代産業装飾芸術国際博覧会
SADのパヴィリオン
「フランスの大使の館」(パリ1925年)

「フランスの大使の館」というのが、SADが博覧会参加に際して設定したテーマであった。ピエール・シャローはコンペの結果として、建築家シャルル・プリュメの担当パヴィリオンで「書架のある執務室」の制作を任されることになった。この執務室についてガストン・ヴァレンヌは次のように述べている。

「フランシス・ジュールダンが手掛けた独創的なスモーキングラウンジは、淡黄色の美しい色調で塗られていて、居心地の良さだけは類がなく、必要なものを何でも揃えている。このスモーキングラウンジは、ピエール・シャローの"書架のある執務室"へ通じている。この執務室は巧妙さと、奇抜さと、大胆さとを備えた傑作である。その巧妙さはめったにお目にかかれるものではなく、その奇抜さには意外性と論理性の両方が満ちあふれており、さらにその大胆さは、実用性に対する鋭敏な感性ゆえに程よく抑制が効いている」*

この執務室に対してはたくさんの報告やコメントがなされたが、そのどれもが褒め称える内容であった。批評家ガブリエル・ローゼンタールは以下のように評している。

「光が差し込んでくる白い円蓋の下で、机が部屋の真ん中に陣取っている。その円蓋は開閉可能な天井で日中は隠れて見えない。部屋の左右では、溝の上を滑らせて動かせる本棚に書物が並んでいる。巧みに考案されたこの可動式本棚によって本来の執務室が外から遮断され、独立した小さな秘書室を2カ所の隅に設けることができる。木繊維が交互になっているヤシ材が、場に応じて大小の材料として使われて全体をつくり上げている。何の装飾も施されていない壁面はこの内装材の下に隠れて見えない。入口のドアには、ブロケード織の絹のドアカーテンが掛かっている。そのドアカーテンの控えめな光沢によって木材の調和がうまく途切れず続いており、よくある図書室のごとくすべての壁が本棚で覆われている。シャローの執務室はこの種の探究でなし得た成果として、最も斬新で最も創意に富んだ成功作のひとつであると考えることができる。そこでは、装飾家としての資質と建築家としての資質が同時に発揮されている。この両方の資質を兼ね備えている点こそがシャローの特権なのだ」**

この円形空間や扇のパネル類は、1923年のサロン・ドートンヌで発表した婦人用の小サロンとともに始まった探究をさらに推し進めて、その内容を豊かにするものであった。シャローのこの探究は、翌1924年に手がけたラニック家のアパルトマンの小サロンでも受け継がれている。1924年の素案を見ると、プロジェクト当初からシャローがこのやり方を選択していたことがわかる***。

この執務室の場合、シャローのこれまでの制作物とは異なって空間全体は閉じていないが、可動式の本棚が「厚みのある壁」の役割を演じている。しかもこれは、技術力の高さの点で、単純な縦パネルの間仕切りをはるかに凌駕するものだ。一方、上述の「円蓋」のほうは完全に閉じるのに必要な数の天井パネルを備えていて、あたかもカメラの絞りのような様相を呈している。

本プロジェクトにはルイ・ダルベ、エレーヌ・ランティエ(エレーヌ・アンリ)、ジャン・リュルサ、及びピエール・ルグランらが協力者として名を連ね、ジャック・リプシッツのブロンズ彫刻も展示されている。なお、全体の構成要素の一部が、1927年に別の家具類を伴ってマルサン・パヴィリオンに再登場した。現在では、すべてが国家コレクションに属していて、パリ装飾芸術美術館で常設展示されている。

*
ガストン・ヴァレンヌ著「装飾美術展、フランスの家具類」、『アール・エ・デコラシオン[芸術と装飾]』、1925年7–12月、p.4。ヴァレンヌの論考1ページ目にはシャロー作品の全体画像が掲載されている。
**
ガブリエル・ローゼンタール著「パリ現代産業装飾芸術国際博覧会」、『ラール・ヴィヴァン』no.20、1925年10月15日、p.17
***
パリ装飾芸術美術館デッサン室の保管資料を参照

053 フランスの大使のための書架のある執務室 | 1925年
撮影：フォトグラフ・リラストリュシオン

第I部　　確立——作風と名声の形成
PART I　　THE CONSECRATION

LA CONSECRATION

体操室の休憩室

パリ現代産業装飾芸術国際博覧会
SADのパヴィリオン
「フランスの大使の館」(パリ1925年)

056 体操室(手前)と休憩室(左奥)
カタログ『フランスの大使の館:SAD』より、
パリ現代産業装飾芸術国際博覧会
1925年、シャルル・モロー出版、パリ

フランシス・ジュールダンはスモーキングラウンジと階上の体操室を手掛けた。その体操室に隣接する限られたスペースに、シャローは休憩室をつくった。簡素なスモーキングラウンジやスパルタ調の厳格さが感じられる体操室とは対照的に、休憩室はいろいろな物が置かれていて活気があり、温かい印象で入りやすい雰囲気になっている。

収納家具、テーブル、スツール(ジャン・リュルサのデザインによる布で覆われている)など明るい色の木製の品々は第1世代の家具類に属しているが、新しい工夫が凝らされているのは、ルイ・ダルベとの協働の成果である吊りベッドと壁の配置である。この吊りベッドは、設置場所と揺れ具合の希望に応じて、留め方にさまざまなバリエーションがある。例えばヴィラ・ノアイユ(シャルル・ド・ノアイユ別邸)の屋根つきの屋外スペースやここのように、ベッドを吊り下げるU字形金具が2つあるもの、ノレ通りのシャロー家のように4つの固定ポイントがあるもの、あるいは、壁に固定した腕木付き支柱にポールを組み合わせたものなどのバリエーションである。

他方、壁の配置に関してもシャローは新たな考案をしている。それはまるで、用途を極限まで突き詰めた造り付け家具のようである。すなわち、ここでは壁の機能が家具の機能を完全に代替してしまっている。この代替原理はあたかも、壁の表面が他から切り離されて自立性を獲得したことに依拠するかのようである。壁についている錬鉄製の構造物には照明器具が組み込まれていて、インテリア用の布地を張ったり絵画を掛けたりできる。シャローは布地と絵画との組み合わせを普通にやっていたのであるが、そうと知らなければ、人々は調整可能かつ移転可能な現代ミュゼオグラフィーの先取りを見出した気になるかもしれない。

055　吊りベッド　透視図｜1925年頃

055

第I部　　確立──作風と名声の形成
PART I　　THE CONSECRATION

058　食堂椅子｜撮影：アトリエ・ピエール・シャロー

057　コロニアルスタイルの住まいの食堂、インドシナ・パヴィリオン、SAD、パリ現代産業装飾芸術国際博覧会、1925年、『アール・エ・デコラシオン』誌｜撮影：フォトグラフィ・ド・レブ

058

057

LA CONSECRATION

コロニアルスタイルの住まいの食堂

パリ現代産業装飾芸術国際博覧会
インドシナ・パヴィリオン（パリ1925年）

「インドシナ・パヴィリオンでは、貴重な木材でつくった食堂を展示しています」。博覧会への参加についてジャーナリストから質問されたとき、シャローはインドシナ・パヴィリオンに関してこう述べただけでそれ以上コメントせず、主要作である「書架のある執務室」のことを主な話題にした*。他方、批評家のギヨーム・ジャノーは、このパヴィリオンに対しては照明器具のことしか関心を示さずにこう発言している。

「アラバスター製プレートでつくられているランプはまず扇状に配置され、次に巨大なバラの花びらのように各面が互いに重なり合っている」**

この作品については、デッサン（その一つはカラー）や写真などのさまざまな資料が今日まで残っている。それら各種の資料間における相違点と共通点を検討すると、シャローの仕事の内容が明らかにできる。まず、厚紙に印刷されたものと1枚の写真との間に類似があってもほとんど驚くに値しない。と言うのも、厚紙のほうは写真からつくられて雑誌などに掲載され、色彩に関する情報の欠如を補う役割を担ったからである。しかし逆に、デッサン間の相違を検討することからは、制作プロジェクトの変遷を明るみにすることができる。

シャローはここのインテリアに純粋さと軽快さをもたらそうとして、ディテールにこだわっている。例えば、4つの天幕の間に見える白い天井から照明器具が吊り下げられている。またこの食堂には、彫刻家シャナ・オルロフの2つの母子像が食器棚両脇の石柱の上に載っているほか、1枚のタピストリーも掛けられている。加えて、ドアと通路は同じ高さで四方の壁をつたっているカーテンで隠されるようになっている。さらには、床には幾何学模様のパターンがある。これを十分に表現するために、カラーの印刷が必要になったのだった（それによって実際よりもよく見えてしまうかもしれないとしても）。

*
ジョルジュ・ルフェーヴル、『ラール・ヴィヴァン』no.12、1925年6月15日、p.28
**
ギヨーム・ジャノー著「パリ現代産業装飾芸術国際博覧会」、『ボザール』no.12、1925年6月15日、p.185

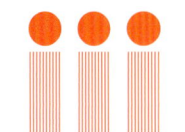

飛躍——インテリアから建築へ
THE APOGEE | L'ESSOR

アールデコ博以降、インテリアの仕事が増えるなかで特筆すべき作品が2つある。「レファンベール夫人」邸のインテリアデザインと「グランド・オテル・ド・ツール」のエントランスロビーの改修である。前者は、親しくしていたモダニズムの建築家ロベール・マレ＝ステヴァンスが、パリ16区に手がけた邸宅である。マレ＝ステヴァンスの代表作となったこの邸宅で、シャローはインテリアの一部を任される。後者では大きな空間を初めて手がけていた。いずれの作品でもさまざまな新しい家具が考案され、インテリア・デザインと建築の融合が図られている。装飾を否定したモダニズムの建築とは異なるシャロー独自の美学が具現されている。

059 化粧台 | 1925–1927年

L'ESSOR

ウルマン夫人の寝室

化粧台と収納家具（1925–1927年）

ref.007

ref.007　収納家具｜1925–1927年
061　化粧台とスツール｜撮影：テレーズ・ボニー
062　化粧台　透視図
063　テーブル　透視図｜1925年

061

062

063

060　化粧台のスツール｜1925–1927年

シャローが携わった20数件のインテリア整備の仕事においては、さまざまなタイプの類型が自然な形で現れている。書斎が男性の顧客との関連が強いのに対して、夫婦の寝室を含めて寝室は女性的であることが非常に多い。そして、ベッド脇の枕元の象徴的な家具は化粧台であり、また必ずそこになければならない家具は収納家具である。

　まず、一般の化粧台の特徴としては、大きくないこと、鏡が付いていること、整理引出しが付いていること、それに自由に物が置ける台が付いていることなどであるが、シャローの化粧台はこれらの特徴を保持しつつも旧来のつくり方から解放されている。すなわち、シャローが顧客のウルマン夫人に提案した化粧台はかなり簡素でまた少々厳かである。奥まで伸びる脚部はシンプルで、なめらかな面である。いくつかある引き出しがアクセントになっている。鏡は、円形、卵形、小ぶりの正方形などの通常の形状は採用されず、化粧台の横幅いっぱいの長方形が用いられている。この化粧台の凝ったところは、天板をなしている木材種のコントラストにあり、カエデ材でできた中央部分が、外周のマホガニー材からくっきりと際立っている。

　次に、収納家具も同じ材種のコンビネーションを採り入れ、外側全体がマホガニー材、内側がカエデ材になっている。こうした優美な調子の対照や、象牙の鍵などのディテールの追求により、収納家具が持つ決まりきった機能性が和らげられている。

　この化粧台と収納家具という2つの純化された家具からは、その後の木と金属を組み合わせた家具が示す先鋭性を予告している。

L'ESSOR

レファンベール邸

パリのマレ＝ステヴァンス通り4-6（1927年）

建築家ロベール・マレ＝ステヴァンスが手掛けたレファンベール邸2階の装飾は、ピエール・シャローに委ねられた。応接間と食堂と寝室は直方体であるが、シャローはそこに曲面や凹凸を導入していく。

まず応接間では、曲面の書架と化粧天井に囲まれた入口をつくるだけにとどめた。しかし、壁に一列に設置した金属製ウォールランプが、部屋の雰囲気をそれとなく引き立たせている。そして、このウォールランプは、天井から吊るされている2つのシーリングライト「フラワー」が生み出す調子とうまく呼応している。

次に食堂では、シャローならではの工夫を天井に加えた。すなわち、幾何学構成を備えた面や辺をたくさん増やし、天井隅のL字形ケースの中にランプ「リュッシュ（蜂の巣箱）」を組み入れている。このL字形ケースは、同じものが反対側にもあってシンメトリーを形成している。

さらに寝室においてシャローは、この長方形のプランの中にしなやかにアーチを描くカーテンレールや、円筒形のクローゼットが演出する曲線を導入した。カーテンの間仕切りがスペースを分離独立させる一方で、クローゼットの突出部が2つの空間の境界をつくっている。クローゼットの外観もこの家具の独創性に見合っている。その独創性について言うなら、クローゼットの内部には鏡、整理ユニット、棚、引出し、及び服を吊るす金具が、軸を中心に回転するドラムの中に一緒に収まっていて、外側の円周上の引き戸がそのすべてを隠す形になっていることである。このクローゼットは、「ガラスの家」の食堂の整理棚や浴室の戸棚を予見させるものである。後者の浴室の戸棚の動作はいっそう洗練されている。

064 食堂 レファンベール邸｜撮影年不詳｜撮影：ジョルジュ・ティリエ

065　寝室　レファンベール邸｜『室内装飾』誌、フランシス・ジュールダン制作、おそらく1929年、シャルル・モロー出版、パリ

L'ESSOR

グラン・オテル・ド・トゥールの大ホール等の改修

トゥール、フランス（1927年）

ポール・ベルンハイムから依頼されたこの仕事は、シャローにとっては、それまでのアパルトマンの内装やサロン全体の空間の提案に比べるとスケールが違っていた。実現すべき改修の計画の複雑さと規模の大きさだけでなく、納入すべき家具類の数の多さからもそう言えた。

この仕事に対する専門誌の取り上げ方も格別で、現在では失われたこの空間についてしかるべく報告している*。ここからはまず、第一に与えられた計画に対するシャローの対応の妥当性が確認される。例えば、技術面では大きな音楽室やロビーでは音響効果が優れていることが必要だったし、空間構成の面では各スペースがうまく連続していたこと、さらに装飾の面ではさまざまな機能に固有の雰囲気が醸し出されていたことが指摘できる。第二に、全体の構成とディテールの両方を同時にこなすシャローの能力が十分に開花している。例えば、2階バルコニーの軒天や天井のディテールに関して印象深い仕事をしたこと、及び大ホールの分厚い欄干に鏡を埋め込んだことがシャローの才能の2つの実例として挙げられる。第三に素材を選択し、組み合わせ、その特性を生かすシャローの腕前がここでも如実に示されている。例えば木材では、壁の外装にはマホガニーのブリケットでモザイクを施したり、銀めっきを施したカエデ材ボードで内壁を上張りし、複数の材木種を組み合わせた幾何学模様で床を仕上げたほか、エレーヌ・アンリの布地、金属やガラスも適宜に活用していた。

こうした名人芸の発揮においては、当時のシャローが専心していた探求の基軸に相当する2つの点が注目に値する。すなわち、可動性（モビリティ）と斬新なガラス使用の2点である。まず前者については、シャローは「書架のある執務室」のために創案した原理に基づいて、扇の可動パネルの仕切りをスモーキングラウンジとバーの間に設置している。この可動性は大ホールの床にも応用されていて、観客の階段席を設けたり舞台を高くしたりできるようになっている。

次に後者について言うなら、格別の研究を要したのはこの大ホールのガラス天井ではなかった。その設置方法は昔から知られていたからである。従って、鏡の象嵌細工だけがそこの持ち味になったと考えられる。他方、壁にガラスを用いることにシャローの独創性が顕著に表れており、報告者によって説明の仕方がさまざまに分かれるほどだった。ある者は曇りガラス、ある者はすりガラス、またある者はマジックミラーだと言った。人々は壁の下地によって与えられるガラスの緑や黄緑の色彩を目の当たりにして、その効果を褒めそやした。美術評論家で詩人のイヴァノエ・ランボソンは次のように述べている。

「人々を取り巻く壮大な海緑色の空間の中におぼろげな光が反射している。それは、夕刻にセーヌ川が橋の下で繰り広げる光に似ている。ピエール・シャロー氏は詩人である。彼は音楽室の理想的な雰囲気をつくり出している。参加者の注意を奪ってしまう恐れのある絵画や彫刻をそこに持ち込む過ちを犯さないように注意しながら、シャロー氏は音楽会にとりわけ相応しい曖昧な雰囲気をつくり上げた。そこでは、なにものにも視界を妨げられることなく遥か先まで見わたせるのだ」**

*
アーネスト・ティスランド著「室内装飾家ピエール・シャローの新作」、『ラール・エ・レザルティスト［芸術と装飾家］』no.83、1928年1月、pp.130-134
イヴァノエ・ランボソン著「トゥールのグラン・オテル」、『アール・エ・デコラシオン［芸術と装飾］』、1928年2月、pp.33-39
ガストン・ヴァレンヌ「グラン・オテル・ド・トゥールにおけるシャローのインテリアコーディネート」、『ラムール・ド・ラール［芸術の愛］』no.2、1928年2月
P.F.「トゥールの近代ホテル」、『アール・エ・アンデュストリ［芸術と産業］』、1928年1月、p.46
『現代美術・装飾業百科事典』vol.1、アルベール・モランセ出版、パリ。なお、この百科事典には、テレーズ・ボニーが撮った写真の重要なセットが掲載されている。
**
イヴァノエ・ランボソン著「トゥールのグラン・オテル」、前掲、pp.38-39

070 『旅行者のホテル』誌、第2巻より、シャルル・モロー出版、おそらく1930年、パリ

第1部　　飛躍――インテリアから建築へ
PART I　　THE APOGEE

L'ESSOR

グラン・オテル・ド・トゥールのための家具

スツール（1927年）

あるフォルムやテクニックからはさまざまなバリエーションが派生するが、シャローの家具類を取りまとめてみても、そうしたフォルムやテクニックのバリエーションが見られるわけではない。そうではなくて、ある個別の注文にふさわしく探求した結果として生まれるスタイルの統一性が見られるのである。

グラン・オテル・ド・トゥールの大ホール等の改修は、それまでの仕事に比べて規模も計画内容も異なっていた。なぜならそこは公共の場であり、扱う空間は広大で多岐にわたり、シャローにとっては初めて取り組むたぐいの空間の用途でもあったからである。家具に関しては、シャローは部屋の目的に応じて対処方法を変えていった。例えば、大ホールのために特別の座席をつくらず、ありきたりの簡単な椅子で済ませた。ラウンジ、食堂、ロビーのコーナーについては、最近制作した家具類を充てた。肘掛け椅子や食卓用の椅子といった新旧の作品を活用したのだった。だから、シャローが新規に家具を創作したのはビジネスラウンジやバー兼スモーキングラウンジに限定されていた。かくしてバーの家具としては、脚が鋼管（スチールパイプ）で座面が木材の背の高いスツールと、堂々たる形状をしたすべて木製の「小さな個別カウンター」からなっている。

机と遊戯テーブルの天板や椅子の座部が分厚い木製なのに対して、それらの脚には軽快な鋼管を使う。シャローはこうしたコントラストを、視覚的な不釣り合いが生じないぎりぎりのところまで追求した。だから、シャローの作品のフォルムには一時代前の影響が色濃く残っていて、当時流行った鋼管製のモダン家具の枠には収まっていない。

形鋼のパーカライジング（鉄鋼の錆止め法）、継手スリーブによる組み立て、及び木材の先端など、ここで使われているテクニックは、鋼管をひじ形に曲げてニッケルめっきする今日からは古めかしいものに映るだろう。おそらく、彼のクリエイティブな作品の進展においては、流行にあまり頓着しないもうひとりのシャローの姿を見出すべきなのかもしれない。

069

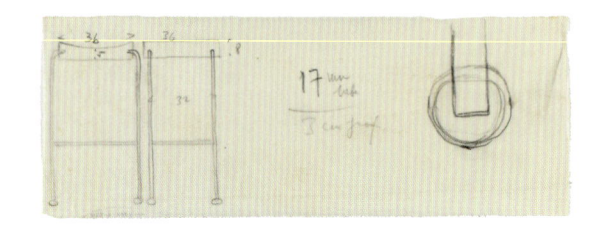

066

069 グラン・オテル・ド・トゥールのバー兼スモーキングラウンジの空間再現、1927年のサロン・ドートンヌにて
066 グランド・オテル・ド・トゥールのためのスツール　立面図、詳細図
067 ハイ・スツール《MT344》| 1927年
068 スツール《EF596》| 1927年

067

068

ヴィラ・ヴァン・ダヴァル南側ファサード｜1993年撮影｜撮影：ジャック・ルピケ

モデルニテ（近代性）——建築の探求
MODERNITY | LA MODERNITE

1927年頃からはシャローにとって建築が研究の新しい土壌となっていく。この年、オランダ人建築家ベルナルト・ベイフットの協力を得て、初の本格的な建築作品を南フランスで2件実現させる。また、ダルザス夫妻が所有するサン＝ジェルマン地区の古い建物の改装の工事許可をパリ市に申請している。のちのガラスの家である。この頃発表した家具は、建築の新しいあり方を探求するなかから発想した点で、それまでの造形とは一線を画している。複数のヴァリエーションが展開され、独創性が際立つようになり、「木と金属の時期」ともいわれる。

LA MODERNITE

ボーヴァロンのホテルの
ゴルフ場クラブハウス

ヴァール県ボーヴァロン、
フランス（1927–1929年）

アニー・ダルザスの伯父にあたるエミール・ベルンハイムは、当時ボーヴァロンのゴルフ場の開発を手掛けていた。シャローが1926年に設計注文を受けたそこのクラブハウスは、1929年初頭に建築工事が開始されている。

キュビスム建築を思わせるクラブハウスは正面が白色で凹凸がない。このクラブハウスは、ロベール・マレ＝ステヴァンスが同じくコート・ダジュールのイエールに建設したヴィラ・ノアイユ（シャルル・ド・ノアイユ別邸）の建築に相通ずる。シャローはそこの屋根つきの屋外スペースを設計するように依頼されたことがあっただけに、ヴィラ・ノアイユを熟知していた。他方、シャローの協力者であるオランダ人建築家のベルナルト・ベイフットが以前に行っていた仕事からの影響も認められる。ただし、ベイフットによるコンクリートは、クラブハウスの持ち味の決定的な影響を与えてはいないようである。なぜなら、イエールのヴィラ・ノアイユと同じく、何よりも大事にすべきなのは美的観点だったからである。

クラブハウスは、それぞれ固有の用途を持つ複数のヴォリュームの並置から成り立っており、集会場とバーが入っている本体（母屋）が全体を見下ろす格好になっている。建物の正面が湾曲しているために、外の風景が大きなパノラマとなって入りこんでくる。シャローは、1列の照明装置を入れる横長ケースを大型ガラス窓の上部に据え、下にはフラワーボックスを設けて、正面に見かけの重厚さを演出している。不釣り合いな正面壁のせいで生じる外観の圧迫感が、ガラス窓の部分が引っ込んでいるために強調されている。こんなふうにつくることになったのは、辺りを草木に囲まれたクラブハウスに目印の役割をもたせるためだったのかもしれない。

更衣室、キッチン、およびボイラー室は、本体（母屋）の裏手にある鉄筋コンクリート造のキューブ状の建物内に収められ、陸屋根の各建物の軒に据え付けられた1列の照明器具が屋外灯になっている。そして、屋根付きテラスがクラブハウス全体をつなぐ役割を果たし、中央に位置する暖炉を起点にして空間が配分される形になっている。この屋根付きテラスはうまく均整が取れていて、重厚感のあるバーを含む本体とコントラストをなしている。

建築史家ケネス・フランプトンはこのクラブハウスを批判的に検討している。

「建築的観点からすると、当クラブハウスの特に尋常ならざるところは、不完全なキュビスム建築のような様相を呈していることである。あたかも、（なんとか）外形を与えようと作者がいささか困惑しているかのように、どの方面からアプローチしようとも常に不均衡になっているのだ」*

しかし、当時の専門誌は作者であるシャローを好意的に迎えて、暖炉がもたらす「申し分なくロマンチックなトーン」や、シャローの感性や、場の尊重といったことを取り上げた**。そして、一般大衆も次の一文と同様に好感を示した。

「シャローのクラブハウスが登場して以来、ボーヴァロンにやってくるゴルフ愛好家（いわゆる"スポーツマン"）たちは、もはや英国コテージ風の山小屋では物足りなくなっている。と言うのも、木蔦や木陰くらいしか魅力がないような山小屋で、どのゴルフクラブも何とか粋なふうを装おうとしているのだから。この点、シャローは出かけていく先々で、人々に自分たちの本当のニーズやスタンスや振る舞いなどを知らしめて、人々の役に立とうとしている」***

*
マルク・ヴェレ、ケネス・フランプトン著『建築家兼インテリアデザイナーとしてのピエール・シャロー［1883–1950年］』、1984年、ルガール／ヴィア出版、パリ、p.238
**
『ラルシテクチュール・ドージュルデュイ［今日の建築］』、no.3、1934年、p.89
***
『ツーリスム』、p.18

102 ボーヴァロンのホテルの
ゴルフ場クラブハウス
『ラルシテクチュール・ドージュルデュイ』
no.3、1934年4月、
アンドレ・ブロック編集、パリ

103 ボーヴァロンのホテルの
ゴルフ場クラブハウス　屋根付きテラス
『ラルシテクチュール・ドージュルデュイ』
no.3、1934年4月、
アンドレ・ブロック編集、パリ

102

103

101 ボーヴァロンのホテルのゴルフ場クラブハウス模型　1:100

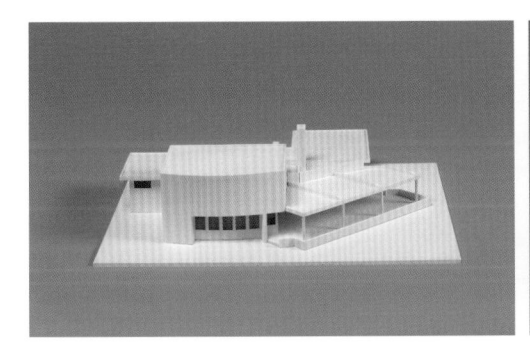

LA MODERNITE

ヴィラ・ヴァン・ダヴァル

ヴァール県ボーヴァロン、
フランス（1927-？年）

ヴィラ・ヴァン・ダヴァルの仕事には謎が付きまとっている。この点に関しては、建築史家たちは何も発言しないか、無関心を装うかのいずれかの態度をとっている。これまでの通説によれば、この仕事はシャローのフランスでのキャリアの後期のものであるばかりか、彼がアメリカに旅立った後にようやく実現したために、事実上、本人のコントロールを離れてしまったとさえ考えられてきた*。

しかし、その後に得られたさまざまな証言や情報のおかげで、今日ではプロジェクトの実情が明らかになっている。第一に取り上げるべきは、妻ドリー・シャローの次の証言である。

「ピエール・シャローは1927年に、エドモン・ベルンハイム氏の自邸とともに、ヴァール県ボーヴァロンのクラブハウスを建てました。ベルンハイム家のおかげで彼は自由に自己表現して、建築家としての夢を実現することができたのです」**

2番目は、ピエール・シャローの仕事場で1928年に雇われた若い女性の証言である。彼女は当時、クラブハウスの模型だけでなく複数のヴィラ（別荘）の模型もつくったことを記憶していた。この証言内容は、ルネ・クラヴォワジエという人物によっても裏付けられている。クラヴォワジエは自身の履歴書に、その頃にシャローの下で研修を行い、クラブハウスとヴィラのプロジェクトに専心したと記していた。さらには、ほかのさまざまな情報源によっても、ヴィラ・ヴァン・ダヴァルとクラブハウスが公式に結び付けられている。例えば、ある写真アルバムの表紙にはヴィラとクラブハウスの両タイトルが付けられており、またある地方刊行物には、「レネス社」という同一の企業が両施設の建設を請け負ったことが報告されていた***。

他方、建築スタイル上の同一性も、ふたつの構想が同じものであったのではないかという説を強化している。もしも、ヴィラ・ヴァン・ダヴァルの構想を10年先、すなわち「ガラスの家」の後に位置づけるならば、シャローの作品展開の中に明らかな不条理を導入してしまうことになるだろう。確かに、仕事の実施そのものは同時進行ではなかったようであるが、それは本質的な問題ではない。現在のヴィラ・ヴァン・ダヴァルをシャローの模型の写真と突き合わせてみると、それが模型に非常に忠実につくられていることがわかる。なるほど、あちこちに幾つかの違いはあるが、いずれも細かい点に過ぎない。一般的に言うなら、こうした変更部分はみな、模型が示していたプロジェクトのクオリティより低い。このことは、階上のテラスのスペースを形づくる間仕切り壁をなくしてしまったことや、大きいガラス窓をやめてしまったことにも当てはまる。

ヴィラ・ヴァン・ダヴァルは2階建てのL字形の本体（母屋）と、それに直交する平屋の翼部からなり、疎と密が組み合わされている。このヴィラにはいろいろな特徴が認められる。例えば、2階のテラスは半分だけ屋根があって残りは閉じている。また、テラスの屋根は長く張り出して開放的な庇になり、雨風をしのぐための保護スペースをつくっている。さらに、屋根を覆うコンクリートがカーブを描いて、下の階のためのスカイライト（明かり取り）のようになっている。

しかし、こうした特徴は必ずしも十分にバランスよく生かされていないようであった。ヴィラ・ヴァン・ダヴァルにぎこちなさが生じているのはそのせいかもしれないが、それは、このヴィラが演じ得た実験的な役割を示すことにもなっている。

---

*
マルク・ヴェレはこのヴィラの建築計画の時期を1937–1939年と推定している。M. ヴェレ、ケネス・フランプトン著『建築家兼インテリアデザイナーとしてのピエール・シャロー［1883–1950年］』、1984年、ルガール／ヴィア出版、パリ、p. 62

**
『ラルシテクチュール・ドージュルデュイ』、no. 31、1950年9月、p. 7にあるドリー・シャローの証言

***
問題の写真アルバムはパリ装飾芸術美術館に保管されている。また、この情報は1929年1月11日付『レ・タブレット・ド・ラ・コート・ダジュール』に記載されている。

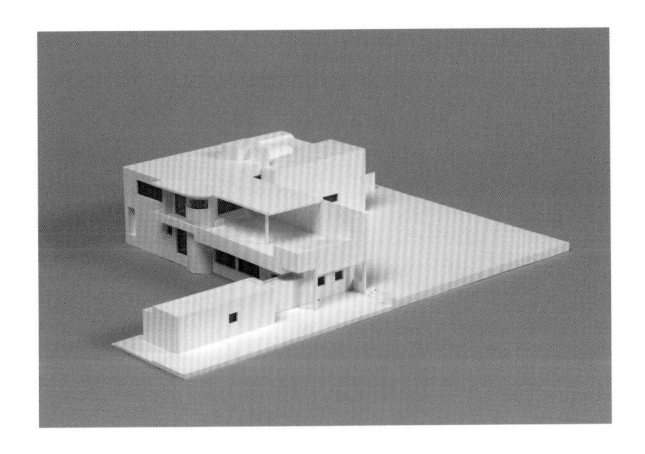

104 ヴィラ・ヴァン・ダヴァル　模型　1：100

106 ヴィラ・ヴァン・ダヴァル西側ファサード｜1993年撮影｜撮影：ジャック・ルピケ

第I部　モデルニテ——建築の探求
PART I　MODERNITY

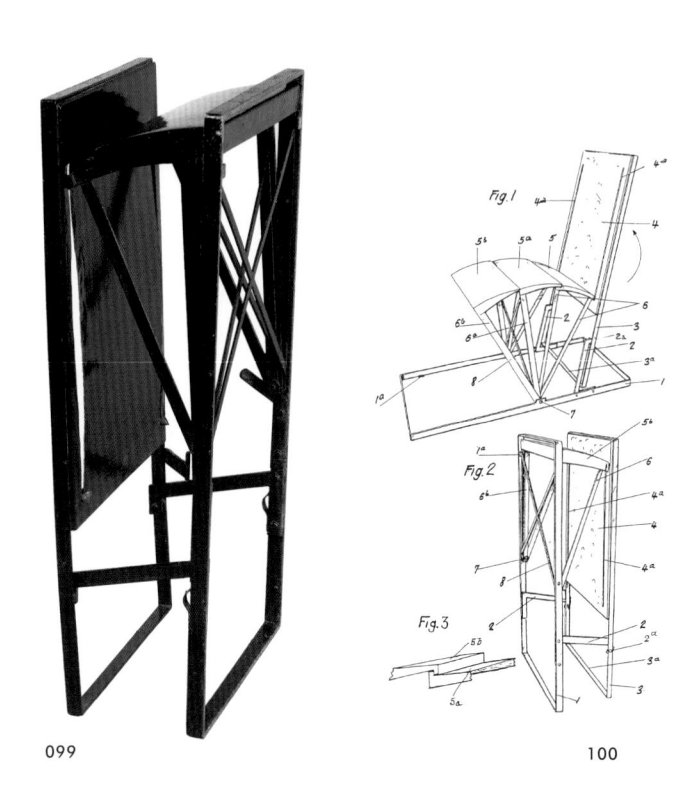

LA MODERNITE

テクニック：金属平板

椅子MC763、MC767（1927年）

シャローが手掛けた大半のインテリアを見ると、錬鉄を用いた装飾部分に関しては金物職人ルイ・ダルベとの協働の成果が表れている。そのテクニックは、幅が狭い平鉄板という単純な素材に依拠するもので、ボーヴァロンのクラブハウス受注に端を発する一連の家具にも生かされている。同クラブハウスの屋根付きテラスは、小テーブルと椅子から構成されている（p.73、図103参照）。

まずテーブルについては、もしも中央の脚がディアボロ（空中独楽）形になるような4つの曲線でできていなかったら、1本脚の小型円卓を彷彿させるかもしれない。テーブルの天板は木製である。

次に椅子は、背もたれが完全に平らで、座面が盛り上がり、前脚が門型のフレーム状の脚が床に接している。椅子のバリエーションとしては、まず同一モデルで折りたたみ式のものがある。その座面は連結した3つのパーツからなり、地面に接しているフレーム状の脚は背もたれと同じ大きさになっている。横から見ると、折り畳むときの動きは扇子に似ているため、シャローは権利保護のために特許登録する際に「扇構造の折りたたみ椅子」という表題をこのモデルに付けた。これらの折りたたみ椅子はすべて金属製であるが、もうひとつの固定式モデルのほうは、皮張りまたは布張りかどうかで違いがある（皮張りや布張りは座部だけにするか、それとも背もたれも含めることもある）。

元となった作品には戸外用家具としての武骨さがあったのだが、その後、特にラ・スメーヌ・ア・パリ新聞本社のロビーなどの改修（p.123、図089参照）を手掛けるようになってからは、シャローはより洗練されたモデルを提案するようになる。例えば、背もたれはフラットのままにしながら、柳で編んだり皮張りにした座部を優美にふくらませることがあり、さらにはこれをベンチや各種の座席にも応用するようにもなっていく。

095

095, 099 折りたたみ式椅子《MC763》｜1927年

100 イギリスでの特許登録書類「扇構造の折りたたみ椅子」｜1927年

099　　　　　　　　　　100

096　椅子《MC767》(固定式モデル) | 1927年
097　椅子《EZ849》(固定式モデル) | 1927年

096

097

098　鍛鉄製腰掛け | 1927年

098

第I部　モデルニテ——建築の探求
PART I　MODERNITY

LA MODERNITE

「木と金属」の時期

「ロベール・マレ＝ステヴァンス」
モデルの机（1927年）

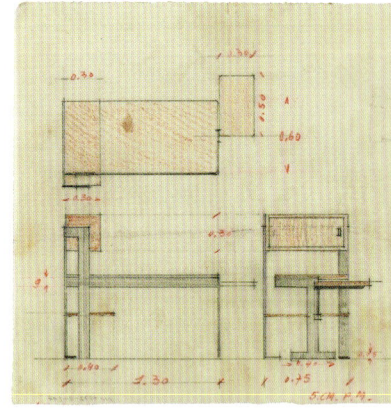

076

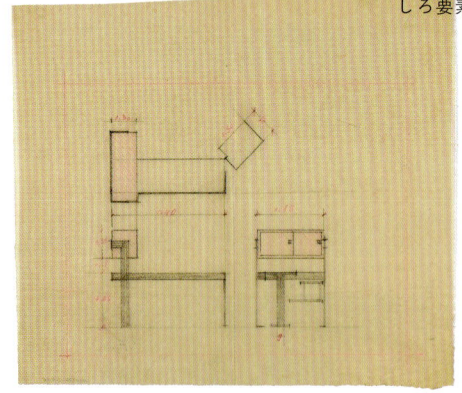

075

076, 075, 074, 073 「木と金属」の時期の机
平面図、立面図、透視図｜1927年

072 衣装整理箱　立面図、透視図｜1927年

071 「ロベール・マレ＝ステヴァンス」
モデルの机｜1927年

「木と金属」という表現は特定のテクニックを示すものではない。そもそも、単に「木と金属」と言っただけでは、それがどんな技術を意味するのかは規定し得ないだろう。この表現は、むしろシャローの家具作品におけるある一時期を示す言い回しである。しかもこの時期は、彼にとっては最もモダンな作風の時代であったと考えられる。

シャローが自身の事務所（パリのノレ通り）のインテリア家具として、金物職人ルイ・ダルベに製作させた机は、錬鉄プレートでくるんだ紫檀の天板でできている。机の一方の側の脚にはT字を逆にした形の金属プレートが使われ、もう一方の側の脚は門型になっていて、机の天板とその上の棚を支えている。この門型の脚にもシンプルな金属プレートが用いられ、その両端を曲げて接地させることで、安定して床に置けるようになっている。また、天板の片端の下に嵌め込まれた回転板によって、反対側の端とのバランスが図られている。

他の家具については多くの異型があるが、ここで取り上げている机の場合はむしろ要素の組み合わせが特徴となっている。すなわち、金属構成の原理をいったん決めてしまえば、机の表面のデザイン、回転板の配置と数量、金属製の棚の大小、あるいは木製の棚の吊り下げの有無については、顧客からの注文に合わせてさまざまなバリエーションを工夫することが可能である。さらには、黒染のブナ材や紫檀といった木材種の選択や、金属のニッケルめっきや黒ワックス塗りの選択の問題もそこに加わるだろう。他にも、顧客次第での注文内容が違ってくる。こうして、顧客ごとに「シャロー」モデル、「フレッグ」モデル、「カプフェレ」モデルなどが登場したうえ、ロベール・マレ＝ステヴァンスのためにも1つのモデルがつくられることとなる。結果として、1927年から1931年までに計25種類ほどの机がつくられていく。

なお、しばしば机に付属するスツールは、座面が木製になっていて、床に接触する部分がT字形の金属プレートが脚の役割を果たしている。そして、スツールの両サイドに付けられた2本の細い金属棒が、座面の張り出し部分を支えるようになっている。

074

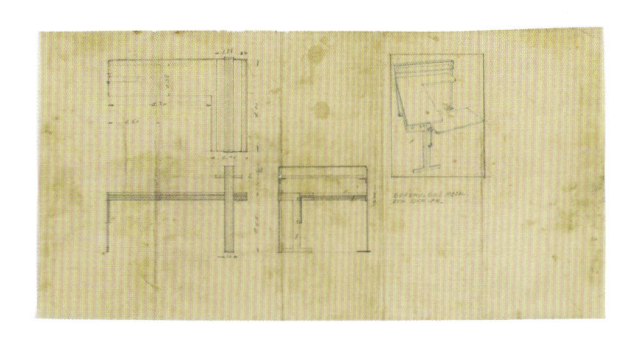

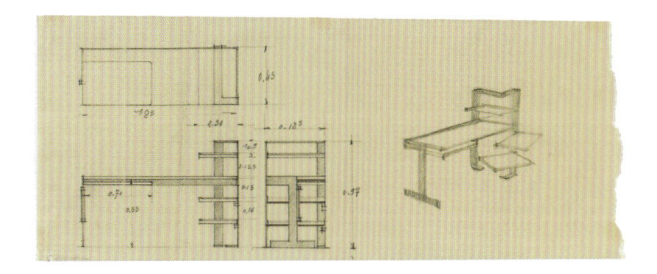

073

072

071

第1部　　モデルニテ——建築の探求
PART I　　MODERNITY

078

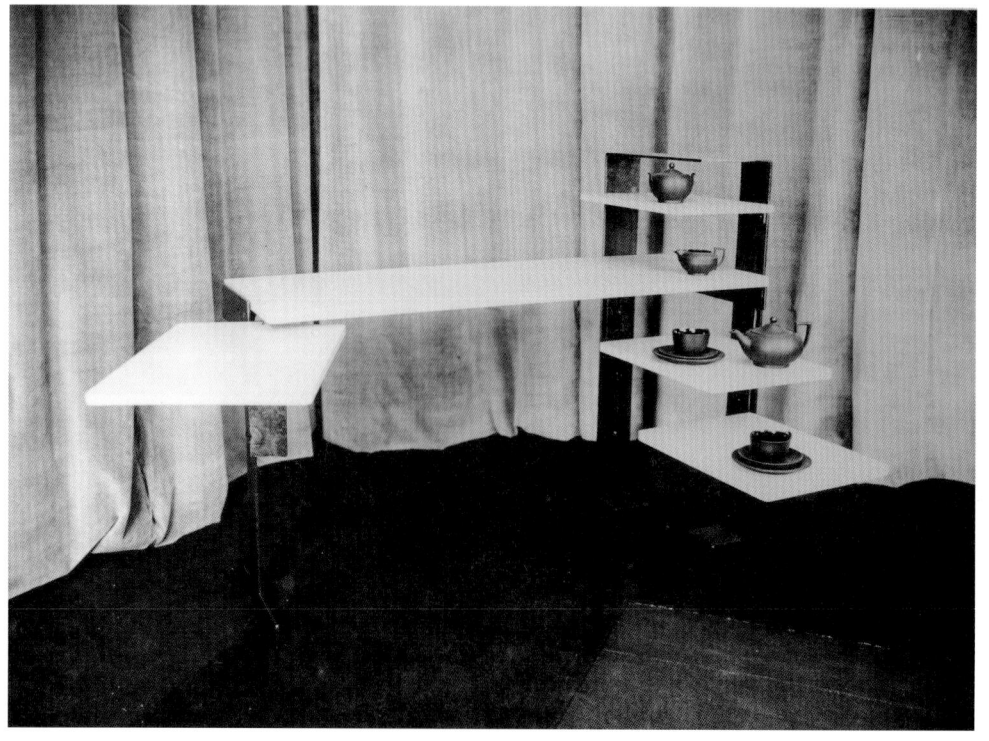

081

078 「木と金属」の時期の机
撮影：ジョルジュ・ティリエ

081 カエデ材の天板と鉄材を用いた
ティーテーブル｜制作年・撮影者不詳

PART

II

第 II 部

ガラスの家──装飾・家具・建築の統合
THE HOUSE OF GLASS

ref.008　ガラスブロック「ネヴアダ204A」
撮影：ジョルジュ・メゲルディトシアン

ガラスの家──装飾・家具・建築の統合
THE HOUSE OF GLASS | LA MAISON DE VERRE

建築家ピエール・シャローの名を歴史に刻んだ「ガラスの家」は、長年の顧客であるダルザス夫妻からの信頼を最大限に活かした改築プロジェクトである。当時最新の建設技術とシャロー特有の「発明」的アイデアを投入することにより、与えられた課題に見事な回答が示されるばかりか、既存の建物は全く異なる姿に変容し、家具やインテリアデザインは、建築へと見事に融合している。図面がほとんど残されていないため、これまで充分に明かされてこなかった設計趣旨を、ここでは同時代の証言も参照しながら解読する。完成したサロンは往時、ダルザス夫妻を中心としてエリートたちの知的交流の場として賑わった。1980年代の保存修復活動を経て、その輝きは今なお失われていない。

ガラスブロック「ネヴァダ204A」

LA MAISON DE VERRE

ガラスの家の成立過程

パリ、サン＝ギヨーム通り、1927–1931年

　ピエール・シャローの代表作であり、20世紀建築史の伝説ともなったガラスの家は、多くの分析や解釈を生み出した。かたやオリジナル資料はなく、その歴史は非常に多くの謎につつまれている。アトリエ・ピエール・シャローのアーカイヴが存在しないこと、ダルベ工房のアーカイヴの中にサン＝ギヨーム通りの現場に関する資料が残っていないこと、ベルナルト・ベイフトを筆頭にシャローの協働者の証言が極めて少ないことが、その原因である。ガラスの家に関する知見は、長らく「現場の分析」から得られたものであった。オリジナル資料の欠落を何とか補うために、ディテールと平面からおこした図面資料の作成が求められた。修復工事の責任者、ベルナール・ボシェが試行錯誤の結果、最も効果的であったのは、このような手段なのである。それは、考古学のように時代を遡るアプローチで、複数の資料（大半は写真）に何度も立ち戻りつつ、実際の敷地調査を繰り返すことで確かめられた。そこで本稿は、シャロー自身の作品に関する言説といくつかの現存する資料を呈示するなかから、ガラスの家の成立過程を描き直していきたい。

　1925年、これはピエール・シャローがガラスの家の「コンセプト」を考え始めた年である*1。おそらくそのはずだが、もしそうでないとしても、コンセプトを考える実際の段階の最初であろうし、時間的にいえば、1925年10月25日付のダルザス氏の所有権証書の事実が裏付けるように、少なくともひとつの考察の前提がこの時期にあったのである*2。ダルザス夫妻はサン＝ジェルマン大通りのアパルトマンを引き払いたいと考えており、サン＝ジェルマン・デ・プレ地区にある、ベルンハイム家が所有する物件の中にある住居を享受する好機を得た。最上階に居住者がいたため、彼らは中庭と背後の庭園の間にある建物全体を手に入れることができなかった。そこで、夫妻は装飾家であり彼らの友人でもあるピエール・シャローに助けを求めた。仮説としては、シャローが依頼されたのは、当初は単なるインテリアデザインだった。果たしてそれは、本物の建築のプロジェクトとなり、そのうえ、シャローが身を投じることになる、最も独創的なプロジェクトとなるのである。

　1927年11月23日付の工事許可申請書が一連の貴重な情報を提供する。まず最初に、平面図の読み取りが住居としてのプログラムを明らかにする。1階には、使用人が使う部屋とダイニングがある。2階部分は、もしリネン室を含まなければ、応接空間だけに充てられている。3階には寝室と浴室がある。次に、この住宅の本質をなす原則がすでに決定されていることが認められる。ひとつは、柱によるスラブの保持という構造である。もうひとつは、2層分の高さのところに3層が構成されているということである。様々な空間の高さに加えて、床と床の間の空間や多種多様な段差が示されており、それらが空間に複雑さと豊かさを授けている。三番目に、ファサードの扱いが注意をひきつける。玄関側のファサードではとりも直さずガラスブロックという、この住宅の決定的な表現が現れている。庭園側のファサードは板ガラスで構成された垂直な壁面を見せている。コンセプトを構想した時のことについて、シャロー自身が以下のように明確に述べている。

　「私は隣接しているふたつの壁の間に建設しなければならなかった——平面は近代的な生活の嗜好とニーズに調和した配置を想定していた。光を可能な限り採り入れる方法はひとつしかなかった。全面的に半透明なファサードを実現すること。厚みがあり表面をつや消しされた大きな板ガラスを使って、私は1927年にテストを開始した。この最初のスタディに私はちっとも満足しなかった。いずれにせよ、特別な方法で暖房と換気の問題は解決されていたので、安全のための小さな開口部だけを残して、窓を排除する基本方針が採用された。私たちが大きな板ガラスという案を捨てて、大きなガラス面を用いる場合の空白感をつくらずに、集合体となったとき無限の表面を与え得る要素（ガラスブロック）をスタディすることを考えはじめたのは、その時である。このささやかな規模では新素材を検討することは望めなかった。既に存在するものの中で、私が選んだのはブリック・ネバダ（ネバダは、1920年代末にフランスのガラスの大企業サン・ゴバン社が工業的に製造していたレンガもしくはガラスブロックの型である）*3 で、これは問題となっている条件に最もよく対応すると思われた」*4

　この「インテリア改修」のための工事許可申請書は、建築審査官（パリ市付の建築家で、法令を順守しているか監視し、建築許可に適合しているか審査する*5）の実地検分の後、以下のような理由をつけて拒否される。

　「……以下の理由による。

　1. 提出された図面には不備があり、各種寸法が不十分で、計画されている工事の実態を評価することができない。不足しているものはとりわけ以下のものである。a：所有物件全体の図面、b：配管図2部、c：変更前の各階図面

　2. 1階と2階の一部の天井高が2.8メートル以下である（1902年政令17条に違反している）

　法規に関する不備に加えて、不明瞭な表現は未完成の状況を確認させるのみである——物置やリネン室の一部の上にある「空隙」の位置のような、統一性の欠如を修正してはどうか」*6

　二番目の計画は1928年8月11日に提出され、8月21日に道路課の上級委員会の意見に従って許可を受ける*7。

　前回の提案との違いは注目に値する。プログラムは進化を遂げていた。1階が全面的に医師の診療所に割り当てられている。1階のサロンと2階のサロン兼ホールというように、たとえそこに応接

108 医師のロベール・ダルザスが所有するサン＝ギヨーム通りの邸宅
通りからの入口を入ったところの中庭に面した玄関側のファサード　撮影：ジョルジュ・ティリエ

109 鉄骨を建てている　建設中のガラスの家　撮影：ジョルジュ・ティリエ

のための空間の配置にためらいがみられるとしても、上階の配置は合理性を増している。階段は確定的な位置を、いくつかの間仕切りは設置する必然性を獲得している。この計画は付属の別棟を中庭側に戻し、主屋とそれの分節で最良の使われ方を見出すことによって、前回の計画より構成が明確になった。ファサードも修正された。庭園側のファサードは、このときからガラスブロックの表面が組み入れ、玄関側のファサードは以前のプログラムでは一律な表面であったが、ここでは一部奥まった箇所が見られる。次第に骨子が明らかになってきており、モデュールを使った建設方法の発想が姿を見せ始めている。プロジェクトのこの進捗状況において、数多くの要素が不確定な状況にとどまっている。図面に描かれている構造体は、コンクリートでの実現を考えたままである。配管と煙突は、それに替わる暖房システムを明示することのないままに消えてしまっている。

工事プロセスを記録した写真は、史実をたどる第二のよりどころとなる。そこには取り壊し、工事の再開、ファサードとフロアプランの完成といった、さまざまな段階が読み取れる。工事現場は訪問者や雑誌の記事をひきつけ、その結果が私たちにいくつかの情報を与えてくれる。『板ガラスとガラス』誌が「ガラスの家」のタイトルで紹介する。その「偉大なるガラスの大壁」は「見た目に軽く」「力強くがっしりしていて」「しなやか」と描写されている。もし、その美しさが魅力的だとすれば、それは精密さを前提として用いられた技術なのである……。

「ガラスブロックの配置については、私は人からはわからないうまいやり方見つけた……ここに最初の結果（写真）がある。しかし、私はあなた方にこの建物全体の写真をまだ公開しないようお願いする。もし必要なら、ガラスブロックの集合体によって獲得されたファサードの断片にしてほしい。重要な複数の要素が今はまだ足りないので、ファサードのすべての要素が装備されたときのみ、ファサードは全面的にはっきり理解できる意味をもつだろうから」*8

この記事は、建物が完成したら、と将来の記事の予告で終わっている。しかし、続編はなく、よって残念なことに建築家本人によるこれ以上のコメントは存在しない。

おそらくシャローによって言及された要素は、ファサードの仕上げに必要な、すなわち、ルイ・ダルベと彼の職人たちの仕事だろう。ひとたびベトン・トランスリュシッド*9（半透明なコンクリート：コンクリートに流し込まれたガラスブロックからなる。ヴォールトや壁やスラブに与えられた名称）を専門とするダンドルー社によってガラスブロックが施工されると、主な工事は金物職人の腕の見せどころとなる。かくして、入口のガラスの箱といくつかの開口部を含む集合体としてのファサードが完成されることになる。同様に、内部では、「家具＝建物」のしかけが次第に空間を構造化していく。ドイツ・ヴァスムート社の建築雑誌は、工事現場の写真の隣に、1931年の秋にサロン・ドートンヌに展示された模型写真と図面一式を掲載した*10。これらの二つの資料（図面と模型）は完成した状態をまだ伝えていない。同様に、一連の3点のデッサン──日付も署名もないが、それらの「オランダ風」の描き方から判断すればベイフットによるもの──は、ついたて式の間仕切りとレールに吊るされ、キャスターで動く大箱といった、日の目を見ることのなかった仕掛けを明らかにしている。

工事はおそらく1932年のはじめか、1931年の年末頃終わっている。当時ルネ・シャヴァンスへの返信のなかで、シャローは自分の意図をはっきり説明している。

「私は居住者と外界の間に、テーブルと必要なベッドを置くだけのテントの布のようなヴェールを提供したかった。私はこのテーブル、このベッド、というよりむしろ、ある現代の家族の家の中の複数戸のアパルトマンを厳密に合理的な条件によって、しかも自然に配置した。他のやり方は自らに禁じた」*11

それ以降、ガラスの家は二重の生き方をするようになる。ひとつは壁の内側のダルザス家の生活の場として、もうひとつは建築の国際的な舞台の最前線としての建物としてである。

*1
「ピエール・シャロー自身によって解説されたガラスの家」『ル・ポワン』誌、コルマール、1937年、p. 51（本書p. 109）引き続きこのテキスト全文を参照のこと。

*2
この資料は、VO（道路課）11組の建設許可申請に関する書類の中に存在する（パリ市公文書館1Fi 455）。

*3
ネヴァダというのは、「レンガ」もしくは「ガラスブロック」の型式で、フランスのガラスの大企業サン＝ゴバン社によって1920年代末工業的に生産されたものである。

*4
M. D.「一軒のガラスの家」『板ガラスとガラス』誌、no.16、1930年6月、pp.19-20

*5
建築家＝道路管理官は、法令順守を監督し、建設許可との適合性を審査する、パリ市に帰属する建築家である。

*6
パリ市公文書館VO11 3266

*7
前掲資料

*8
M. D. 引用記事（注4）

*9
半透明なコンクリートというのは、コンクリートの中に流し込まれたガラスブロックからなる、ヴォールトもしくは垂直・水平の壁に与えられた名前である。

*10
Lonia Winternitz, «Glas/das Haus eines Artes in Paris/Architekt: Pierre Chareau, Paris», Wasmuths Monatshefte, nov.-déc.1931, pp. 497-498.

*11
ルネ・シャヴァンス「ガラスの新しい技術と応用」『アール・エ・デコラシオン［芸術と装飾］』誌、1932年、p.312

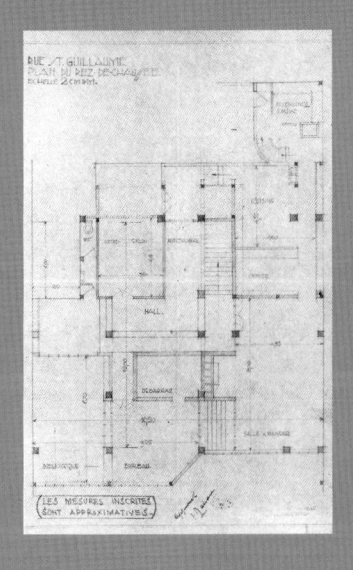

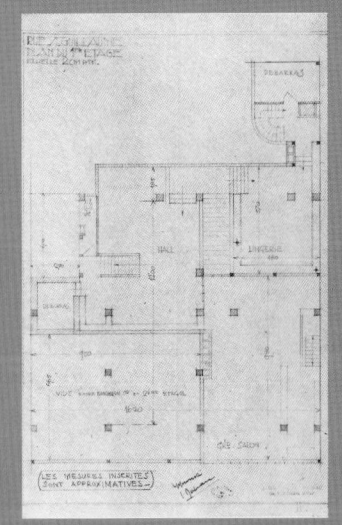

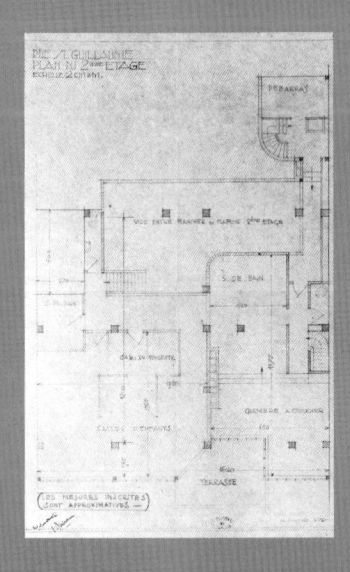

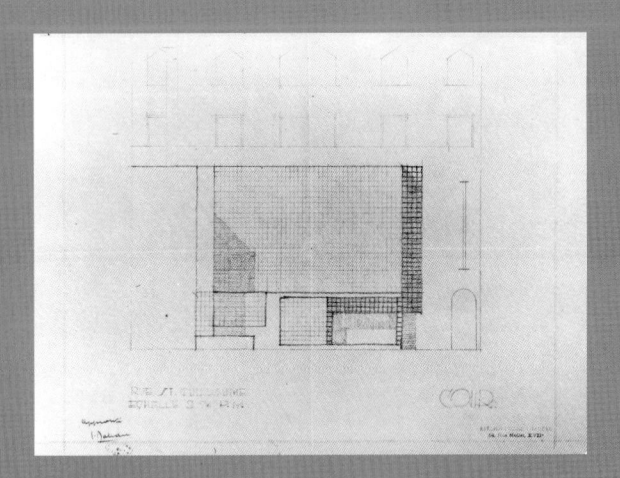

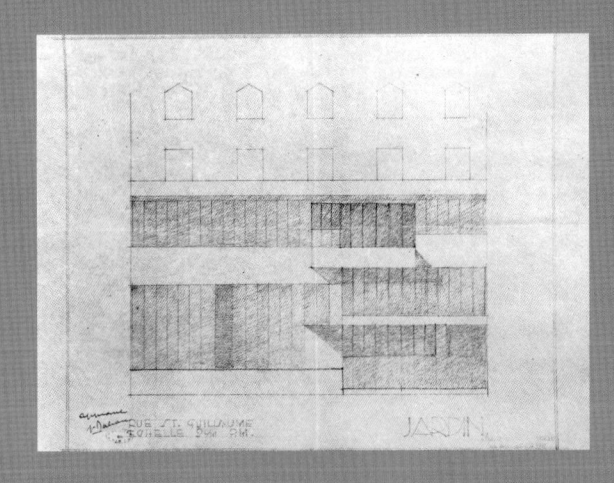

132–136 ガラスの家
第1案の建築許可申請図面　1927年
アトリエ・ピエール・シャロー

134　1階平面図
135　2階平面図
136　3階平面図

132　通りからの入口を入ったところの
中庭に面した玄関側立面図
133　1階庭側立面図

第II部　　　ガラスの家──装飾・家具・建築の統合
PART II　　THE HOUSE OF GLASS

111　竣工間近のガラスの家　2階サロン｜撮影：ジョルジュ・ティリエ

124　3階廊下の書棚が仕上がったところ｜撮影：ジョルジュ・ティリエ

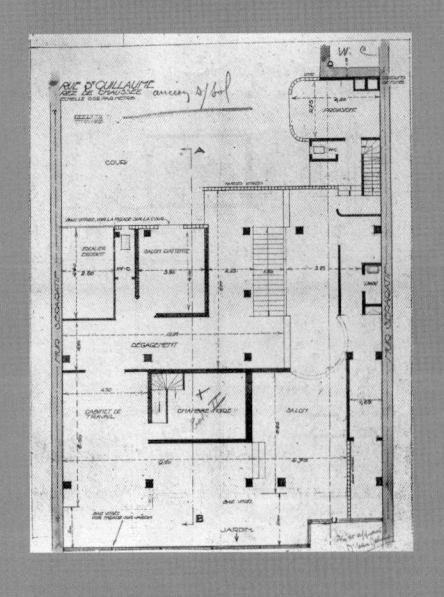

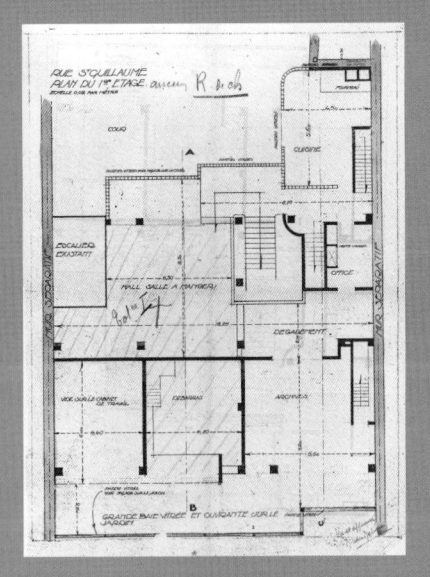

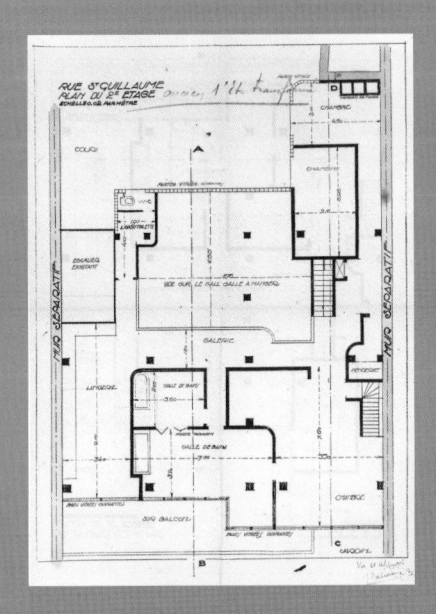

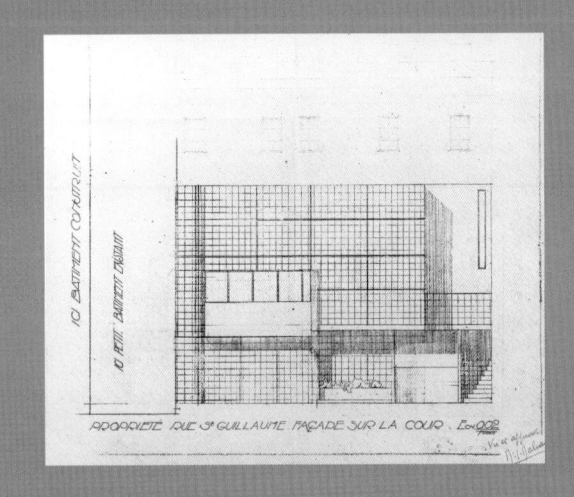

137–141 ガラスの家
第2案の建築許可申請図面 1928年
アトリエ・ピエール・シャロー

139 1階平面図
140 2階平面図
141 3階平面図

137 通りからの入口を入ったところの
中庭に面した玄関側立面図
138 1階庭園側の立面図

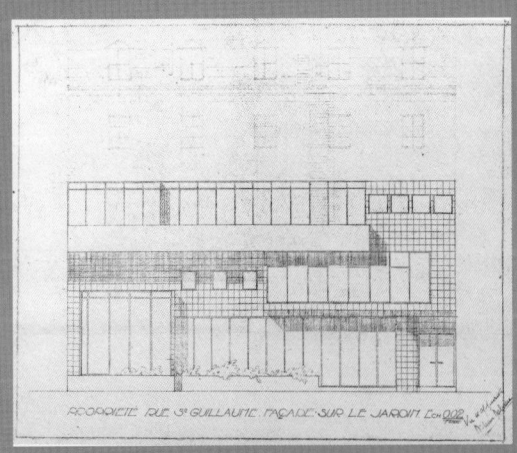

第Ⅱ部　ガラスの家――装飾・家具・建築の統合
PART II　THE HOUSE OF GLASS

142-145 ガラスの家 実測図 1985年
実測図製作:ベルナール・ボシェ

142 配置図
143 1階平面図
144 2階平面図
145 3階平面図

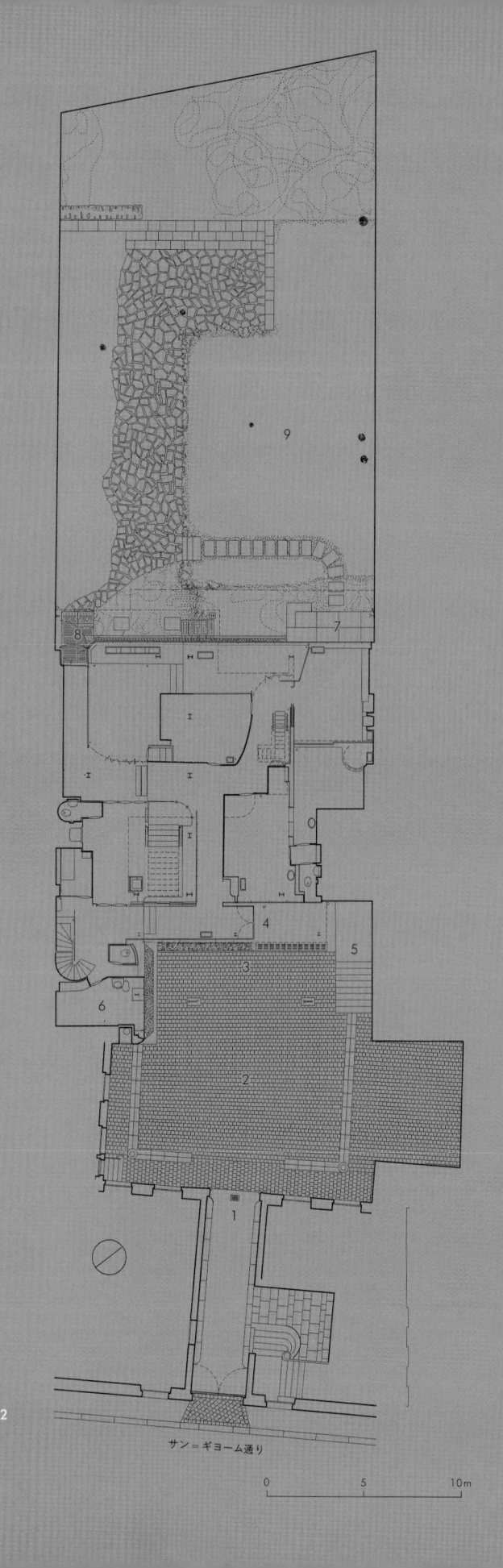

1 通りからの入口
2 中庭
3 ガラスブロックのファサード
4 玄関
5 上部アパルトマンへの入口
6 サービス棟
7 診察室のテラス
8 庭園への出入口
9 庭園

サン＝ギヨーム通り

0 5 10m

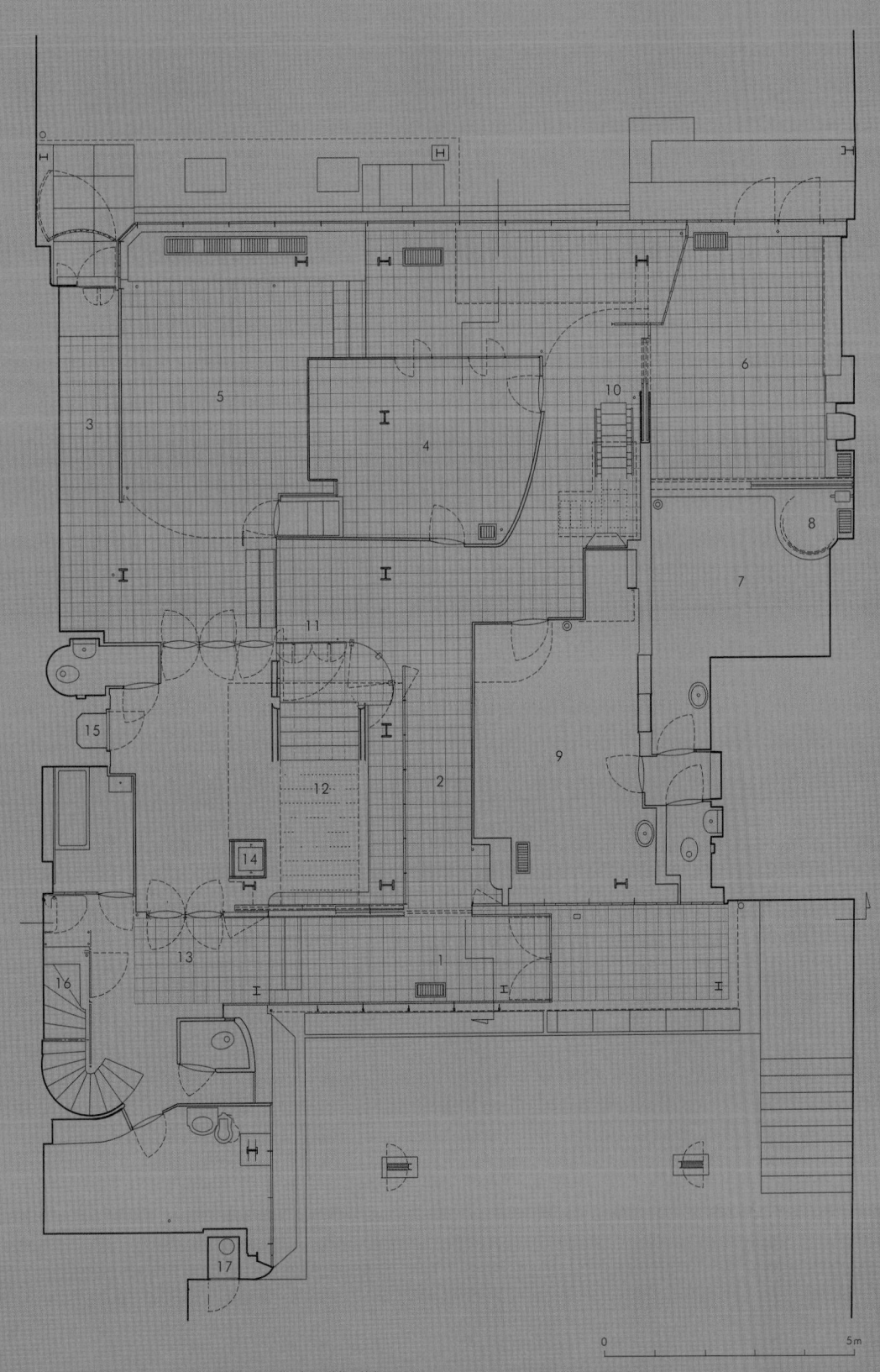

1	玄関ホール	6	診察室（問診室）	11	主階段入口	16	サービス棟階段
2	中央廊下	7	検査室	12	主階段	17	ごみ捨て場
3	庭園への廊下	8	患者の更衣スペース	13	使用人専用出入口		
4	受付	9	処置室	14	運搬リフト		
5	待合室	10	医師の書斎への専用階段	15	エレベーター		

第II部　　ガラスの家——装飾・家具・建築の統合
PART II　　THE HOUSE OF GLASS

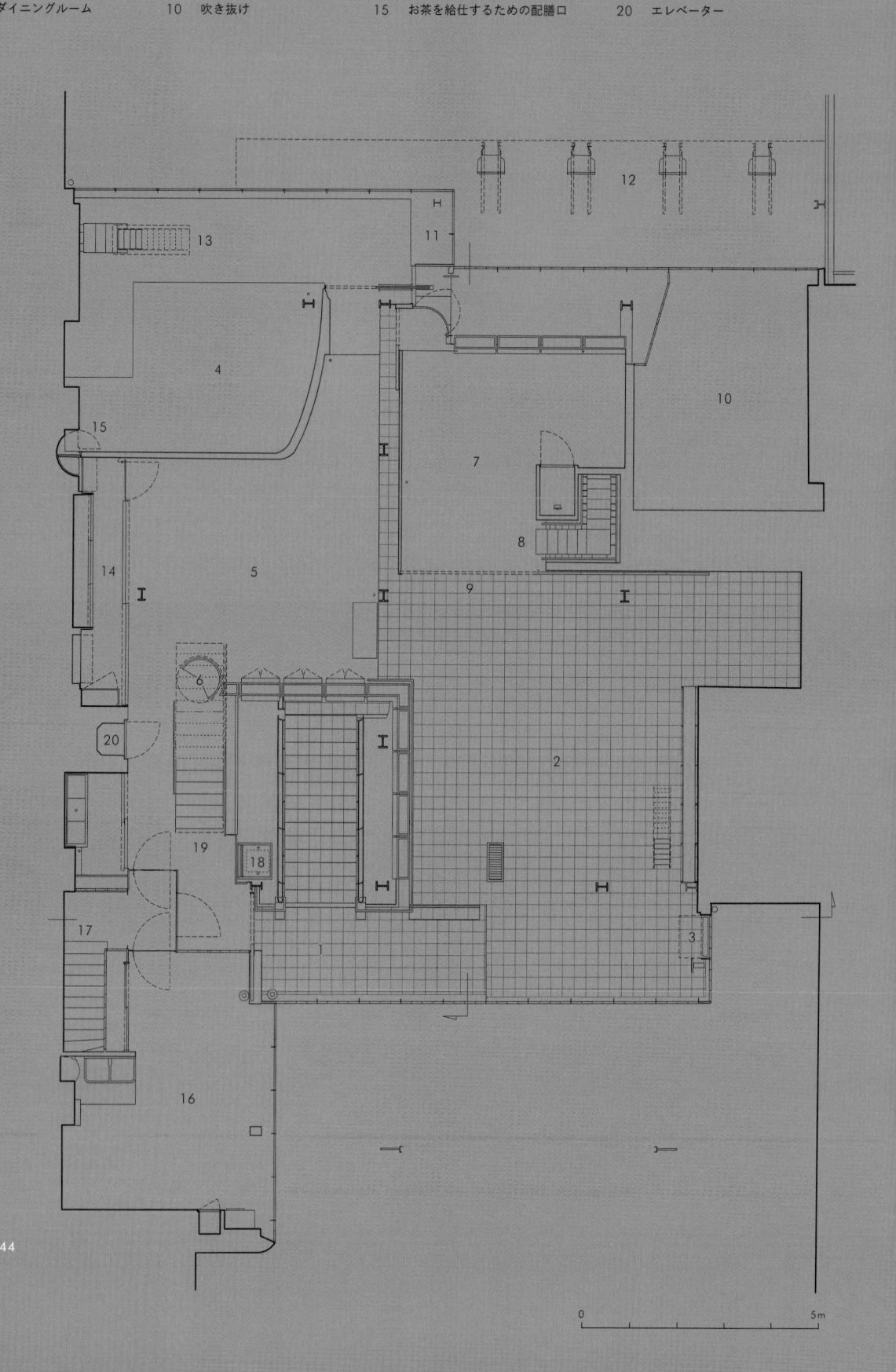

1	主階段踊り場	6	整理棚	11	温室	16	台所
2	大サロン	7	書斎	12	投光器と外部はしご	17	サービス棟階段
3	換気ガラリ	8	診察室からの階段	13	主寝室へと続く収納式の階段	18	運搬リフト
4	夫人の小サロン	9	サロンと書斎の間仕切り	14	収納ユニット	19	3階へ続く階段
5	ダイニングルーム	10	吹き抜け	15	お茶を給仕するための配膳口	20	エレベーター

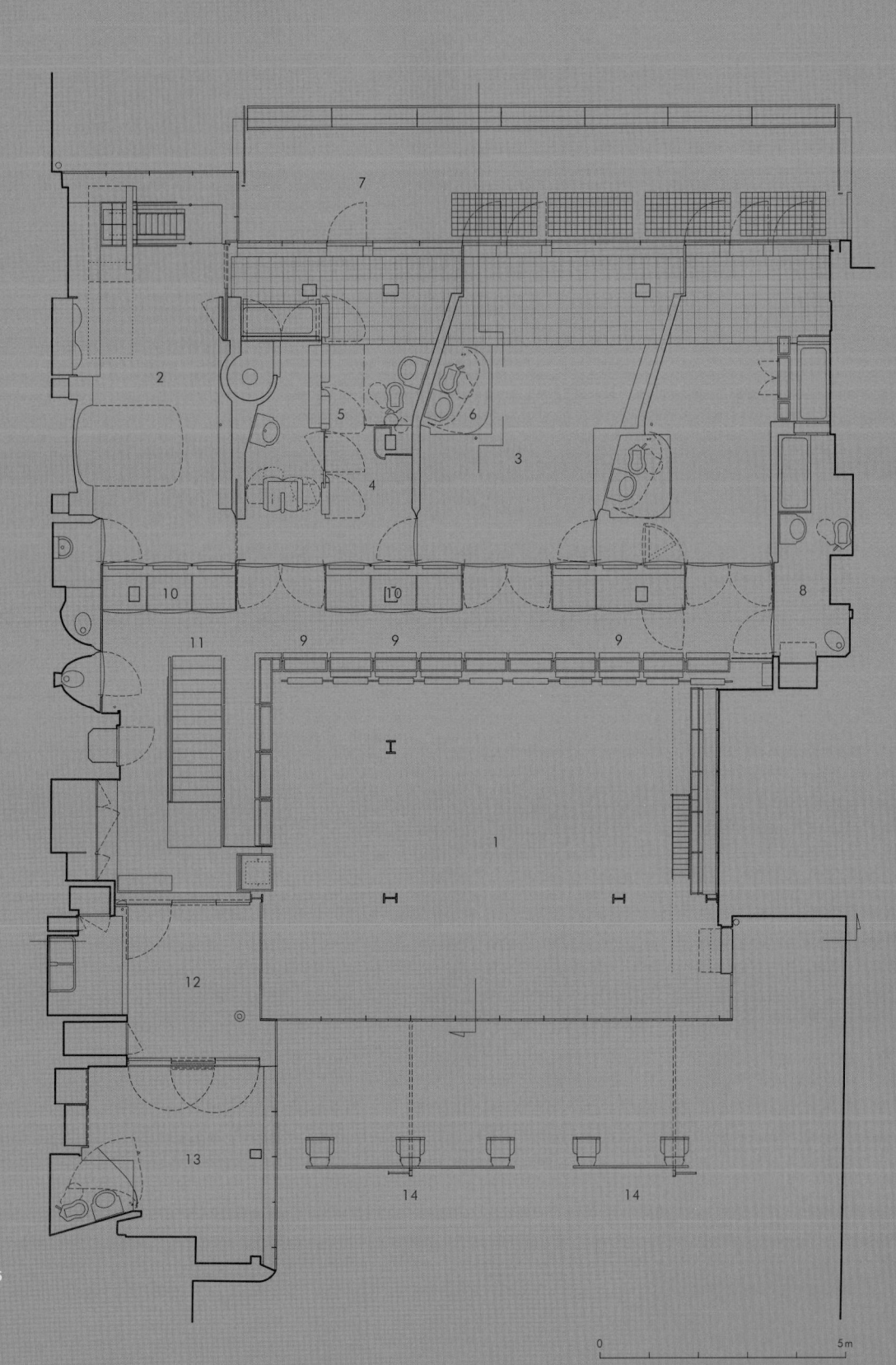

1	サロン吹き抜け	6	寝室内の洗面スペース	11	2階へ続く階段
2	主寝室	7	テラス	12	家事室
3	寝室	8	客用浴室	13	使用人居室
4	主寝室浴室	9	サロン側の書棚	14	投光器と外部はしご
5	浴室収納棚	10	二重扉構造のクローゼット		

第II部 ガラスの家——装飾・家具・建築の統合
PART II THE HOUSE OF GLASS

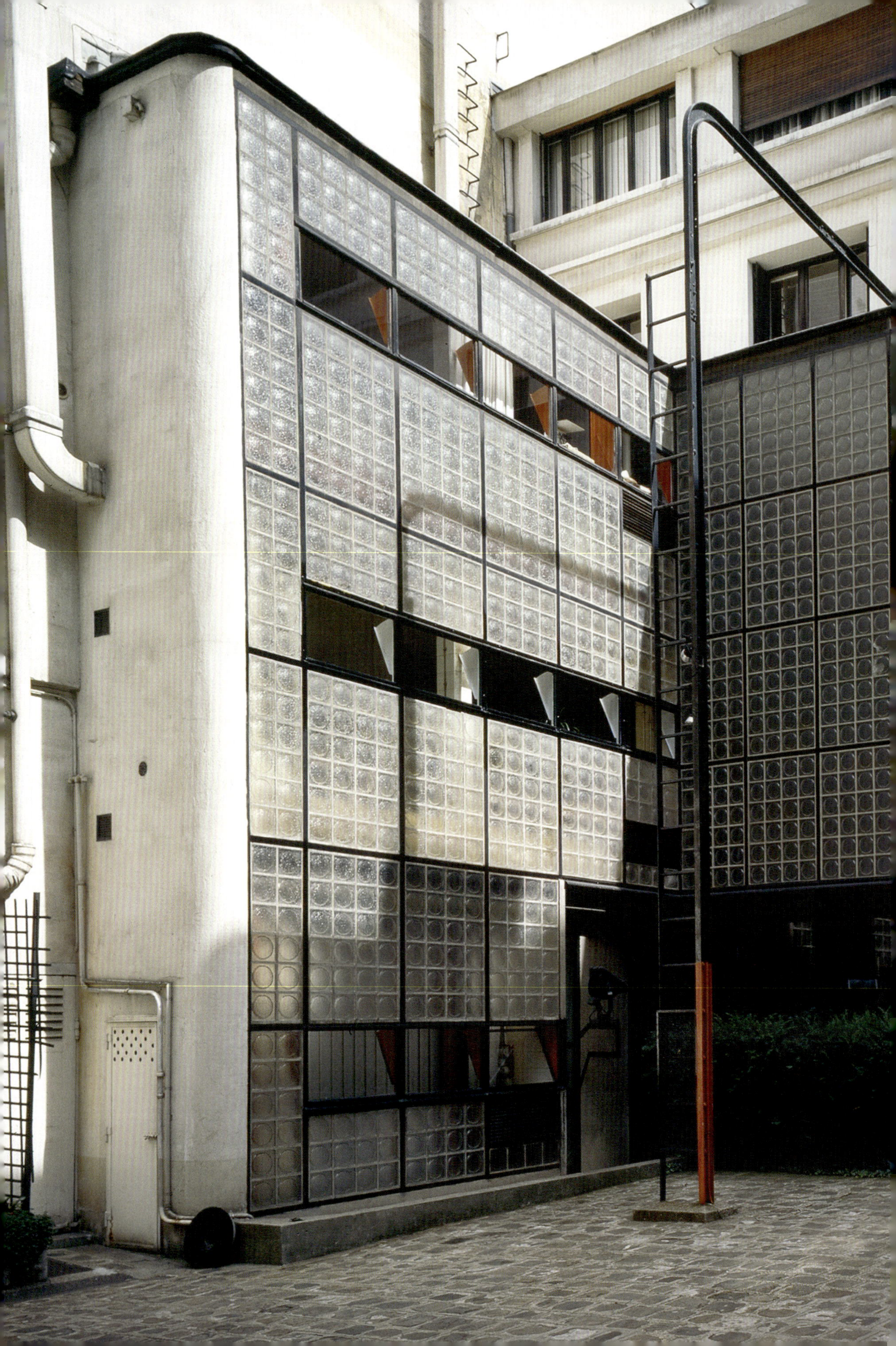

147 玄関側ファサード、右側に上部アパルトマンへの出入口｜撮影：ジョルジュ・メゲルディトシアン

LA MAISON DE VERRE

ガラスの家――平面計画について

パリ、サン・ギヨーム通り、1927-1931年

『ラルシテクチュール・ドージュルデュイ［今日の建築］』誌（no.9, 1933年）において、ポール・ネルソンがガラスの家の理論的分析を試みる一方で（資料1）、ジュリアン・ルパージュ（建築史家ユリウス・ポーゼナーのペンネーム）は訪問を基に観察記を記している（資料2）。それでもなお、ガラスの家は、場所として直感的に把握することが難しい。それほど独特で複雑なものなのである。たとえその空間と設計の豊かさを説明できなくても、描写というものはぜひとも必要である。ふたつのことがガラスの家の成立過程の基礎を築いている。つまり、住居に仕事場（診療所）を付け加えることと、既存の建物の2層であったところを3層にすること、である。

ピエール・シャローが依頼を受けたときに見せられた建物は、サン＝ジェルマン地区の一軒の小さな伝統的な邸宅だった。通りには複数階の集合住宅がそびえ、この集合住宅のファサードにある専用の大きな開口部を通って中庭に入る。邸宅はもともと、中庭と背後の庭園の間にある。中庭には、建物本体の左脇に小さなサービス棟が位置する。シャローは、矩形のフロアと屋根裏部屋がある高層階を維持しつつ、新しい空間をつくらなければならなかった。

通り側から集合住宅を通り抜けて中庭に出ると、ガラスの家の全体像に出会う。視線は突如としてガラスブロックのファサードに捉えられる。1階の壁面も同様にガラスであるが、ガラスブロックの表面とは対照的に、軽くて繊細な土台という印象を与える透明な板ガラスでつくられている。サービス棟もまたガラスブロックで覆われているが、用途を考慮して窓が配されている。開口のない巨大なガラスブロックの壁面は、おそらく近代建築における最初の開口ゼロのファサードのうちのひとつである。建設当初、この半透明なコンクリート（ガラスブロックのパネルの技術）は、セメントの滑らかな表面になっていた。1950年代の改修で、玄関側のファサードは改修され、金属製の骨組みが目に見えるように残され、黒く塗られた。ガラスの家の上方に伝統的な2階分の空間があり、その時、2層目は少し後退し、屋上テラスが見えるところに取りつけられた。ガラスの家の上にある階には、かつても今日も、建物の右にある階段を利用する。

ガラスの家の入口の開口部は脇を向いているので目立たない。3種類の呼び鈴が、医師への、使用人への、家人への、と訪問者を区別する。診療所がある1階は多様な動線によって構成されている。患者は受付へ直接進み、診察室とさまざまな検査室に呼ばれる前に、待合室で待つ。診察後に患者は受付の前を通り、来た道を引き返す。これは受付が中心軸となる周回コースである。医師は、全くもって軽やかな金属製の専用の階段を使って2階にたどり着くことができる。使用人たちは家の横にある彼ら専用の動線をもっており、黒御影石に覆われた階段を利用する。庭園にアクセスできるのも同じ側である。一方、荘厳な3つ目の主階段が訪問者を1階から2階へ誘う。玄関と階段を一列の動線上に並べる古典的な配置とは反対に、この階段は玄関のある中庭側のファサードに振り向くことを強いる。そこで客人は階段を上り、正面のガラスブロックによって拡散された光にふいにとらわれる。この金属製の階段はそれ自体傑作である。それは、ガラスの宝石箱の中、側面の強化ガラスと扉の透明なガラスの中にある。実際、診療所からの分離を強調するために、階段の上り口は折りたたみ式のパンチング・メタルによって透明性を減じることのできるふたつのガラス扉が進入をコントロールする。これらの扉の大きさは、ほとんど取り外しのできる間仕切り壁といえるほどである。ひとつは平らで、もうひとつはすばらしいカーブをもつ間仕切り壁である。階段の段は蹴込板のない踏板だけで、2本の金属製のレールの上に置かれていて、浮いているような印象を与える。上りきると、あらためて人は振り返ってサロンを発見する。

このフロアは応接のためのもので、大小のサロンがある。大きい方は、アヴァ

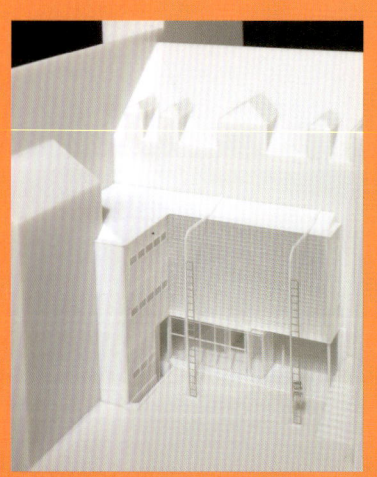

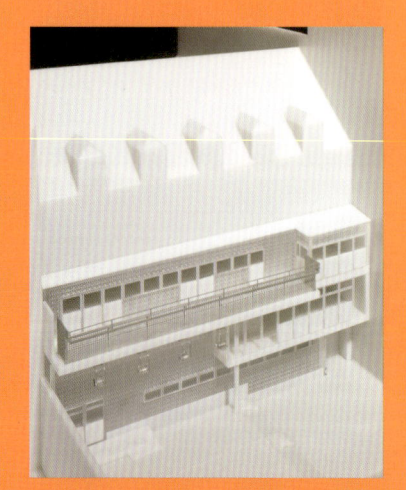

107　ガラスの家　模型　1：100　2006年

156　2階サロン｜1993年撮影｜撮影：ジョルジュ・メゲルディトシアン

159　2階サロン｜1993年撮影｜撮影：ジョルジュ・メゲルディトシアン

166 2階食堂｜1993年撮影｜撮影：ジョルジュ・メゲルディトシアン

168 2階小サロン（夫人居間）、上階の寝室と行き来するための収納可能な鉄骨の階段が見える｜1993年撮影｜撮影：ジョルジュ・メゲルディトシアン

ンギャルド映画の上映やコンサートの場所として使用できる。小サロンは夫人が友人を招いたり、ダイニングルーム（唯一、シャローのデザインではない家具）はディナーに使われたりする。このダイニングルームは目にふれにくい廊下とパントリーの連続によって、サービス棟に位置する台所につながっている。主人もまた、もっと私的に使える空間を所有している。この主人の書斎と大サロンの間には、レールの上を滑る間仕切りがあり、それが開放されたときには庭園側から玄関のある中庭側まで広々と見通しのよい眺めが提供される。サロンはそのような延長がなくとも、吹き抜けによる2倍の階高と面積のおかげで、家の中で最も広い空間である。もっとも明瞭に構造体が見えるのがここである。金属製の柱が3層分の高さを貫いている。これらの柱はその頂部においてガラスの家の上に載る既存建物の構造を支え、各階の平面も支えている。柱は赤と黒に塗り分けられている。赤は鋲打ちされた鉄の形鋼に塗られた塗料であり、黒はこれらの柱の側面を覆うことになるスレート板の色である。パンチング・メタルの黒色、床のゴム材の淡いベージュ色、ジェラルミン製の表面の銀灰色、木製の大箱のオレンジの木の色、ガラスブロックの光の青みがかった色、しかし同様に家具や衝立や絵画や大きな書棚に収納されている本の背表紙の色彩もあり、柱の存在感は、使用されたさまざまな材料のすべての色彩によっていささか損なわれている。

言われているように、この半透明なファサードには開口部がない。ひとつの窓も開口部もないので、外を見ることができない。そこで、換気が問題になるわけであるが、それについては、機械主義者の装置が解決する。ハンドルによって操作される2枚の重ねられた金属製パネル（換気ガラリ）が、求めるだけの空気の流れをつくれるように、ヴォリュームの上部に設置されている。ガラスブロックのファサードの大きさは、内部空間すべてにおいて、メタリックな支柱の存在感を見るものにおしつける。そしてさらに、赤という色が垂直のメタリックな要素を性格づける。1950年代の改修時のガラスブロックは1930年代のそれと比べて、より青みがかった色と表面のより細かい粒によって識別される。そこで、透明な板ガラスとガラスブロックを組み合わせている庭園側のファサードは、より強い黄緑の色合いを見せる（これはガラスの中に含まれている硫黄の経年変化によるものである）。小サロン、つまり夫人用の居間では、ガラスブロックは使われていない。庭園に面している窓は当初のものである。工業製品の車両の窓枠の上を、特設の窓台の中からガラスが上下して滑るようになっている。ここで最重視されているのは、快適さへのこだわりである。冬には、置き敷きのカーペットがスレート板の床の上に敷かれる。カーテンレールには垂れ布とレースのカーテンが重ねられる。小さな暖炉が温度というよりはむしろ雰囲気を温め直すためにそこにある。この部屋には2つの劇的な小道具がある。すぐ目につくのは、上階の寝室と行き来するための、収納可能な金属製の階段である。もうひとつは、全くこっそりとしたものだが、部屋の一角にある配膳口で、これは魔法のようにお茶を出してもらうためのものである。壁には芸術作品が飾られており、特筆すべきはジャック・リプシッツのレリーフである。

3階に続いている唯一の階段はマホガニーの板でできた踏板と蹴込板をもつ。3階はプライベートなフロア、つまり寝室がある。それはサロンの大空間の上にある、巨大な中2階のようにみえる。このフロアは、ムーブル＝イムーブル（家具＝建物）の手法で空間を構成するピエール・シャローの仕事ぶりをもっともよく示すものである。この原則は、各寝室に通じる廊下に現れている。この廊下にはサロン側から見れば大きな木箱と手摺となる棚である。寝室側から見れば、部屋の間仕切りを形成するクローゼットである。扉が同じような外見を持って繰り返されることで、この組み合わせに特徴を与えている。扉は金属製で、強度のために膨らみを持ち、黒く塗装されている。寝室では、壁も同じものになっている。というのも、これらのクローゼットは「二重扉構造」だからである。つまり、衣類は廊下側から使用人が整えて並べ、寝室側から各自によって取り出される。各寝室に浴室があるが、子どもの寝室では部屋の中にあり、主人の寝室では、寝室に隣接して独立して設けられている。ダルザス氏の寝室の家具は、サン＝ジェルマン大通りのアパルトマンにあったもので、シャローが最初に依頼された品は、新しい環境の中に統合されることになった。可動式のタンスの腰高の回転する間仕切り、浴室のさまざまな空間を形成する、つや消しされた金属製のすべては、この家具のクラシシズムと対照をなす。ここでは衛生と収納整理というテーマがシャローをさらなる発明と洗練へと駆り立てている。3つの寝室と浴室は互いにクローゼットの長さ分ある廊下を介して行き来が可能で、さらに建物の横幅分の長さがあり、庭園に張り出しているバルコニーへはどの部屋からも出入りすることができる。裏にあるこの小さな庭園から今日私たちが得られる眺めからは、往時の構想を思い描くことはできない。とりわけ樹木が大きく育ち、地面のデザインはほとんど消えてしまった。

庭園側のファサードは中庭側のそれとはかなり異なっている。開口部はガラスブロックではなくなり、その後ろで展開する用途を明らかにしている。患者を待合室から診察室へと導く1階の横連窓。夫人の居間に接し、完全なガラス張りの小さな温室につながる2階の張り出し窓。寝室のフロアではバルコニーの存在によって後退しているように見えるが、ガラスブロックの格子の中に規則的に窓と窓付き扉がうまく収まるように並べている。夜間、ガラスのファサード越しに内部を照らすように、大きな投光器がバルコニーの下から吊るされている。中庭には、投光器を支えるためにファサードから離した金属製の2つの大きな梯子がある。一日の終わりには、ガラスの家は魔法のランタンのようになり、夜が訪れれば外から照らされて、この家は生き続ける。

152

152　パンチングメタルとガラスの扉の向こうに大階段が見える
撮影：ジョルジュ・メゲルディトシアン

154　大階段をサロンへ上がる
撮影：ジョルジュ・メゲルディトシアン

164　2階サロン、正面の書斎との間の仕切りが解放された状態
撮影：ジョルジュ・メゲルディトシアン

164

| 101 | 第II部 | ガラスの家──装飾・家具・建築の統合 |
| --- | PART II | THE HOUSE OF GLASS |

165

171

102

151

172

173

177

165 2階書斎	151 エントランス	128 電気設備盤　撮影者不詳
撮影：ジョルジュ・メゲルディトシアン	撮影：ジョルジュ・メゲルディトシアン	129 統合されたスイッチとコンセントパネル　撮影者不詳
171 3階主寝室	172 3階主寝室浴室	130 電話が取りつけられたスイッチパネル　撮影者不詳
撮影：ジョルジュ・メゲルディトシアン	撮影：ジョルジュ・メゲルディトシアン	
	173 3階子供部屋、左手の金属製仕切りの中には洗面スペースが隠されている	
	撮影：ジョルジュ・メゲルディトシアン	
	177 庭園側のファサード	
	撮影：ジョルジュ・メゲルディトシアン	

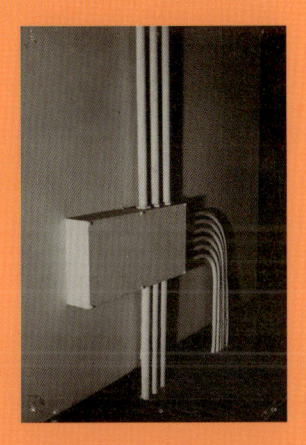

128

129

130

114　3階の家事室からサロンを見下ろす｜撮影：ジョルジュ・ティリエ

125　2階サロン
3階廊下の整理棚の背面が見える｜撮影：ジョルジュ・ティリエ

資料1　サン＝ギヨーム通りの住宅
ポール・ネルソン

　今日の時代は生活に新しい感覚と反応をもたらした。しかし、建築は、それを体現できるほどにはいまだ十分成長していない。というのも、建築はディテール、ファサード、金物、材料あるいは形式、たとえば窓が水平か垂直かで、その建築が何ものであるかが決定されるわけではないからである。大時代的な作風を粉飾するためにうわべばかりの「近代的な」お飾りを目にしたり、実際には見るべきものは何もない、偽広告のような、いわゆる「純粋な」建物を見るのはがっかりするものである。現代の建築には他にやるべきことがあるのだ――たぶんより地味にはなるが――建築家の哲学的感性が、この新しい生活の物理的・精神的プログラムを打ち立て、それを構想として表現することを可能にするだろう。そして、建設のための技術的な知識によってこの構想は実現し、機能するようになるだろう。こうしたことが本当であると示せる機会をパリの一人の医師がシャローに与えた。
　労力の軽減は、この新しい生活の極めて重要な特徴である。一時代を画した自転車による直行の手段以来、人間は機械的な手段によって自らの労力の軽減を推進した――電話、テレグラフ、自動車で二次元の征服を、飛行機、ラジオ、テレビに至って三次元の征服を成し遂げた。そういったなかで、住宅は生活を濃縮する機械とならねばならぬ。今日の人間は、空間だけではなく空間の中の動きというものもよくわかっている。建築家に人々が求めるものを満たせるのは、もはや平面図や断面図ではなく、第四の次元、つまり時間というものが作用してくる。相対的な時の流れのなかに回遊するような空間を創造しなければならない。この4つ目の次元に敏感にならなければならない。サン＝ギヨーム通りの住宅は、この感覚を掻き立てる。
　空間を創造しうるためには、まずそれを限定することから始めなければならない（窓、もしくは透明な壁は、外界と直接つながることになり、空間の印象を消してしまう。それゆえに窓は機能の求められるところに、大変慎重に用いられなければならない）。そこで、すりガラスブロックによって区切られたこの空間の中にある、静的なものと動的なもののコントラストによって生まれた第四の次元を高く評価しなければならない。建築における静力学とは不動で永遠であるはずの骨組みである。可動壁、家具、階段その

104

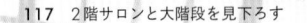

他による水平と垂直の配置によって表現されるダイナミズムは、骨組みから完全に独立している。柱は、規則的に置かれた石標であり、機能の配置をすりぬけて不規則に回遊する道筋を測ることができる。

シャローの住宅は静的なものではない。この住宅は写真的ではない。映画的なのだ。それを味わうには、空間を回遊しなければならない——回遊することによって、今日の人間は空間に結びつけられるものである。この住宅に足を踏み入れると、人はまず他の惑星に移住したような奇妙な感覚を覚える。そして、その空間に慣れ、理解すると、ここに住みたいと思う。そこに完全にはまりこむ。そこで生きたいと思う。

この住宅は建設された。この住宅は機能している。この住宅は抽象的な理念をふりかざしているわけではないが、うまくいっている。壁が空間をしっかり保っている。引き戸が滑る。漏れというものがない。空気調節が機能する。寒さや暑さでくたばりそうには思えない。この住宅は現実のものである。

この住宅はひとつの出発点として重大である。技術の課題に挑み、小さなディテールに至るまで勇敢にそれらを解決した。純粋に審美的な探求は目的ではなかった。しかし、不思議なことに、技術的な研究によってのみ、この住宅はシュルレアリストの彫刻を凌駕したのである。カルダーやジャコメッティならそれを作品とみるかもしれない。主階段の前の吊られた回転扉は、全くもって美しいシュルレアリストの彫刻である。金属製の物入れも同様である。それはなにも「芸術のための芸術」としてやろうとしたものではない。

「近代建築」は死にかかっている。それは文学や音楽でよりうまく表現されるロマンチックな感傷的なものになってしまった。いまや、工学技術に重きをおいた建築が登場した。新しい生活様式が要求するものと、建設のための本物の知識だけを頼りにする建築が登場した。シャローは限定する術を心得ていた。それゆえにシャローは美しいものをつくれたのであり、本物の建築のための出発点に立っているのである。

初出:『ラルシテクチュール・ドージュルデュイ［今日の建築］』no. 9, 1933年11–12月号

資料2　**訪問観察記**
ジュリアン・ルパージュ

　ガラスの家の明確な思考を平面図や写真によって出版物の中で説明するのは、不可能ではないにせよ、とりわけ困難なことである。レンズでも鉛筆でも捉えることのできない、2つのことがある。まず、空間。それは絶えず生成し、訪問者が歩みを進めるにつれ変化する。そしてディテール。これが空間を生き生きとしたものにする。自分でも驚いたのであるが、モノクロの静止画の写真を見ても、絶え間のない変化のなかに生きているように見えるこの住宅が、たくさんの骨で継ぎ合わされた有機体であることに気付かなかったのである。

　これは単に、明確に規定された住宅に付随する実用的なディテールの問題ではない。逆に、すべてはディテールの「継ぎ手」を目立たせるために考えられ、静的な機能すらもメカニックな働きに翻訳されている。主階段は、1階の中央廊下と大サロンをつないでいるのだが、まるで梯子のようにかけられている。建築家はこの吊りの部分を見せるように心配りした。吊られた収納棚も間仕切りの一部である。パントリーからお茶を運ぶための夫人の寝室の小テーブルは、壁のくぼみの中で回転する半円形のものが考案されている。これは全く異なった目的の2つの空間を効果的でさりげなくつないでいる。おそらく、裏板のない棚でも同じことはできよう。しかし、この建築家はそれを使わなかった。この住宅は生き生きとしたメカニズムで振動している。例えばアルミニウムの軽やかな軸の周りを回るパンチング・メタルの覆いが寝室内の水まわりコーナーを隠す。金属で覆われた壁的な要素は、硬い木製の2列のレールの上を滑り、2つの居室の間の開放をガラス、パンチング・メタル、分厚いカーテンによってあらゆる度合に調節できるようにしている。可動式の足場の上を滑るベッド、潜望鏡のように吊られた小さな船階段。精密につくられたこれらの道具は主寝室と夫人室をつなげている。

　この気まぐれな梯子だけではなく、この住宅には4つの階段がそれぞれ固有の方法で考案されている。すでに「モニュメンタルな梯子」については述べた。金属製の腕に固定されたこの階段の踏面はプラスチックゴム製の床材で覆われ、主要な居室ではすべて使用されている。鉄の透かし細工の階段もある。それは医師の書斎に通じている。プライベート用の階段は暖色系の色調の寄木張りで覆われている。パントリーから寝室へ上っていく階段と、もうひとつはコンクリート製のサービス用階段である。

　いたるところで気づかされるのは、機能を可視化することへの配慮、その機能の可能性までも表現することへの配慮、所有者の現実的なニーズを満たすだけでなく、潜在的ニーズにも応えることへの配慮である。たしかに、洗練されたメカニズムで、あらかじめそれらのニーズを満たしながら、所有者がまだ気づいていない新しい欲望を生ぜしめるための配慮がある。そして建築家は惜しむのである。「教養があっても、この家族はまだこの住宅のリズムで暮らしてくれてはいない」と。奇妙だが、重要な告白である。つまり、この住宅はほとんど独立した存在と

して、まるで機械のように自分の規律を所有者に押し付けるのである。

「機械」という言葉は、どこか冷たく、うんざりさせるようなものを想起させる。この住宅の中には、そんなマシニスム（機械信奉）は存在しない。すべての設備は人を脅かすようなものとは無縁である。器具は、とても軽やかに扱われており、その作用があまりに強調されているので、これらは道具というよりむしろ器官なのである。夫人の寝室にある古い家具を隠す、アルミニウム製の格子をご覧あれ。それらがほっそりとした軸で回転するところを。パンチング・メタルが美しくつくられているところを。人は、気持ちよい道具を操作することを好むものだ。人は、建築家のあまたの奉仕者たる器官に対する愛の中に導かれるのである。私たちはすべすべした縁取りのある、弧を描く鉄の薄板だけで構成された扉に魅了される。そのリズムは寝室の前にある長い通路を生き生きとさせる。目立たない錠を上に押し上げながら、扉を開ける。そして、鉄の扉と木の扉の間につくられた優雅な靴の棚を、喜びをもって発見する。そして木の扉は、クローゼットを中に隠してもいる。

私はそのような設備、すべて美しく人間的な道具の魅力を際限なく挙げることもできる。しかし、私は読者がこの住宅が実利的なディテールの集積だとみなすことを恐れる。それは違う。この住宅は逆にひとつの明確な構成であり、その生命の中心は大サロンである。ここからすべての部分が特別の目的に向かって広がっていく。ダイニング、パントリー、台所の領域は大サロンの一方の側に目に見えないように占めている。家族の領域は3階の廊下から階下を見下ろすメタリックなタンスの後ろに隠されている。最後に、診療所の領域だが、これは一階の一番広い部分を占めていて、医師の診察室を介して、玄関ホールと連絡している。

この大サロンのガラスの壁に向かって側壁のない階段を上ると、空間は変貌する。人はある非常に強い、ほとんど荘厳ともいえる印象から逃れられない。この印象は、建築家がこの空間をつくるために使った、かなり特殊な2つの方法によって強調されている。寝室が並んでいる3階の廊下へ上がる階段は、この大サロンの中にはない。二つの階の間の連絡は、つまり隠されたままなのだ。3階は吹き抜けに面していて、大サロンの中にある。劇場のバルコニー席のように。それでこの大サロンは「玄関ホール」の性格とは随分異なった性格を保っているのである。

夜間は、屋外に設置された投光器でガラスの大きな壁を介して照明される。ガラスの大きな面は、かくして光を拡散する性格を保つ。

驚くべきことに、建築家はこの住宅の半透明のガラスブロックの中に多かれ少なかれ、透明なガラス窓も併用しながら、寝室では親密で自由で住みやすい性格を、患者の待合室ではパブリックな場でありながら内省的な性格を、診察室では正確で科学的な性格を、庭の上に吊られた夫人用の居室では優しくフェミニンな

112　2階小サロン（夫人用の居間）上階の寝室と行き来するための収納可能な鉄骨の階段が見える│
撮影：ジョルジュ・ティリエ

115　3階主寝室浴室の収納棚とついたて│
撮影：ジョルジュ・ティリエ

資料2　訪問観察記
ジュリアン・ルパージュ

性格を感じさせる術を心得ていたのである。

　読者は、断面図や写真をじっくり検分することで、これらの可能性に気づき得るだろう。そして、大サロンの半透明の壁が、透明なガラス板とは全く性質を異にするため、外から見たとき大サロンの中がどうなっているのか、想像したくなるにちがいない。最後に、この独特の作品から得られる不思議な体験について、もう一度指摘しよう。この作品は建築本体と同じくらい、すべての大企業を排除して、職人による綿密なディテールを実現した。建築家は「ある工業的標準化の視点から職人によって実現されたモデル」としての住宅を性格付けた。標準化というこの厄介な問題はさておき、私たちはこの住宅のすべてにおいて、非常に職人的なエスプリを認めるのである。そして私たちは、建築家の仕事にはこのエスプリ（それが工業化を導くものであるなら）が大変必要なものであると信じている。

　そして、この情熱的な職人＝建築家、ピエール・シャローは完璧を追求するあまり、私たちが親しんできた伝統的な厳格な建築のあり方から逸脱する。私たちは所有者についての一文、所有者が住宅のリズムの中で生活していないという一文を先に引用した。

　この住宅を訪問するなかで、私たちはこの住宅の従属的な部分が住民の新しいニーズを喚起するまでに自律的であることに気づいた。しかし、建築家としての仕事というものは、新しいニーズを創り出す方向に向かうものではなく、むしろ目の前のニーズを厳しく定義し、率直に（できるだけ率直に！）満足させるものなのだと私は信じている。

　神経を高ぶらせる都市生活の一日を終えて帰宅するとき、少なくとも家の中にいるときには、人間の生活というものはすべての複雑さから解放されているものだということを、私たちは喜んで確認したい。つまり、私たちは食事をする。私たちの曽祖父の代と同じようにテーブルのまわりに、椅子に座って食べる。食事マシーンのようなものではなく、カップや取り皿、スプーンを使って食べるのである。このような私たちの生活における分断を、二元論と形容してもよい。そう、私たちはこの二元論を受け入れよう。私たち建築家特有の務めは、生活をそのようなものと認識し、自身も参加している現実の生活にひとつの形態を与えることであると認めよう。ところが、空想家は全く別のことを考える。建築における空想主義の時代は終わったと断言することを恐れるのはやめよう。

　このことはピエール・シャローの努力の興味深さを半減するものではない。ひとつの見事な作品が実現されている。ひとつの貴重な経験がつくり出されている。しかしそれに加えて、ひとつの問題、私たちの職能の問題が提起されているのである。

初出：『ラルシテクチュール・ドージュルデュイ』no.9、1933年11–12月号
ジュリアン・ルパージュは建築史家ユリウス・ポーゼナーのペンネーム

資料3　ガラスの家
ピエール・シャロー

　私はしばしばこう言われるのを聞いた――「住宅は飛行機ではないし、大型客船でも、実験室でもない。機械の神の横暴に屈するより、家の守護神を信仰していた方がずっといい」

　ガラスの家は現代生活に横たわるさまざまな問題を解決しようとする試みであるが、その解決方法は何よりもまず人間的なものでなければならず、実際に居住すればそれが納得できるはずである。

　この住宅は1925年に計画され、1931年から住まわれ、今日ではやってきたことに確信をもつようになった。

　建築はひとつの社会的な芸術である。それは同時に、すべての芸術を包括するものであり、人間の総体の発露である。何百万もの人の声を聴き、理解し、苦悩を共にし、苦しみを取り除くために闘うことでしか、建築家は創造することはできない。建築家は人間が叩き上げた鉄を使い、人間を未来へと誘う。建築家は人間というものの過去を知っているからである。実に、建築家は人間のためにしか生きないのである。

　人間は秩序を求める。人間はより少ない労力で物事を実現させ、時間を支配したいと望む。私たちの研究は、そのお手伝いである。

　半透明のファサードは、ガラスのためのガラスではない。17世紀の古い館（14×14メートル程度）の基礎の上に建設されたこの建物の平面図をじっくり眺めれば、古い邸宅の普通の階高の窓は3分の1の光を奪っている。より決定的なひとつの証拠（それはひとつの試練でもあるが）は、住宅の計画が決まったとき、ここは庭園に囲まれていた。

　竣工が近づいてくると、ある噂が流れる。家に沿ったロマンティックな庭園が消え、そのうちに高さ25メートルの壁が視線を閉じるというのではないか……庭園側のファサードは永遠に暗がりの中におかれるかもしれない、と。さてところが……私にとってこれは断じて重要であると言わなければならないのであるが、何も変わっていないのである。光は以前のように至るところに差し込んでいる。しかも、私の協力者で友人のベルナルト・ベイフットの計算によれば、私たちは都市計画のために無駄になっていた土地の25-30パーセントを取り戻すことができたのである。

　人間は孤独も望むが、心地よく集まることや、たやすく移動できることも望む。空間の再編成と今日の技術の適切な採用によって、すべては住宅のなかに与えられる。

　半透明のファサードを採用しようとしまいと、それでもなお問題は残る。住宅、そして都市計画には、時代が、そして人間的尺度がはたらいている。

　すべての現代的な建築の解決方法は、これらの基本的な関係に配慮しながら創造されることになろう。

初出：芸術文学雑誌『ル・ポワン』no.2、1937年

110　3階の庭園側ファサードを内側から見る　建設中のガラスの家｜撮影：ジョルジュ・ティリエ

126　1階庭園側のファサード　竣工時のガラスの家｜撮影：ジョルジュ・ティリエ

077 『家具』序文、『今日の国際芸術』
vol. 7、おそらく1929年、
シャルル・モロー出版、パリ
（書影はp.114参照）

資料4　『家具』序文

『今日の国際芸術』vol. 7より

INTRODUCTION

〈国際現代家具〉というタイトルを付けた作品を紹介するにあたって、取り上げるべき作品の選択基準がいかにも恣意的で、明らかに非常識ではないかといぶかる読者諸氏がいるかもしれない。すなわち、世間で代表的な家具として認められているものをほとんど考慮せず、あまつさえ第一人者たちの傑作さえも無視しているのではないか、と。だが、もちろん私は、家具づくりの第一人者たちに対しては最大の敬意を持っている。したがって、ここで私が強調したいポイントは、「非考慮」や「無視」などといったこととは別次元の話である。

　思うに、そもそも動産に分類される家具は"動かせるもの"であって、この点をわきまえて本来の建築と関係づけることなくしては、きちんと考案することは不可能である。

　この「本来の建築」は、今まさにその黎明期にある。

　家具と建築との関係をうまく見定めることは必ずしも容易でなく、矛盾をはらむことも珍しくない。

　我々に感動を与えてくれるのは新たなイメージだけである。

　　　　　　　新たなイメージは新境地を開く。
　　　　……それは旧いイメージを打破する……
　　　　　　　それは我々の想像力を誘発する。
　　　　　　　我々を無限の希望で満たし、
　　　　　　　我々の心の中に熱い信念をかきたてる。

私は当該の家具様式の形成要素をことさら分析するまでもなくある種の金属製家具の貢献が最も大事だと考えている。なぜなら、金属を利用することによってのみ、望ましい新たなイメージが形づくられるからである。そのイメージはいかなる偏向や固執もないために、我々の想像力の発揮に不可欠な心の休息をもたらすだけでなく、それによって我々が待ち望む将来の創造開花を準備することにもなるはずである。

　我々の想像力のために必要な心の休息（それは有用性に満足することで得られる）。

　新境地を開いたり、旧いイメージを打破したりする新たなイメージが次々と生起すること。それこそは、我々がその偉大さを簡単には理解できないような豊かな時代の到来の確かな兆候である。

　私が第一人者たちの傑作や一般の家具をあえて割愛してしまったことをどうかお許しいただきたい。

　私としては、こうした新たなイメージを取りまとめることによって、「人生」という唯一かつ共通のゆるぎないの使命のために、世界中に散らばって仕事をしている仲間たちを多少とも紹介できるならば望外の喜びである。

ピエール・シャロー

110

PART III

第 III 部

苦難の時代——不況下の模索と支援
THE DIFFICULTIES

新天地を求めて——新たな展開
IN EXILE

1階庭園側の出入口｜1932年撮影｜撮影：ジョルジュ・ティリエ

論考　1930年代：ピエール・シャローとUAMの10年
ジャン＝フランソワ・アルキエリ

マルサン館で1930年に開催された、近代芸術家連合（UAM）*1 の最初の展覧会の折、ピエール・シャローは招聘アーティストとして参加し、家具（本棚、金属製フレームの事務机、ジャン・ブルクハルトのラグ、ワックス磨きされたマホガニーでできたキャビネットにジョイントで接続した円形のローテーブル）を展示する。これらの家具は、見た目も技術も変化に富んだ非常に個性的な造形芸術で、家具メーカー・トーネット社の影響を感じさせるル・コルビュジエ、ピエール・ジャンヌレ、シャルロット・ペリアンの家具の均質性にも並ぶものである。この展覧会の後、シャローは全会一致でUAMのメンバーに推薦される。

この一大イベントは装飾家のモダニズム（デコラトゥール）の潮流を示すもので、彼らは同時代の人々に生活の枠組みに新しい要素を提供し、社会の技術的進化に適応した日常のかたち（オブジェ、家具、建築）をつくりたいと思っていた。「贅沢品の製造」という国の伝統を支持する者と、近代精神と大量生産の工業化のしくみによって具現化された進歩を擁護する者との間の対立を、この展覧会は鮮明にしたのである。フランス社会のふたつのビジョンの間には深刻な軋轢があった。これが経済危機にあった1930年代初頭の状況である。

UAMとドイツ工作連盟とは、1930年6月の芸術家装飾家サロン（SAD）への参加の時点から対立していた。ドイツ工作連盟とは、バウハウスの校長であったヴァルター・グロピウス率いるドイツの装飾家・建築家のアヴァンギャルドの一派である。専門性対洗練、集団対個人。ドイツとフランスの対比は鮮明である。この対比が、UAMの展覧会において、フランスの今日の装飾家グループがドイツの建築家によってなされた努力と同等のものを生み出す能力があり、最も進歩的で、最も大胆であると批評家に認めさせることになる。

1929年、UAMの最初の方向性は、シャルル・モロー社の『今日の国際芸術』シリーズ20巻のアルバムの編集と時事報告書の出版によって示された。各巻にはUAMの各メンバーによる序文があり、テーマごとにフランス国内外の事例が選ばれ掲載されている。シャローは第7巻『家具』の序文を担当している。

より明白なUAMのキャンペーンとしては、ロベール・マレ＝ステヴァンスが率いた1930年3月の、『ラ・スメーヌ・ア・パリ』という新聞の発行元のオフィスの改修がある。忠実な共働者たち、ガラス芸術家のルイ・バリエや彫刻家のマルテル兄弟とともに、マレ＝ステヴァンスはファサードを手掛ける。装飾家たちが家具、室内装飾、照明といった空間一式を分業でデザインする。このようにして他の幾人かのなかで、シャローは受付のホールと編集部室を、家具デザイナーで建築家のフランシス・ジュールダ

077 『家具』、ピエール・シャロー編、『今日の国際芸術』vol.7、
おそらく1929年、シャルル・モロー出版、パリ（序文はp.110参照）

ンは重役室を仕上げる。

　批評家たちは揃って、この最初のデモンストレーションを応用装飾芸術の模範的な成功例とみなし、作家たちの改装技術の高さ、想像力、近代的な生活の枠組みにおける快適さを扱う能力へ賛辞を呈している。

　UAMの成立と並行して、1928年6月、スイスのラ・サラ城での会議をきっかけに、国際的な理論討議の場となるCIAM（近代建築国際会議）が組織される。国レベルでは、近代建築運動の活発なスポークスマンであるアンドレ・ブロックが、1930年11月に建築雑誌『ラルシテクチュール・ドージュルデュイ［今日の建築］』誌を創刊する。この雑誌は、フランツ＝フィリップ・ジュールダン、オーギュスト・ペレやCIAMやUAMに属するアヴァンギャルド、シャロー、アンドレ・リュルサ、ロベール・マレ＝ステヴァンス、ガブリエル・ゲヴレキアン、フランシス・ジュールダンといった、モダニストの大物の後見者たちによって構成される委員会を頼りにしていた。

　1931年のUAMの2回目の展覧会で[*2]、シャローは再び家具とジャン・ダルザス医師のためにパリで建設中の建物の模型を出品した。この建物は、建築家ベルナルト・ベイフットと金物職人ルイ・ダルベとの協働である。その後にも、この模型は何回か展覧会に出品されるが、これが「ガラスの家」の初公開である[*3]。しかし、この作品についての批評家のコメントや分析は、『ラルシテクチュール・ドージュルデュイ』誌の特集の出版を待たねばならない。ヴァルター・グロピウスによるベルリンのジーメンスシュタット団地（1929年）の写真を見たとしても、その模型はエレガンスと透明性の繊細な魔力の限りをふりまいている。その他にも外国からの招聘作品があり、ウィレム＝マリヌス・デュドック、アルベルト・サルトリスに加え、サンテリアの「新都市」（1913年）も紹介されている。

　ジャン・カルリュ、ロベール・マレ＝ステヴァンス、シャルロット・アリクスと同様に、この展覧会の後、シャローはUAMの委員に選ばれる。シャローは方向性を決定するための討論を望み、個人の展示をやめて、集団としてプレゼンテーションすることを主張する。

　装飾芸術中央連合（UCAD）の後援を受けて、1932年にマルサン館で3回目の展覧会が開催されたのは、不穏な政治情勢と世界恐慌というコンテクストのなかである[*4]。図案家による共同プレゼンテーション以外は、やはり経済的な理由によって個人展示の原則が継続される。シャローは家具と補足でボーヴァロンのホテルのゴルフ場クラブハウスの写真を展示する。

　1930年代のもっとも優れたスペシャリストを結集した図案・広告部門では[*5]、ソ連のアーティストの参加とジャン・カルリュのポスター「国家の軍備縮小のために」（1932年）について、美術評論家チエボー＝シッソンの中傷記事「芸術再編におけるソビエト社会主義共和国連邦とドイツの工業」が書かれることになり、UCADによるポスターの撤収という事態が引き起こされる。

　UAMは返答する権利を要望し、UCADからの財政的独立を公に宣言し、「我々の会員は、自らの芸術を広める以外の目的を追求しない」と主張する[*6]。UAMはまたUCADに対し、マルサン館での展示中止を引き起こし、将来の展覧会を不可能にしてしまったポスターの再展示も要求する。

　1932年、ポール・イリブとギュスターヴ・ウムデンシュトックは弁明書（『豊穣擁護。職人仕事の擁護』）を出版した。それがさまざまな攻撃に対応するため、UAMにひとつの宣言文を書くきっかけとなった。『アール・エ・デコラシオン［芸術と装飾］』誌の経営者であるルイ・シュロネが、その宣言文の著者である。

　1933年の4回目の展覧会[*7]では、建築部門にかなりの部分が割り当てられた。それでも、シャローは高級家具一式（ソファー、本棚、大きな収納家具兼本棚、エレーヌ・アンリの大きな明るい色のラグ）を展示するのみであった。批評家はテーブルの天板が花を飾れるように切り取られた金属とガラスのテーブルを記憶にとどめた。

　建築のウルトラモダンな傾向は、写真と平面図と模型で示される。例えば、ロベール・マレ＝ステヴァンスによるクロワのヴィラ・カヴロワ、ル・コルビュジエとピエール・ジャンヌレによるアルジェの街の都市計画、ジョルジュ＝アンリ・パンギュッソンによるサン＝トロペのホテル・ラチチュード43、ポール・ネルソンによるリールの大規模病院施設、アンドレ・リュルサによるヴィルジュイフの学校とその家具、アントニオ・サルトリスによるルチエの教会がその例である。

1934年7月、宣言書『近代芸術のために、現代的な生活の枠組みを』を出版した際、UAMはパリ16区のマレ＝ステヴァンス通りで展覧会を企画する。この機会に、ジャン・カルリュ、ジョルジュ＝アンリ・パンギュッソン、アンドレ・サロモンは、形態を単純化すること、より多くの人々のニーズと希望を定義し満足させることの必要性をUAMとして再度明確にする。そして、今日的な審美の動向を社会の進化へ適用することだけが、この景気後退の時期を克服することを可能にするともはっきりと述べている。宣言書は誹謗中傷者の言い分に逐一回答しているものの、かといって曖昧さの全くない、理論的な説明を生み出すことには成功していない。

1934年にジョルジュ＝アンリ・パンギュッソンが委員に任命され、『ラルシテクチュール・ドージュルデュイ』誌の援助を得て、企業経営者と芸術家の距離を縮めるための活動に着手する。複雑な企画は成果をあげることはなかったが、UAMのなかで考え得る合意の条件は整えた。

　UAMの最初の協調的な関係が具体化するのは、「サロン・デ・ザール・メナジェ」（生活芸術展）の役員のポール・ブルトンが、住宅展の企画をUAMと連携している『ラルシテクチュール・ドージュルデュイ』誌に任せたときである。この新しい舞台によって、ようやくすべての人の手に届きやすい工業生産という目的をもち、住宅、家具、機能をもった場所について再考し、大衆に訴求することが可能となった。1934年の最初の展覧会*8では、建築写真や模型が展示され、シャロー、レイモン・フィッシャー、ル・コルビュジエ、ロベール・マレ＝ステヴァンスが紹介された。1935年には*9、シャローとルネ・エルブストによって「装飾家のギャラリー」と題された2回目の展覧会が企画される。そこでは、手ごろな価格の量産品のコレクションが提案される。金属を使った家具で参加した企画者たちの他には、ロベール・マレ＝ステヴァンス（煉瓦製の暖炉）、フランツ＝フィリップ・ジュールダンとアンドレ・ルイ（暖炉まわりのインテリアデザイン）、アンドレ・リュルサ（台所）、ピエール・バルブ、ジャン・ギンスベルグ、ジョルジュ＝アンリ・パンギュッソン、ルイ・ソニョといった、UAMメンバー全員が参加する。

ふたつめの協定は、電気中央局や照明技術者のアンドレ・サロモンの仲介によるもので、マルセル・ロッシュによって企画された2回目の「サロン・ド・ラ・リュミエール」（光のサロン、1934年）にUAMの参加を提案するものであった。パリ電力供給会社の建物の中で開催された1935年の3回目の「サロン・ド・ラ・リュミエール」*10にも再び参加が実現した。こ

187 エレーヌ・アンリ（ピエール・シャローによる下図に基づく）
織物見本｜1925年頃

188 エレーヌ・アンリ｜織物見本｜1925年頃

ref.009 ― 1935年のパリ万国博覧会における写真展示板｜撮影：L.V.グレゴリウス

090　アパルトマンの改装　模型

のサロンでは3フロアにわたって、建築家と装飾家（アルシテクト デコラトゥール）と技術者（アンジェニウール）の緊密な協働から生まれた最新の成果が公開されている。ロベール・マレ＝ステヴァンスとアンドレ・サロモンはUAMのすべての芸術上の専門分野を紹介している。ステンドグラス、彫刻、絵画、宝飾品、金銀細工品、シャローの光る本棚、カッサンドルとジャン・カルリュの光るポスター、ル・コルビュジエとピエール・ジャンヌレの夜のアルジェのジオラマといった作品で、どれも光の適用例として作品にしたものである。

鉄利用のための技術局（OTUA）の顧問であるルネ・エルブストは、客船用のより耐火性の高い客室を実現する金属性部品を造船業者に提案するため、OTUAの同意を得てUAMに助言を求める。6つの提案のうち[11]、4つは企業家の全面的な協力を得て実物の家具を装備して実現したもので、1934年のサロン・ドートンヌで展示され、UAMの毎年の共同展覧会が行えるようになった。この「技術」分野は、フェルナン・レジェの装飾的な絵画のようなより芸術的な専門分野によって補完される。それらの計画案は「パリ国際航海サロン」（1935年）とガリエラ美術館で開催された「旅行への招待」展（1936年）でも部分的に繰り返し展示されることになる。これらの計画案は批評家の歓迎を受ける。一般の人々の目にも海上火災を避けるための効果的な対策と映るからである。

OTUAは、学校家具の計画案があった1936年の協働の経験を、1937年のサロン・ドートンヌとサロン・デ・ザール・メナジェに引き継いだ。

1937年のパリ万博[12]の準備は1932年4月、有力な芸術家団体の参加交渉によって始まる。少数派で思想的に対立関係にあるUAMの代表者[13]は、提案された方向性に賛同することを非常に早い時期に拒否し、交渉から離脱する。UAMがこの国際的な行事の枠組みのなかで、どのようなかたちで参加すべきか討論を行うのは、1935年のはじめを待たなければならない。UAMは毎年の展覧会に使えるパヴィリオンの建設のための助成金を獲得しようと目論む。決定機関との連絡全般を担当したルネ・エルブストが、技術的問題の解決と予算の獲得のために政治的に難しい環境（集会、ストライキ、国民議会選挙の準備）のなかで交渉を進める。1936年4月のフランス人民戦線政府の成立は、共同的な社会・文化の思想によって支えられたUAMの社会参加に有利にはたらく。

1936年1月、ジョルジュ＝アンリ・パンギュッソンは、セーヌ川岸にフランツ＝フィリップ・ジュールダンとアンドレ・ルイとの協働でUAMのパヴィリオンを、ジャン＝シャルル・モルーは庭園を担当して建設することを仲間から任された。目標は、建物のコンセプトからメンバー全員の作品のプレゼンテーションまで、1934年の宣言書のなかで定義さ

083

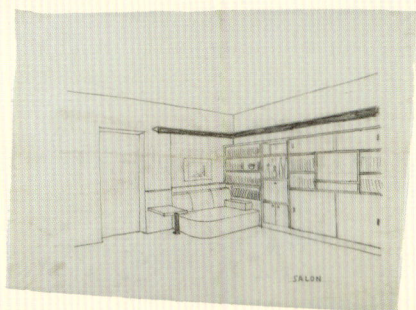

085

086

087

083, 085-087 サロン　透視図

084　子供部屋　透視図

れたUAMの精神を、模範的な方法で明示し表現することである。

建物の全体的な様相と空間の属性を決定する、ふたつの方針が、展示のために採用される。ひとつは、フランシス・ジュールダンによって提案された「バザール」（上質な日用品のコレクション、手ごろな値段のハンドメイドもしくは工業製品）型の共同の展示スペースで、もうひとつは家具などのひと揃いの作品のギャラリー（作家ごとの個人展示）である。目を引く金属を使った構造の露出、ピロティのある建造物、アクセスのスロープ、階段（ジャン・プルーヴェの受付ホールの大階段）、ファサードの透明性、ポール付きの案内標識といったパヴィリオンの建築上のディテールの扱いは、建築の新たな近代性の特徴的な兆しを明らかにした。

こうして1937年の万博は、第二次世界大戦前のUAMメンバーの最後の共同の一大行事となるのである。

戦争がUAMとシャローの関係を完全に断ち切ったわけではなかった。フランスの国土解放の後、1945年1月26日のUAMの臨時総会において、議長のロベール・マレ＝ステヴァンスは、ピエール・シャローのニューヨーク滞在について言及する。ガブリエル・ゲヴレキアンとジャン・カルリュはアメリカから帰国すると、シャローの近況を伝える。シャローの仲間は皆、全員揃って彼の早い帰国を願い、はたらきかける。しかし、帰国はずっと延期された。

1949年、パリの国立近代美術館（現・装飾美術館）において、1925年の博覧会で展示された「フランスの大使の館」の執務室を構成した作品を集めた展示室の公式な開場式があり、厳かなオマージュがピエール・シャローに贈られる。装飾芸術の発展におけるシャローの影響を証明する作品群だからである。この展示は、ダルザス夫妻、エレーヌ・アンリ、ローズ・アドラー、美術館学芸課、ルネ・エルブストの貴重な協力のおかげである。

「親愛なるルネ（・エルブスト）へ

君を助けてくれている皆へ、どれほど私が彼らに心から感謝しているかを伝えておくれ。それから、私がもっと手紙を書かないとしたら、それは多くの場合、手紙を書ける時には、疲れが出て、書くのに必要な力が消え去ってしまうから、ということも伝えておくれ。本当にありがとう。みんなに感謝している。　あなたたちのピエール・シャロー」*14

シャローの没後、究極の感謝のしるしが、一冊のモノグラフ『ひとりの発明家、建築家ピエール・シャロー』である。このモノグラフはシャロー夫人が保存していた資料をもとに、1954年にUAM会長のルネ・エルブストが発表したもので、序文をフランシス・ジュールダンが書き、サロン・デ・ザール・メナジェとUAMが協力して刊行したものである。

*1
装飾芸術博物館、マルサン館、パリ（1930年6月11日–7月14日）
*2
ギャルリー・ジョルジュ・プティ、パリ（1931年5月27日–6月18日）
*3
同年のサロン・ドートンヌへ第二の模型展示、その後1933年にギャルリー・ヴィニオンで、1934年にギャルリー・カイエ・ダールで展示
*4
装飾芸術博物館、マルサン館、パリ（1932年2月4日–3月7日、3月17日まで期間延長）
*5
ジャン・カルリュ、ポール・コラン、カッサンドル（別名アドルフォ・ムロン）、シャルル・ルポ、シャルル・ペイニョ
*6
『フランスの企業』誌、no.1、1932年2月25日、p.9。UAMの返信を参照のこと
*7
ギャルリー・ラ・ルネッサンス、パリ（1933年5月30日–6月28日）
*8
住宅展——第11回サロン・デ・ザール・メナジェ、グランパレ、パリ（1934年2月1日–2月18日）
*9
第2回住宅展——第12回サロン・デ・ザール・メナジェ、グランパレ、パリ（1935年1月31日–2月17日）
*10
第3回サロン・ド・ラ・リュミエール、CPDEビル、ロシェ通り40番地、パリ（1935年10月11日–11月3日）
*11
ブレ社、カレックス社、クリーグ社、ジヴィ社と協働のルネ・エルブスト、ピエール・バルブとロネオ、ガスコワンとジャン・プルーヴェの建設事務所、ロベール・マレ＝ステヴァンスとフランボ社はそれぞれ協働して展示した。一方、ピエール・シャローとG.H.パンギュッソンは実物大の模型を展示した
*12
近代生活における技術と芸術の国際博覧会、パリ、1937年
*13
ロベール・マレ＝ステヴァンス、ルネ・エルブスト、ジャン・フケ
*14
ルネ・エルブスト『ひとりの発明家、建築家ピエール・シャロー』サロン・デ・ザール・メナジェ–UAM出版、パリ、1954年、p.12を参照のこと。

181　ピエール・ヴァゴ「パリのある個人邸」、ポール・ネルソン「サン・ギヨーム通りの住宅」、
ジュリアン・ルパージュ「訪問観察記」が掲載された『ラルシテクチュール・ドージュルデュイ』no. 9
1933年11–12月号、アンドレ・ブロック編集、パリ

VI 苦難の時代 —— 不況下の模索と支援
THE DIFFICULTIES | LES DIFFICULTES

アメリカで始まった世界恐慌はたちどころにヨーロッパへ達し、1930年代のフランスは不況と大量の失業者で経済は逼迫する。加えて、社会主義の勝利、ファシズムの嵐、再び忍びよる世界大戦への不安で人々の生活は荒んでいき、シャローの活動範囲もじりじりと狭まっていく。フランス建築界では装飾家芸術家サロン（SAD）の旧勢力に代わって、マレ＝ステヴァンスを会長に近代芸術家連合（UAM）が結成され、1928年にはル・コルビュジエらを中心に第1回近代建築国際会議が開催された。フランスの建築専門誌『ラルシテクチュール・ドージュルデュイ［今日の建築］』が創刊されたのもこの年である。シャローはこうした活動に全般的に関わり、周囲の支援で辛うじて仕事を続けたが、実現作はわずかである。

LES DIFFICULTES

ラ・スメーヌ・ア・パリ新聞本社

パリ、ダサ通り28番地（1930年）

この新聞社の社屋改修の仕事は近代芸術家連合（UAM）が推進していたものである。シャローは入口、玄関、ロビー、および編集室を手掛けるように招かれた。

　シャローが参加したことによって、ふたつの特徴的な方向性が顕著になった。第一は金属部品だけを使うことで家具と装飾の統一性が確保された点であり、第二は実際よりも広く感じられるようなヴォリュームの処理が行われた点であった。棚、植物のプランター、照明器具、可動式間仕切りに加えて、棚板、椅子、腰掛けなどもルイ・ダルベの工房でつくられたものである。シャローはボーヴァロンのゴルフ場のクラブハウスのために考案した金属製の椅子などをここでも利用している。しかるべく付属品を取り付けたり、中に詰め物をしたり、外装をアレンジすることによって、屋外用の家具からの用途変更が図られた。ただし、これらの家具は専門誌の関心をほとんど引かず、むしろ非難するような論調さえあった。アーネスト・ティスランドは次のように評している。

「そこに置かれた幾つかの椅子は、つい数カ月前にシャローがサロン・ドートンヌに出品したものであったが、我々はその椅子に関して当時から彼を批判していた。問題の作品は独創的だといえば確かにそうではあるが、特に便利で使いやすいわけでないからである。その点は既に指摘したことであるから、ここではあえて繰り返す必要はあるまい。しかしそれはそれとして、シャローが"ラ・スメーヌ・ア・パリ"で実現した高雅なインテリアコーディネートにおいては、これらの椅子が最高の効果を発揮していることを認めないのは不当であろう」*

こういう批評の一方で、モールスキンのついたてや天井は、「まるで底なしの湖の中のようにさまざまな物が映っている」などと言われた**。ついたてや天井の表面をミラーのように煌めかせれば奥行きを感じさせることができ、床の各所に違った材質を使えば仕切りなどを設けなくともスペースを差異化することが可能となり、さらには、さまざまなヴォリュームが相互に嵌め込まれているように演出によって空間にゆとりを生み出すことも不可能ではない。シャローはこうしたテクニックを駆使しながら、社屋の実際の狭さをものともせずに、そこに「まれに見る偉大さを刻印する」***ことに成功したのだった。

*
アーネスト・ティスランド著「"ラ・スメーヌ・ア・パリ新聞本社"における現代芸術家たち」、『ラール・ヴィヴァン［生きている芸術］』、1930年5月1日、no.129、p.362
**
P. L.「"ラ・スメーヌ・ア・パリ新聞本社"の新オフィス」、『芸術と芸術家たち』、no.106、1930年、p.244
***
『ラール・ヴィヴァン』所収、アーネスト・ティスランドの前掲稿

088

089

088, 089 ラ・スメーヌ・ア・パリ新聞本社、ダサ通り

088 『商店の外観と内装』誌より、シャルル・モロー出版、パリ、撮影年不詳
089 編集室廊下、ラ・スメーヌ・ア・パリ新聞本社│『アール・エ・デコラシオン』誌、1930年

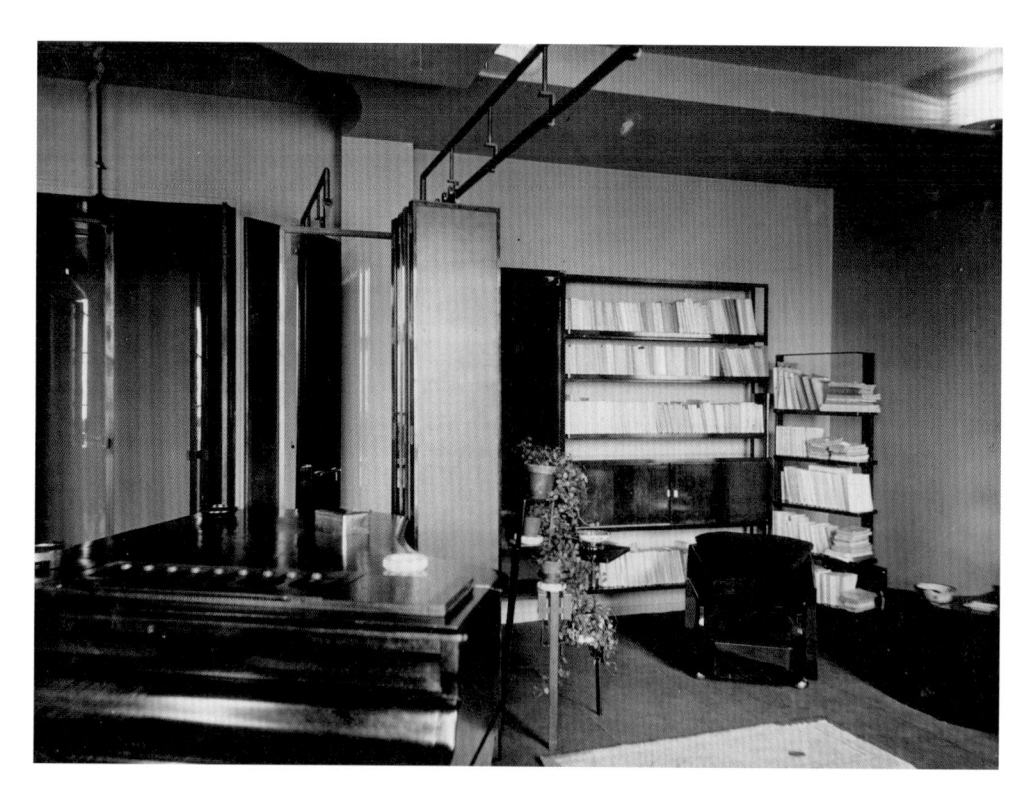

091

LES DIFFICULTES

D. ドレフュスのアパルトマン

パリ、ル・タス通り9番地（1932年）

1930年頃、シャローは非常に大きなアパルトマンの改修を依頼された。これに関してある批評家が次のように述べている。

「つまり現代のインテリアの要諦は、単にどんなカーペットや壁の絵を選ぶかということではない。何よりもまず空間の配分や配置の問題なのだ。具体的には、古いアパルトマンのすべての間仕切り壁をとっぱらって、できるだけ広い単一の部屋にする。それから、元々あったさまざまな用途の部屋をその広大な空間の中に配置し直す。ただしその際は、せっかく見出した広い空間の利点を損なわないように気を付けなければいけない。そこで、可動式の間仕切り壁の役割を果たす背の高いついたてや、間仕切りした空間の独立性をより完全に確保できるガラスの隔壁を巧みに利用する（ガラスにすれば、部屋を一望できるという魅力的なポイントを台無しにすることはない）。かくして、室内装飾家としての役割と建築家としての役割が統合するわけである」*

ここでは、シャローが探求した可動性（モビリティ）の考え方がさまざまな仕掛けによって展開されている。すなわち壁に取りつけた引き出し、むき出しのレールで吊り下げた引き戸、回転する戸棚、丸みをつけた2枚扉のガラス戸（「ガラスの家」で使った方式と同様に上部に回転軸が付いている）などである。ついたては確かにパネルを蛇腹折りにしてはいるが、その設置方法はむしろ可動式の間仕切り壁に近い（金属製の細い横棒にレールを吊るしている）。要するに、スペースの区分がしかるべく保持され、柔軟性と透明性が追求されているのである。

この批評家はさらに次のように付言している。

「シャローは、石や金属の単なる壁の上の淡い色でさえ、そっけない印象を与えないことに成功している」**

*
ピエール・ミジェヌ著「P. シャローの2つインテリアコーディネートについて」、『アール・エ・デコラシオン［芸術と装飾］』、1932年、p.130
**
同上 p.132

091, 092　可動式のついたてのあるドレフュス夫妻の
アパルトマン内装｜撮影：アトリエ・シャロー

LES DIFFICULTES

M. ファーリのアパルトマン

パリ、ラファエル大通り（1932年）

批評家ピエール・ミジェヌは次のように評している。

「こうした建築的な構成においては、たんす類も素材、レリーフ、及び色合いの点ではコーニスや円柱と同じ価値を持つ。その反面、鉄もガラスも昔ながらの建築資材としての有用性、すなわち"固定パーツ"としての有用性から脱却し、"可動パーツ"であるところの家具類の仲間に加わって、石（壁類）と木（椅子やテーブル）を連結する役割を果たすようになる」*

暖房ラジエーターの前の回転棚や、ボールキャスター付き可動ローテーブルなどはその好例である。ミジェヌによれば、シャローが「最も偉大な新機軸」に突き進むことができたのは、やはり鉄とガラスのおかげであった。ミジェヌは次のように言葉を続けている**。

「シャローは M. ファーリの応接間でそれをやったわけであるが、まったくもって、部屋の真ん中にガラス戸を設置してしまうことほど冒険的な試みはないだろう。なにしろ、そのガラス戸は一辺だけしか壁に接しておらず、もう一方はあたかも"宙ぶらりん"になっているのだから。そして必要とあれば、広げたついたてをそこに繋げて部屋をふたつに分けることができるようになっている。いずれにしても、注目すべき結果を考えれば、こうした大胆な試みも悪くない」

実際にはガラスの間仕切りはカーテンで覆い隠せるが、ついたてのほうはスペースを完全に囲ってしまうことはない。というのも、3つの細いV字形金具に引っ掛けられている空中レールが、部屋を横断しきらないまま宙に浮いているからである。この結果、可動部分と固定部分との対照、透明性の競合、および左右の円弧の戯れによって、風変わりな性格がこの空間に付与されている。とりわけ応接間の中央に食堂を設けるシャローの配置方法は、まさに風変わりな性格というにふさわしいであろう。

*
ピエール・ミジェヌ著「P. シャローの2つのインテリアコーディネートについて」、『アール・エ・デコラシオン』、1932年、p.130
**
同上 pp.131–132

094 応接間と食堂（中央）、ファーリ家のアパルトマン、ラファエル大通り｜撮影年・撮影者不詳

LES DIFFICULTES
近代技術としての「モダンな鋼管」

コート掛け（1932年）

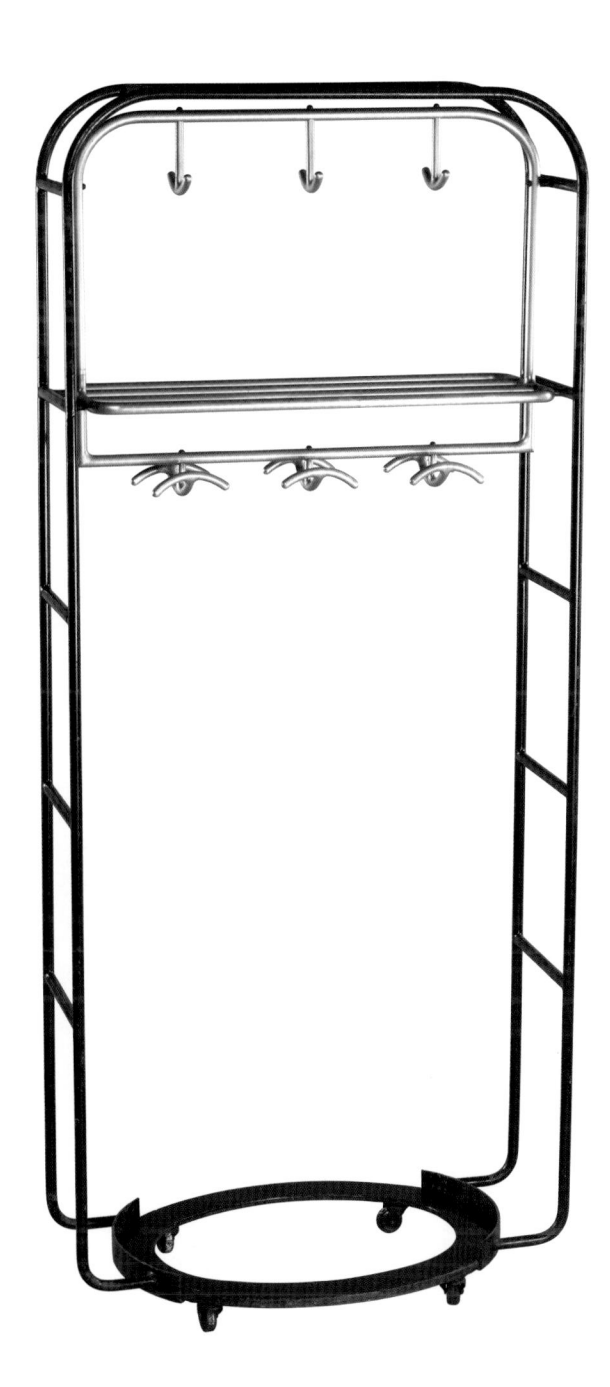

シャローは、幾つかの大きくはない作品に鋼管（スチールパイプ）を使っているに過ぎない。しかも、多くは付随的な家具に属するもので、キャリアの後半以降に制作している。この事実を考慮に入れるなら、シャローは鋼管利用の"革命"にはほんのわずかしか参加しなかったと認めるべきである。

マルセル・ブロイヤーやミース・ファン・デル・ローエといった海外の巨匠に加えて、アイリーン・グレイ、ルネ・エルブスト、ジャン・ビュルカルテ、ル・コルビュジエ、ピエール・ジャンヌレ、及びシャルロット・ペリアンらフランスの仲間たちが鋼管の利用を拡大させたにもかかわらず、シャローは奇妙なほど慎重な姿勢を保っていた。その背景としては、シャローといわば一心同体の関係にあった金物職人ルイ・ダルベが、ひとつのノウハウに縛られずに新たな技術要件に対応できるようなパートナーには恐らくなり得なかったことが挙げられよう。

ガラスの家のために考案したコート掛けは、シャローの最終の創作期を代表する作品である。それは、ダルザス夫妻ために新たなインテリアを完成させた時期であった。このコート掛けがそのような状況でガラスの家に納まることになった理由のひとつは、使用の必然性から来る施主側の注文があったからである。しかしもっと重要なことは、その美学、その技術が、ガラスの家の建設プロセスと直接に結びついていたからである。言うならば、このコート掛けはよそからたまたま持ってきたものではない。それは控えめながらも、ほかの何にもましてガラスの家の"化身"のような存在だったのである。

さて、このコート掛けは自立性と可動性を備えた家具として考案されている。楕円形の金属プレートによるベースには４つのキャスターが付いている。鋼管製のフレームは角を丸めた縦長の直方体になっている。フレームに取り付けられている帽子棚とフックも鋼管でできている。ベースとフレームは黒塗りであるが、帽子棚などにはジュラルミンが使われている。すなわち、家具としての機能部分はくすんだ銀色になっていて、周りの支柱部分からくっきり浮かび上がっている。

183　ガラスの家のコート掛け｜1931年頃

第III部　苦難の時代――不況下の模索と支援
PART III　THE DIFFICULTIES

LES DIFFICULTES

ヴィラ・ティンタ・マニス

イヴリーヌ県バゼンヴィル、
フランス（1937年）

シャローは友人仲間の一人であった舞踏家ジェメル・アニクのために、1935年に彼女が購入した土地に別荘をつくった。しかし、小品であったことから、シャローはこれについて黙して語らなかったどころか、自分の作品であることさえ否認していたという臆説も流れた。ところが、シャローの死後ほどなくして妻のドリーは、建築専門誌『ラルシテクチュール』に対して、自分の夫がこの家を手掛けたとあっさり認めたのであった。かくして当別荘は、ルネ・エルブストがシャローの没後に編纂した書物に掲載されている*。

ただそれにしても、1937年頃に竣工した別荘は写真に撮られることが一切なく、何らかのかたちで専門紙誌に取り上げられることもなかった。このことは、シャローのいかなる家具や建築の仕事にも当てはまらない異例の事態であった。

確かに、建物の構造（木造の柱と梁）、全体の空間構成（ありきたりな階ごとの部屋配置）、及び屋根（シンプルな屋根葺き）のいずれを見ても、シャローが手掛けたと思わせる要素は存在しない。強いて言えば、幾つかの細かい点だけが注目されるのみである。すなわち、ウッドウール（木毛材）のパネルを正面に使っていること、ドアや窓枠をそれぞれ化粧ボルトで固定していること、さらには、壁から少し張り出した窓が外開きになっていることである。しかしながら、これらの点も、古めかしくて無粋な建物の様相を変えることはできないだろう。なにしろ、この建物は明らかに節約を追求しながら設計されたのであるから。

他方、この計画では、複数の証拠が明らかにしているように、スイス・ヴァレー州の伝統建築の影響が見てとれる。シャローは計画実施の少し前にスイスに滞在し、その伝統建築を観察する機会を持った**。当別荘に見出せる木材の骨組み、石造の基礎、及び階上へのアクセス方式などの由来は、この点を踏まえて理解されよう。

*
『ラルシテクチュール・ドージュルデュイ［今日の建築］』、p.31、1950年9月、7頁にあるドリー・シャローの発言。及び『考案者としての建築家ピエール・シャロー』、ルネ・エルブスト他編著、サロン・デ・ザール・メナジェ［家政サロン］出版、近代芸術家連合、1954年

**
クリスチャン・ルブレットが取りまとめたルイ・モレの証言による

191, 192　ヴィラ・ティンタ・マニス
（舞踊家ジェメル・アニク別荘）

191　模型　1:100

184 デザートテーブル　透視図｜1932年
186 手紙用具入れ｜1930年頃
185 フルーツ皿（果物掛け）｜1930年

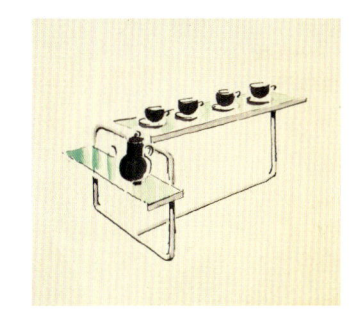

184

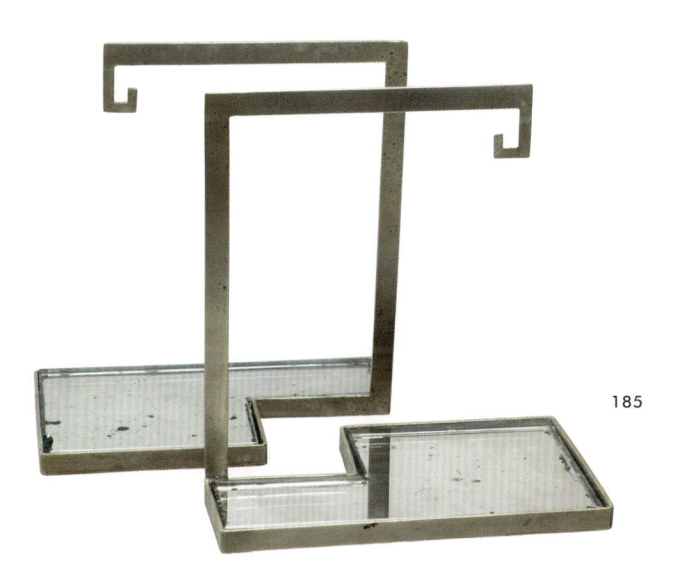

186

185

LES DIFFICULTES

小品

フルーツ皿（果物掛け）（1930年頃）、
手紙用具入れ（1930年頃）、
ファイアースクリーン（1924年頃）、
暖炉用スコップと薪挟み（1924年頃）

シャローは1924年頃、パリのシェルシュ＝ミディ通りに店舗「ラ・ブティック」をオープンした。ここにやってくる顧客たちに各種の作品を見せたり、大型の写真アルバムにまとめた自分の制作物を示したりしたのである。また、こまごまとした実用品や装飾品も販売した。シャローは自分がデザインした暖炉の付属品として、格子、暖炉のスクリーン、たきぎ台、薪挟み、スコップなどの暖炉用金具をダルベの工房でつくらせた。つまり、ここでもまた、シャローの独創力はダルベの製作ノウハウによって支えられていたわけである。これらの製品のデザインは洒脱でラインもモダンであった。

他方、シャローは、ジャンヌ・ビュシェが店に隣接する建物に自前の画廊をオープンするまでの間、彼女が企画する美術展を「ラ・ブティック」の店内で開催した。「ラ・ブティック」は、あらゆる種類の鏡、植木鉢入れ、プランター、スタンド灰皿など錬鉄製の小品を販売するのに都合がよかった。そして、1930年代の半ばにはさらに凝った作りの別の製品も登場するようになった。例えば、ラッカー塗りの単純な金属プレートとインク壺からなる手紙用具入れである（ただし現在インク壺は付いていない）。この金属プレートは折りたたんで、手紙を書くための各種の便箋、封筒、メッセージカードを入れることができるようになっている。また、いっそうユニークなものとして、コンソールテーブルや食卓を飾るための果物掛けがある。この果物掛けは日用品というよりも、むしろ室内装飾の様相を呈している。細い金属線にサクランボやブドウの房が掛けられる。そして、果物掛けの各支持台を覆う鏡に果物の姿が優美に映るのである。

こうした小品の販売は、妻のドリーがつくるクッションの販売とともに、当時の経済不況下においては、本格的な注文の欠如をかろうじて補っていたのであった。

第III部　苦難の時代──不況下の模索と支援
PART III　THE DIFFICULTIES

190 パリ市内のショウウィンドーの計画 『ブティックと商店』より、ルネ=エルブスト監修、1929年頃、シャルル・モロー出版、パリ

vii 新天地を求めて──新たな展開
IN EXILE | L'EXIL

フランス国内にレジスタンス運動が広がっていく第二次世界大戦前夜、シャローもまた危機感を募らせる。1940年渡米、新大陸は晩年の10年間の生活と活動の基盤を提供する戦時中のシャローはアメリカにあってもフランスの国威を掲揚するためのプロジェクトに貢献している。そして戦後の数少ない実現作からは、住まい手の現代的なニーズ、経済的条件、環境との関わりへの配慮といった新しい課題に取り組む建築家像が浮かび上がってくる。現存するわずかな手がかりから、シャローが目ざしていた方向性の全容をうかがい知ることは難しいが、工業技術と斬新な造形を巧みに組み合わせ、新しい建築のあり方を追求していく創造力が健在なのは確かだ。

195 ロバート・マザウエルの住居兼アトリエ
『ラルシテクチュール・ドージュルデュイ』no. 30、
1950年7月号より、アンドレ・ブロック編集、
パリ、撮影：ロニー・ジャック

L'EXIL

ロバート・マザウェルの住居兼アトリエ

ニューヨーク州イースト・ハンプトン、アメリカ（1947年）

当時、まだ若い画家だったロバート・マザウェルは次のように語っている。

「この家は本当に独創的でした。地面より1メートル近く掘り下げた床は、冬至には真南の陽を浴びるようになっていました。建物の南側正面のほとんど全部が、下見板張りのように重なり合う小さなガラス板でできていました。シャローは、同じようなガラスの重ね方を採用している近くの温室をあらかじめ観察して、これなら絶対うまくいくと大いに満足していました。南側の壁が大きなガラス張りになっているおかげで、暖房費はほんのわずかで済みました（確か月額12ドルくらい）。セメントの床は冬には快適ではありませんでしたが、自分たちにはフローリングやタイル張りにするだけの予算はありませんでした。家を建設するためには松の木を何本も切り倒さなければならなかったわけですが、切り倒した松の幹がまだ地面に転がっているのを見て、ある日ふと名案が浮かびました。これを挽いて厚さ数センチの輪切りにしてから、パテを使って輪切りをつなげ合わせて床材にすれば味のあるインテリアになるだけでなく、歩きやすい床をつくることもできるのではないか、と。それで、早速そうすることにしたのです」*

この住居兼アトリエの姿を見た人にとっては、建造物の主要部分がプレハブの仮兵舎を転用したものだという事実を、マザウェルが全く話題にしていないことが奇異に思われるだろう。実際、仮兵舎から転用されたために、建物の異形は忘れがたい印象を与えている。

1950年、当住居兼アトリエを人々に紹介した筆者不詳の一文は、設計者シャローが提出した生の仕様メモをそのまま掲載している。シャローは建物の構想にあたって、一般的な工業部材を使うことを主張したのであった。これについてはメモに次のように記されている。

「戦時中の米軍避難施設クォンセット（かまぼこ形のプレハブ建築物）がその可能性を提供。（a）軍事行動が終結した時に一掃すべき在庫の中にクォンセットを発見。（b）骨組みのアーチ形小梁が見事（材質は曲鉄板）。その形状により内側と外側に鋲が固定可能。（c）波板でできた屋根カバーで骨組みを覆い、依頼に応じて内壁を断熱防音処理。（d）クォンセットの直径は約6メートル。約3.6メートルのユニットごとに売られているためそれぞれを接合」**

上の仕様メモには、規格化した工業製品が当時いかに一世を風靡したかがよく示されている。シャローは所与の構造をうまく生かすために、まずは各所の寸法を決めることから始めた。すなわち、内部スペースのうち長さ18メートル分を住居に充て、長さ10.80メートル分をアトリエに充てた。次に、地下1.20メートルまで床を下げ、クォンセット全体をフラッシング（雨押えの金属板）の上に載せた（この2つの作業によってもう1層ができる）。さらに、幅10.80メートル、高さ3.60メートルの大窓を南側に設け、あたかもサンルームのようにした。

このように仮兵舎をしかるべく転用するためには、繋ぎ小梁を各所に配置するとともに、大窓全体に補助の木組みを取り付ける必要があった。シャローは完璧な立体の中に非対称性をつくり出し、単なる反復を心地よいテンポに変換することによって、あっという間に最適解を示したのであった。

*
1984年8月5日にクリスチャン・レプレットがとりまとめた記録文書より抜粋。ニューヨークの「ディーダラス財団」及びクリスチャン・レプレットの快諾により本稿転載。原文の仏訳はジネット・モレル

**
「ロング・アイランドの画家のためのサマーハウス、建築家ピエール・シャロー」、『ラルシテクチュール・ドージュルデュイ』no.30、1950年7月号、p.51

193, 194　ロバート・マザウエルの住居兼アトリエ
193　模型　1:100
194　『ラルシテクチュール・ドージュルデュイ』no.30、1950年7月号より、アンドレ・ブロック編集、パリ｜撮影：ロニー・ジャック

L'EXIL

「ワンルーム」の家

ニューヨーク州イースト・ハンプトン、
アメリカ（1947年）

シャローは、ロバート・マザウェルから譲り受けた土地にこの「あずまや」を建てた。これは、シャローが手掛けた住居兼アトリエ建設に対して画家マザウェルから支払われるべき謝礼の一部を受領する便法であった。この点に関連して、マザウェルは当時金銭的に困っていたことや、シャローとの間にコミュニケーションの問題があった（互いの言語にそれぞれ不案内であった）ことを明かす一方で、顧客としてはシャローの仕事に満足していたと述懐している*。

この「ワンルーム」の家は簡略につくられたものではあったが、それでもふたつの象徴的な意味合いを持っていた。第一に、シャローにとってこれは、自分自身が使うために設計した唯一の住宅だったことである。そして第二に、未完成に終わったにしてもこの家はシャローの"終の住処"になったことである。

家の正面は、コンクリートとレンガをラフに積み上げている。ブロック層を交互に重ねていくありさまが内壁にむき出しになっていることから、モルタルなどによる壁の仕上げを省こうとしていたことがうかがえる。建物の中に数多くある開口部は、扉がガラス製のフランス窓になっている。このフランス窓は壁の外側にじかに設置されて、外に向かって開く点が特徴である。また、雨水などの浸透を避けるために少し張り出している。構造壁も間仕切りもない建物の中は、暖炉、ボイラー、トイレ、シャワー、及び簡易台所を一緒に含む機能ユニットが中心を占めていて、その周りでは、シンプルな竹のすだれや可動パネルがスペースを区切っている。

ミニマリズム（最小限主義）とブルータリズム（ブルータルな手法を用いた表現主義）を体現する「ワンルーム」の住宅は、数年後にル・コルビュジエを南フランスのカップ・マルタンでカバノン［休暇小屋］の制作にかりたてたのと同様の欲求に基づいている。

*
1984年8月5日、クリスチャン・レブレットがとりまとめた記録文書より

196 「ワンルーム」の家
（シャロー自邸）アクソメ図

L'EXIL

ラ・コリーヌ

ニューヨーク州スプリング・ヴァレー、
アメリカ（1950年）

ピエール・シャローの最後の作品となった小さな住宅「ラ・コリーヌ」は、彼がアメリカ亡命中に作品を残そうという最終的な試みを意味していた。目立たないこの作品は、女性ピアニストのジェルメーヌ・モントゥーと女流作家のナンシー・ローリンという2人の依頼主の証言によって、忘却の彼方から救い出された。しかし、建物が現存していないため、コメントなしの写真によってのみシャローの年譜の中に登場する*。

"田舎の隠れ家"というコンセプトや、資材を用いるという点では、舞踏家ジェメル・アニクの別荘をまず引き合いに出さざるを得ない。しかし、ここアメリカは"こけら葺き"（屋根板）と"上げ下げ窓"の国なのだから、アニクの別荘のつくり方とは自ずと異なった。他方、ピアノを置く部屋の音響効果を良くし、かつ、この仕事場を他から遮断した空間にするというふたつの明快な条件が、「ラ・コリーヌ」の建築上の決め手となった。例えば、五角形の部屋のさながらドーム風の天井によって優れた音響効果が得られた。

この部屋は建築計画上の要所であるがゆえに、そこから諸室を配置していった。そして、シャローとしては、角部屋をたくさんつくるという事態に正面から向き合わざるを得なくなった。おそらくこういう特性があるために、1950年代初頭にあってさえ、この建築プランにモダンな効果が付与されたと言えよう。

しかしながら、この「ラ・コリーヌ」にあっては、各空間のつながりに関して不手際なところがどうしても目に付く。この点は、ボーヴァンのゴルフ場クラブハウスをつくる際にシャローが遭遇した困難を想起させずにはおかない。しかしインテリアに関しては、とりわけ壁の使い方でシャローらしい自在さを発揮した。例えば、第一に厚い壁につくり付けた棚、第二に部屋の壁伝いのベンチ、暖房ラジエーター、及び壁に組み込んだ照明器具、そして第三に防音壁の機能を果たす奥深いクローゼットなどに見てとれる。

*
「アメリカにおけるフランスの家」、『アール・エ・デコラシオン』no.27、1952年、p.4, 25。
「ガラスの家」史料館

197

196, 197 ラ・コリーヌ
（ジェルメーヌ・モントゥーと
ナンシー・ローリン邸）
196 模型 1:100

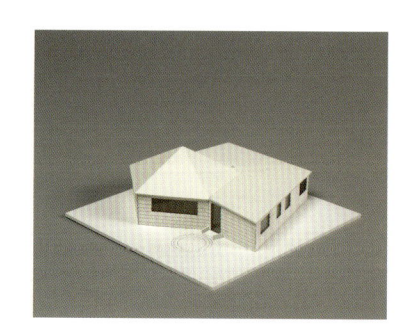

196

Pierre Chareau

Pierre Chareau, architect of the House of Glass:
A Modernist in the time of Art Deco

ARTICLES

DOCUMENTS FROM THE 1930s

NOTICES

Articles

translated by Anna Knight from French to English

p. 17

Pierre Chareau:
Modern, Resolutely Modern

OLIVIER CINQUALBRE

For a long time and still today, the *Illustrated Petit Larousse*, the reference dictionary of French schoolchildren, had an entry on Pierre Chareau. Though very succinct — specifying that he was the author of the Maison de Verre [House of Glass] in Paris — it contains a biographical error in stating that he was born in the city of Le Havre. Chareau was in fact born in Bordeaux. Elsewhere, he is attributed a ship-owner father, when in fact his father was a wine merchant. These would be very minor details, if it were not for the fact that they betray a certain ignorance about his life, despite the fact that his work has been acclaimed. This constitutes a paradox that the historiographer has not yet broached. A life lived for 67 years, begun in the late 19th century, surviving the First World War for 5 years in uniform and ending after the Second; at the same time, a dazzling career spanning the twenties, brutally interrupted by the economic crisis without ever really being able to be revived, whether it was in France or in exile in New York. It was this work that was hailed by the critics of the era that virtually faded from view with the death of its author, and which was only to resurface again in the late 20th century through a building scrutinised by generations of students and architects, as well as furniture design that continues to ignite the passions of collectors.

Since a bona fide biography still remains to be written, it is the evolution of this body of work, the affirmation of a style, the inventiveness of forms, the natural and subtle shift in his research from furniture to interior design, and more rarely, from the latter to architecture, that forms the subject of this presentation.

Regarding the elements of public records, we note his birth in Bordeaux on 4 August 1883; the establishment of his family in Paris in around 1893 (he was therefore not a young provincial type who had come to the capital for his career); his wedding, at the town hall of the 17th arrondissement, to an English school teacher Louisa Dyte, known as Dollie, on 11 July 1904; his enlistment in 1914 in the artillery squad and his demobilization in 1919.[*1] As for his education, Chareau did not apparently receive it from a school. "At the age of sixteen, Pierre Chareau was hesitating between painting, music, and architecture. Opting for architecture, he worked for a year under the guidance of a fine arts professor," according to his wife's testimony before she passed away[*2]: twice, in 1900, he sat entry examinations for admission to the École Nationale des Beaux-Arts, in the "architecture" section, without success. Pierre Chareau is therefore not, as has often been written, a certified architect. His training took place within a furniture company, Waring & Gillow, an English firm established in Paris. He joined the company in 1903 as a tracer, and became head draughtsman in 1914. The references from Waring & Gillow show productions of considerable importance, interior design for hotels, theatres, and luxury liners; the production, in a classic style, presents a range of stylish furniture with a strong English influence.

THE EARLY YEARS

It all started for Pierre Chareau after the war. After those years of horror, nothing could ever be the same again: Chareau embarked on a new life of creation, as an independent, in his own name. He became known in 1919 through his first commission, which he presented at the Salon d'Automne. This was the interior design of an apartment situated on Boulevard Saint-Germain, and the rooms that he chose to present at the Salon before definitively installing them were the young doctor's office and the bedroom. The critics didn't say a word about it and were far from imagining that Chareau's destiny had been set in motion. His clients were a young couple, Doctor Jean Dalsace and Annie Bernheim, whom Dollie and Pierre Chareau were very close to, since Dollie had been Annie's English tutor in her youth. They were the ones who introduced him into vast family and social circles that would later prove to be a source of many of his future commissions: Edmond and Émile Bernheim, Hélène Bernheim, Edmond Fleg, and the Teplansky, Lévy, Dreyfus, and Grumbach families. Again, it was Jean and Annie Dalsace who would later become the clients of the Maison de Verre and who would provide such unfailing support that they can be considered to be the designer's patrons.

After this first showing, Chareau would go on to do many salons. Each year, he presented his new designs at the Salon d'Automne and the Salon des Artistes Décorateurs. These were events that became regular from the outset, in which he exhibited the furniture and interior designs that his clients commissioned. Bedroom, bathroom, dining room, office, children's play area, young man's bedroom, office: he launched into all the rooms of a home, searching to update forms and norms, to explore new materials, and suggest new arrangements. The period was sumptuous, and his imagination was fertile. The critics knew a good thing when they saw it and began to follow his work from then on, either supporting it, or, if they were reticent, nonetheless praising it. "Pierre Chareau does not so much seek originality and rare forms as he does the production of ideas that he has consolidated about architecture, through studies and research into the solution of the problem of the present time. His concern for construction allows him to avoid sentimental absurdities. He is a lover of fine materials, using them judiciously and with acute awareness of their constructive or decorative possibilities: mahogany, rosewood, white cedar, ash, or sycamore, he knows all of their practical virtues as well as the psychological virtues of such species. He draws charming harmonies and dissonances from them. But his audacity draws the line at absurdity. Pierre Chareau remains a builder. In his furniture, volumes and planes create lines through subtle interplay. Although they no doubt constitute the furniture that appeals the least to us in the three rooms for a villa that he is exhibiting this year, the vast corbelled bed and armchair, whose curves appear to be seen through photographic deformation, strike me as highly characteristic of a discipline of mind that never fails to move us and demand careful attention on the part of the beholder."[*3] "His concern for construction [...] Pierre Chareau remains a builder [...]": the terms recur in appraisals by the same authors, and among others: "Chareau has ideas, productions that are often successful, and an obvious sense for well-built designs."[*4] A builder: the term is important, as it distinguishes Chareau from decorators. Of course, when he applies himself to the room of a house, he intervenes on all of the surfaces, choosing the colours of floor and ceiling coverings, using wallpapers and weaves (he designs the patterns), furnishing the space with his creations, and presenting the works of his artist friends here and there. But the design of his furniture and layouts is exempt of anything superfluous, of any add-ons. The style is pared down, the structure of the furniture is underlined, and the lines are sober, accentuating the materials used. The wood species may be highly prized and precious, the cabinetmaking is of a very high quality, and the furniture remains no less singular, pushing the limits of prevailing forms of Decorative Art.

From this effervescent period, other important elements should be retained. The first is that when Chareau first emerged on this creative scene, he became acquainted with strong personalities such as Francis Jourdain or Robert Mallet-Stevens and thenceforth belonged to their circles. He found himself by their side at every available opportunity. He then introduced designers Eileen Gray and Hélène Henry into these circles. He worked with artists Jean Lurçat and Jacques Lipchitz. His furniture, through its originality, contributed to worlds such as the sets of the film by Marcel L'Herbier, *The Inhuman Woman* (1924).

The second element was his crucial meeting, most likely in 1922, with Louis Dalbet, a wrought-iron craftsman in Paris. Trained at the Emile Robert Studio (where Jean Prouvé also later completed his apprenticeship), Dalbet was an excellent craftsman and he and Pierre Chareau very quickly became inseparable. Chareau found in him the man capable of translating the forms of his inspirations into metal, such as the "Nun", the lamp with supple lines, which only a firmly established level of expertise would be capable of producing. He also found in him an entrepreneur who was willing and able to follow him as a designer: while the Dalbet Studio forged all kinds of lighting elements (table, wall, and suspension lamps, among others), the alabaster slabs that equip these lighting fixtures were cut on site, to form various kinds of 'lampshades' (a cutting machine had been especially acquired for the purpose).

This period also saw Chareau invest in a distribution "tool", by opening a store known as "La Boutique", at 3 Rue du Cherche-Midi, in Faubourg Saint-Germain. He was thus able to permanently display his designs to potential clients, present photo albums of his productions, become the publisher of younger talents such as Jean Burkhalter, or organise artists' exhibitions in association with Jeanne Bucher who opened her own gallery just next door shortly afterwards.

Finally, Chareau's growing reputation is reflected by the publications of the time. The period of glowing or sceptical Salon reviews gave way to that of articles that were by then exclusively devoted to him: *Mobilier et Décoration d'Intérieur* for its first issue in late 1922, or *Art et Décoration* in which, in May 1923, Gaston Varenne penned "L'Esprit Moderne de Pierre Chareau", and also in May 1923, *L'Art et les Artistes* with a contribution by Maximilien Gauthier: "Art Décoratif: Pierre Chareau" (1924), not to mention a recurrent presence in the magazine *Les Arts de la Maison* directed by architect Jean Badovici. It was in its pages, in early 1926 that one of Chareau's major commissions was published, the design of the Lanique apartment in which he focused for the first time on sculpting the space by introducing mobile, fan-shaped walls. Between its completion (dating from 1924) and the publication, there was a brief hiatus. Between the two, the 1925 Exposition was held.

RECOGNITION
———

The Exposition Internationale des Arts Décoratifs, Industriels et Modernes de Paris [International Exposition of

Modern Industrial and Decorative Arts] was incontestably Chareau's hour of apotheosis. Among the modernists, who took advantage of this occasion to battle against tradition and classicism, he was present by way of three contributions. In the pavilion of the Société des Artistes Décorateurs, entitled the "French embassy", he produced the "Office-Library", his main piece, and a delicate little day room, as an extension of the physical training room by his friend Francis Jourdain; and the Indochina pavilion featured his dining room. His participation earned him the Legion of Honour. The office of the "Office-Library" design was acquired by the Musée des Arts Décoratifs: it was the first of Chareau's furniture designs to enter a French public collection, accompanied the following year by an armchair. The exhibition of his work brought him new clients such as Madame Errera from Brussels, Armand Moss, and many others. He was often solicited to give interviews. Pierre Chareau thus accepted an interview with Georges Le Fèvre, as had his famous colleagues Follot, Ruhlmann, Jallot and André Groult, before him. "If the decorative arts were to hold a congress of its key contractors, Pierre Chareau would most likely occupy a seat in the second-to-last bay on the far left. His uncompromising principles coupled with a calculated and consistently intriguing sense of audacity make this artist a leader who could be referred to in the corridors in hushed tones as a 'likely candidate'. He is a man of average height and broad shoulders. He has a clear blue gaze. His greying hair is retreating from his temples. Quick-witted, his mind is always bubbling with energetic thoughts. He sets out his doctrine: " — The relationship of furniture to decoration. A man who takes it upon himself to produce a table, an armchair, or a wardrobe must be an architect above all. The harmony of the whole is always what is most attractive. Whether you work in white wood or Macassar ebony, the discipline must remain the same. I was commissioned to produce a room, at the Embassy, that is a kind of private office-library. Unlike what may've been expected of me, I used extremely rare woods that are nigh impossible to find, yielding to a kind of creative exaltation that encouraged me to produce a real 'folly'. But when you consider that the same white wood would have been too expensive for the poor... you are able to let yourself go, for once, and leave the earth."*5

Following the virtue of craftsmanship that the critics had acknowledged, it was now his virtue as an architect that Chareau wished to affirm. Elsewhere, in response to an investigation by Guillaume Janneau concerning "tomorrow's home", he specified: "The plan of a real construction requires a professional: that's the architect's job. The interesting part is to transmit general ideas. The application of these must be freely interpreted. You need to allow room for the builder's initiative. The architect's task should be limited to providing, in a certain sense, the algebraic solution to a set program, allowing the executing party to carry out the calculations: apparently, this is how the medieval method worked. We must respect and stimulate the practitioner's creativity: in construction, as in furniture-making, a craftsman makes discoveries that the author of the plans hadn't imagined. We must return to this collaborative formula. An architect is not a tradesman, but a mathematician and philosopher: an inventor of plastic combinations and not a mason. Our immediate ancestors wanted to merge the two, and subordinate art to professional skill. Art is the mind, and nothing can replace it."*6

CHAREAU'S RISE TO FAME

After the exhibition, Chareau's activity continued to expand. He became a highly sought-after decorator, undertaking a number of interior design projects. As a furniture-maker, he was also well known, and continued to innovate. Chareau saw himself as an architect and was offered the chance to build.

Among the interior commissions Chareau was honoured to receive, two in particular draw our attention. The first was that of the design of a whole floor of Madame Reifenberg's mansion, built by Robert Mallet-Stevens in the street that bears his name, in the 16th arrondissement in Paris. Chareau created the reception rooms and the bedroom of the lady of the house; the other rooms on the other floors were assigned to a number of other colleagues. Unlike some of the Parisian apartments that he had previously worked on, the latter was a modern building. He therefore did not need to reinvent volumes and flow, or introduce a sense of contemporaneity through partitions and various other devices. Here, he only had to shape the space slightly. In order to mark out the entrance to the lounge, he lowered the roof; elsewhere, he sculpted it with recesses to accommodate light fixtures (long "beehive" inclines in alabaster); in Madame Reifenberg's bedroom, he delimited the sleeping area and that of a small lounge using a curved curtain rail hung from the ceiling; he covered the walls and ceiling of a gallery in wood, accentuating the cabinets used to store the scores of his musicologist client. The second commission, from the Bernheim family, was for the interior design of the reception rooms of the Grand Hôtel de Tours. This production was a first for Chareau, particularly owing to its size and public character, which were different from the scale and private nature of his previous operations. Through his work on various spaces, qualifying and differentiating their uses, Chareau arranged an impressive array of furniture and lighting in the rooms based on their functions: it thus represents a veritable catalogue of his production. Whenever the right pieces were not available, he created them especially. Hence the bar stools and tables were tailor-made, as were the writing cases of the small correspondence lounge: they are original models with a special feature in that their bases are made from solid black tubes. This was the first time that Chareau used metal in this way, which, as ever, was created by Dalbet. But Chareau did not put the cart before the horse, and his tube is not the one that modernists later raised to the status of an icon.

It was nonetheless through his use of metal that Chareau innovated in his furniture design and radically transformed his aesthetic, which occasionally left commentators speechless. "He is fond of the raw material with which machines are forged. Not resting on his laurels — given the ingenious furniture systems he has devised, such as the large corner divan that invites us to either chat or take a nap, while also serving as a bookcase and shelf, or the semi-circular dressing table, the extremities of which give rise to a series of tablets extending into a fan — he likes to strengthen wood using iron and steel. Crude iron feet support the top of one of his desks, conveniently extended into a T-shape to the right of the occupant. The left side contains a kind of steel chest, replacing traditional drawers. Is this the way of the future? Are these the characteristics of tomorrow's furniture?"*7 Chareau's use of metal in his furniture was therefore disparaged; the severity of steel and the rigour of the geometric lines were denounced. This was due to the fact that the shift away from his former production was radical. His past furniture could be stripped bare of superfluous decorative elements, aim for a functionality attaining the level of a dogma, and could be perceived as emanating from an architect — they nonetheless fell within a kind of continuity of genre, with its series of evolutions, from their construction through to the phases of refinement.

With his "wood-metal" series, Chareau's work departed entirely from his contemporaries, whose productions are now described as Art Deco, but also from those of the modernists, given the extent of originality and personality of his signature style. It is the design of the furniture, their composition and lines (mainly applied to desks, dressing tables, and laundry hampers) that propels them into the modern world, since their production is based on traditional techniques. It is precisely this point of difference that makes them so powerful and amplifies their intrinsic beauty. On the one hand, their pure lines attain an absolute minimalism: planes are the predominant feature, whether horizontal or vertical, multiplied and combined. This is perfectly perceptible in the preparatory drawings that contain strict elevations, like those of a building. On the other hand, unrivalled singularity and poetry arises from his confrontation of materials: the coarseness and austerity of the metal slats, showing highly visible marks from the impact of hammer blows right up to the joins, contrasting with the elegance of the wood that, present in the form of simple boards, relies entirely on the quality of the species used. The shift in architectural paradigms towards furniture is undeniable. Critics spoke more of structure than base, with the metal slat laid on the floor spanning the full length of the furniture.

THE ARCHITECTURE

At the same time, Chareau started to work in the field of architecture. There again, the Bernheim family was his client. Between the commission, the project, and the completed result, the timing varied depending on the various cases and in this case, the effervescence of Chareau's work was so intense that several projects were undertaken simultaneously. For a better understanding of his work, it is important to bear in mind the mutual influence of his research and the range of solutions available, by taking into account the completion dates of his productions, one after the other.

On the Côte d'Azur, between Saint-Raphaël and Saint-Tropez, Chareau devised and built the Clubhouse du Golf Hôtel de Beauvallon in 1927. While it was not his first architectural project, it was the first to be built. It is certainly modest in size and very unusual in its functions, with a bar, a main hall with a terrace, and a cloakroom, but it was nonetheless his first work. Chareau adopted the modernist aesthetic in his own way, using reinforced concrete, visible beams, a smooth façade, and horizontal openings. He also created a family villa nearby that adopts the same canons. These beginnings were marked by a certain clumsiness: here, the proportions were not well balanced, there, the piles were too thin, and there again, certain layouts could have been simplified. Nevertheless, these buildings have a certain stature and are by no means a blight among the productions of his modernist counterparts. Architecture had become Chareau's new field of research, and like elsewhere, he did not make easy choices. This awkwardness might even thwart an interpretation currently in circulation, regarding the authorship of Chareau's architectural works. Dutch architect Bernard Bijvoet, an associate of Johannes Duiker (1890–1935) in Holland, worked with Chareau. Given Bijvoet's level of experience, it would be hard to understand this state of affairs if Chareau had not been at the helm and fully involved. However, it would also be incorrect to see Bijvoet as simply an executing architect. It was apparently a true collaboration, and we can form the hypothesis that Bijvoet was able to suspend the baggage of his training in the face of the self-taught architect's creativity.

Following the 1925 exhibition, Chareau nonetheless did not desert the trade fairs and exhibitions. On the contrary, he increased his level of participation: the interior design of the Hôtel de Tours was thus revealed at the 1926 and 1927 Salons d'Automne. He regularly exhibited in Parisian galleries and also abroad from then on, in New York and Leipzig in 1927. The same year, he filed a patent for a "folding fan-shaped chair". His furniture appears in a significant way in two films *Le Vertige* (Marcel L'Herbier, 1926) and *La Fin de Monte-Carlo* (Paul Pougy, 1927) and in 1929, he designed the sets for the three-act comedy by poet and playwright Edmond Fleg (his friend and client), *Le Marchand de Paris*, presented at the Comédie-Française. But from then on he focused solely on architecture, the architecture he was making and the architecture being made around him.

As a friend of Robert Mallet-Stevens, Chareau also became a friend of Le Corbusier. He visited the Weissenhof of Stuttgart in 1927 and was able to appreciate, among many others in this avant-garde estate, the two houses designed by Le Corbusier and Pierre Jeanneret. In 1928, they participated together in an exhibition at the Georges Bernheim Gallery and met in June at the Château de La Sarraz in Switzerland for the first meeting of the CIAM [International Congresses of Modern Architecture]. While Chareau was one of its founding members, it was clearly at Le Corbusier's invitation, as he chose the members, distancing a French rival (Mallet-Stevens) and confronting another (André Lurçat). This co-opting bears witness to the esteem that he had for him, seeing in him if not an equal, at the very least someone who was not a competitor, and this occurred at a time when Chareau was not yet able to boast of his masterwork, the one named Maison de Verre from the outset. The building consent was effectively given to Monsieur Dalsace on 21 August. The design phase was long (possibly almost 3 years) and the building was to take just as long. We know that Le Corbusier visited the construction site, was particularly interested by the façade in glass bricks, since he had also experimented with these on a smaller scale, during the same period, for the Swiss Pavilion of the Cité Universitaire de Paris. While a number of articles related the building site while it was under construction — particularly in the specialised press relating to glass — after its inauguration, articles abounded, in France and abroad, in architectural periodicals as well as those dedicated to decor. Critics from both disciplines shared an interest in it: the Maison de Verre was indeed a 'total artwork'. It is also possible to hypothesise that, in order to satisfy the strict requirements of the program, both on the surface and in terms of its organisation, in the qualities of volumes and the comfort of the facilities, Pierre Chareau, armed with his clients' complicity, transformed a commission for interior design into an architectural creation. But it was certainly this architectural work that gave its creator a new status; it was this work that was first published in *L'Architecture d'Aujourd'hui*, in 1933, prior to the Clubhouse the following year, despite the fact that it had sprung from the earth beforehand. Chareau exhibited the photographs and a spectacular model of the Maison de Verre at every available opportunity. Chareau thus became an architect from then on, a modern architect in a class of his own, and recognised as such by his peers.

REVIVAL

At the time that the architect was completing the Maison de Verre, the decorator presented two interior designs that were also lauded by the press.[*8] Both are Parisian apartments and were associated by critics since they are both so representative of Chareau's style at his apogee. Without a common yardstick with the volumes of the Maison de Verre, each space here was divided into sequences, bounded by light or glass mobile partitions and thus likely to be able to be combined as required. These two productions contemporary with the Maison de Verre mark the end of a bountiful period of commissions: the economic crisis that began in the United States had reached Europe and the conjunction of the two phenomena now appears to be the consequence of one on the other. The subsequent years were difficult for Chareau. It was impossible for him to participate in an architecture competition or receive a public commission in this restrictive period: he who had made a name for himself as an architect without formal training, he who remained modern while the "return to order" dominated. All that was then open to him was to participate in the various UAM [Union of Modern Artists] events, which he joined after its foundation, those of the magazine *L'Architecture d'Aujourd'hui* of which he was a member of the patronage committee, or those of the OTUA [Technical Office for the Use of Steel], which organised an annual competition and exhibition on a theme, from the cabins of luxury liners to buildings with steel frameworks, or school furniture. With a young Swiss man, Louis Moret, he attempted to find clients in the latter's region of Le Valais: it was no more than a stopgap solution. In all these years, Chareau only built a modest country house for a friend, Djemel Anik (1937). Chareau lived by his wits, requesting the aid of the authorities, obtaining a state purchase of the model of the Maison de Verre. Yet the recognition of both his peers and the authorities was manifest. In 1935, at the Brussels International Exposition, he curated the architectural section of the French pavilion. But it was the Paris Exposition in 1937 that put him back in the public eye somewhat, and earned him some grants. There, he was elected spokesperson for the Groupe Mobilier [Furniture Group], presenting furniture at the uam pavilion that was acquired by the state, along with others by the City of Paris, and exhibited a model in Le Corbusier and Pierre Jeanneret's Pavillon des Temps Nouveaux. Chareau was made an Officer of the Legion of

Honour. He was a member of the acquisitions commission of artworks for national museums. In 1938, he received an artist's grant for the commission of a set of furniture destined for the interior design of the director at the French Minister of Foreign Affairs, and for his participation alongside Francis Jourdain, Louis Sognot, and Jacques Adnet for the interior design of the office and reception hall of the administrator of the Collège de France. 1939: the mounting danger was palpable in the correspondence that Dollie and Pierre Chareau maintained with Louis Moret. In July 1940, Chareau left France for the United States, via Morocco and Portugal.

In New York, he participated in all kinds of patriotic events during the war years: the operation "Free French Week", the "France for Ever" exhibition (1942), the interior design of *La Marseillaise*, the canteen of "France Libre", and the organisation of the reception of Général de Gaulle by France for Ever (1944). After the war, he remained in New York, continuing to organise exhibitions dedicated to French art, but his activity was very limited. Two architectural productions emerged from these difficult years, one for painter Robert Motherwell in 1947, the other, a modest construction, for musician Germaine Monteux and writer Nancy Laughlin in 1950. Chareau died on the 24th of August in that same year. The studio-home for Motherwell was to become the designer's swan-song. Owing to budgeting constraints, he had recuperated and transformed an industrial military construction into an appropriate living and work space, and thus once again demonstrated his inventiveness. Inventiveness is doubtless the keyword in defining his œuvre, as testified by the tribute paid to him by his friends from the uam in 1954, by way of a publication launched by René Herbst and aptly entitled "An inventor, architect Pierre Chareau".

—

Notes

[*1] This information was retrieved from the municipal archives of Bordeaux and the Archives of the City of Paris.
[*2] Dollie Chareau, *L'Architecture d'Aujourd'hui*, n° 30, July 1950, p.51
[*3] "Pierre Chareau", *Mobilier et Décoration d'intérieur*, n° 1, November–December 1922, p. 27.
[*4] Gaston Varenne, "Le mobilier et l'art décoratif", *Art et Décoration*, December 1921, p. 182.
[*5] Georges Le Fèvre, "À l'Exposition des arts décoratifs. Déclarations de quelques décorateurs", *L'Art Vivant*, n° 12, 15 June 1925, p. 28.
[*6] Guillaume Janneau, *Formes Nouvelles et Programmes Nouveaux*, Paris, 1925.
[*7] René Chavance, "Les Cinq", *Mobilier et Décoration*, July 1928, p. 50.
[*8] These were the apartments of the Dreyfus and Fahri families.

p. 35

The 1920s: Pierre Chareau, among Artist Decorators

Elise Koering

"Pierre Chareau accumulates the virtues of a great artist and a great technician."[*1] Less than five years after his first dispatch at the 1919 Salon d'Automne, he is even for some the "best" of the "interior designers at all of the decorative art exhibitions".[*2] Since he was fortunate enough to be held in high esteem, Chareau crystallises his contemporaries' desire to witness the emergence of a new decorative language, in which "new lines that were totally foreign to Louis XV or Louis XVI or other degenerate styles" would abolish "the modern cliché of festoons, sculpted wooden acorns, and arched table legs". Chareau thus represented an alternative and above all, a site of projection for those hoping for the emergence of a "20th century French style".

His age — he is from the *elder* generation comprising Francis Jourdain, Robert Mallet-Stevens, Le Corbusier, or Eileen Gray — and his atypical professional experience with an English furniture company, coupled with his late appearance on the Parisian scene and his unique production, confers a special status on him among Parisian decorators. In 1923–24, Chareau was considered to be a representative of the new modern generation, but above all he was seen as an initiator and even as an inspiration. The critics hailed his influence, thus no longer hesitating to see him as a leader, like Maurice Dufrêne or Paul Follot. For instance, he was the only *Modernist* to express himself in the pages of *L'Art Vivant* in 1925[*3] assuming a leadership role, according to Le Fèvre's own words, complete with disciples, followers, and even those that some considered to be plagiarists.

At the time of the 1925 Exposition, the curator of the Musée Galliera, Henri Clouzot, and the inspector of Monuments Historiques, Guillaume Janneau, took stock of French decorative art and attempted a short-sighted analysis of its origins. For the two men, the productions of the year 1925 revealed two tendencies.

Born in the early 1910s, the first current brings together Ruhlmann, Süe and Mare, and Groult. Qualified as *Neo-traditionalism*[*4], this trend wanted to break away from Art Nouveau and propose creations freely connected to the past: "to maintain the well-crafted tradition while updating it".[*5]

The second trend is the fruit of a determined consideration of the modern world and its upheavals. *Total Modernism of 1919* or *Futurists of 1919* for Clouzot, the *Modernist Group* or the *School of 1919* for Janneau, this trend was apparently not affirmed until 1919. It constitutes a reaction to *Neo-traditionalism* as soon as it "liberates itself of any past formulae and, through new economic and domestic conditions, strictly produces original forms."*6 According to Janneau, it is the decorative transcription of the modern world and its "psychological stimulants".*7

In 1919, Chareau received his first interior design commission for an apartment and exhibited for the first time at the Salon d'Automne. In 1919, Gray created her first decorative works for an apartment for Juliette Lévy, and exhibited for the first time in France since 1913.*8 In 1919, Legrain had already reformed bookbinding; a year later, he exhibited for the first time at the Salons and prepared to renovate the rooms of Jeanne Tachard's residences.

Chareau, Gray, and Legrain thus imposed a new language that was distinct from the French tradition; for Janneau and Clouzot, they make up the *School of 1919* that created *Total Modernism*. In their view, this language favours sober lines, simple geometric forms and harmonious proportions; it gives precedence to the constructive aspect over the decorative dimension, to the projected overall construction over the design of the isolated, practical and rational object, which represents a whole within itself. It is devised in accordance with the "new needs" engendered by modern existence.

The three designers stand out in equal measure through their desire for research, inventiveness, and creative flair. Lovers of rare materials, they dare to make new associations, playing on contrasts and textures that are often captivating. Their aesthetic breaks away from French styles. Gray and Chareau's English experience and the three designers' interest in the artistic avant-garde, as well as in primitive or oriental arts, denote a certain kinship. Gray and Legrain's work in particular evokes far-away or imaginary territories, or by-gone eras.

All three excel in the art of creating atmospheres, which are often distinctively poetic or magical. Gray composed for J. Lévy's home an "ensemble as beautiful as a poem"*9 ; Chareau transformed the ballroom of the Grand Hôtel de Tours into "a vast dingy space [...] in which imprecise lighting is reflected, similar to that trained on the Seine under the bridges, in the evening."*10

The ingenuity that they demonstrate is thus placed in service to a creative spirit liberated of the past and is above all the bearer of solutions adapted to the new realities of modern life. Humanity and human needs, as well as "tastes and habits"*11 , remain the principal concerns of Chareau, Gray, and Legrain whose sensitive creations are opposed to both traditionalism and functionalist radicality.*12 Yet does this undeniable community of likeminded spirit and research allow us to compare them to the point of proclaiming the existence of a *School* as Janneau does?

By referring to a *School of 1919*, Janneau betrayed his desire to band together a number of independent decorators in order to form a distinct group with a leading figure at their head. For him, this leader was Chareau.*13 In 1928, from which point he was labelled *architect*, not only Chareau conserved his status as trendsetter, but he was also then able to take pride in being the leader of a school of thought bearing his name. *The Pierre Chareau School* emerged from his "somewhat surprising considerations of a decorative and pictorial nature" which earned him, in Janneau's eyes, the support of "marvellous talents", the "first graduates" being Legrain and Gray. "Disciples, not of the aesthetic", but "of the poetics" of Chareau who, despite his "considerations" was able to become an architect. The other two could not however lay claim to the same status, remaining "purely decorators" according to the critic, who thus made fresh inroads into his reductive classification operation.

In reality, an enlightened analysis of the evolution and œuvre of each denies the existence, even on a virtual level, of a constituted group and therefore a shared decorative formula, but also refutes Chareau's role as leader of the School.

Others understood this*14 ; the respective works of Chareau, Legrain, and Gray excel through their profoundly individual and recognisable character. Furthermore, excluding Gray from the category of *architects* as Janneau does, demonstrates a misunderstanding of the work of someone who, like Chareau and Legrain, devises furniture and space holistically and creates dynamic spaces for active bodies. This lack of understanding is all the more surprising in that, on that date, Gray, like Chareau, was working on a construction site in the south of France.*15

Thus Chareau is less the leader of a school in his name than a figurehead for a generation of artist-decorators of the so-called Modernist trend, and he could above all be considered to be an "audacious mover and shaker".*16

On several occasions, the decorator played the role of organiser or promoter within an informal group of artists who, from time to time, coincided with the key precepts of modernity. While they shared the same desire to build a world in harmony with modern humanity, in general terms, these creative artists stand out through the identity and originality inherent to their respective work.

In this way, in 1924, according to the press coverage of the time, Chareau brought together a dozen "major" artists at the Salon des Artistes Décorateurs for the stand entitled *The Inviting Intimacy of a Modern Apartment*. We can observe immediately that the works shown by these "leading men [and woman]" cannot be amalgamated, owing to the fact that each is derived from eminently personal research and aesthetics.

Although Chareau was officially behind this gathering that delighted the majority of commentators and even caught the attention of Le Corbusier*17, it must be concluded that he acted exclusively here as an initiator and federator, without playing in the slightest the role of artistic guarantor of an event only reflecting his talent and influence. It is the diversity and creative singularity of the forces present that give life to a gathering in which the abstraction of a Gray cohabitates with the "grand tradition" of a Ruhlmann whose presence here surprises the critics. His work is indeed very far removed from that of Mallet-Stevens for instance, who, in the same period, invited a number of exhibitors of the Salon to join him.

In Hyères, the architect was involved in the design of the Vicomte de Noailles' villa. Admirer of artists' and artisans' associations such as *Wiener Werkstätte*, lover of community construction sites and a true team leader, Mallet-Stevens solicited friends and associates [18] to bring a total modern artwork to life. Here, the most innovative architect-decorators proposed works or devised complete layouts. While Jourdain equipped the walls with minimalist clocks, Theo Van Doesburg coloured "the flower room", Van Ravesteyn designed a guest room, Djo-Bourgeois produced the dining room, and Gabriel Guévrékian created a Cubist garden. Chareau, for his part, designed the master bedroom and a surprising outdoor bedroom with a metal swing bed, with sliding window walls.

Often at the side of Mallet-Stevens, Chareau was present at a number of major modern and less modern *decorative* events of the 1920s. He had a considerable presence at the 1925 Exposition. The author of lighting for Mallet-Stevens' Tourism pavilion, he exhibited notably alongside Mallet-Stevens and Jourdain at the *French Embassy* of the SAD. While the former devised a hall, the latter designed a smoking room based on his *unfurnished* principles and a physical training room to adjoin Chareau's day room.

Despite the federating personalities of Chareau and Mallet-Stevens, the Exposition deplored the absence of modernists, such as Gray, whose absence remains unexplained today. There was great disappointment in the *Modernists*, a negligible turnout at an event entirely dedicated to contemporary decorative arts in a traditionalist vein, mainly targeting the elite. Jourdain, the defender of social art, condemned the exposition, which he deemed "without scope" or "meaning". [19] In a state of mind identical to that of 1924, Dominique, Legrain, Jean Puiforcat, Raymond Templier, and Chareau decided to hold a joint exhibition at the Musée Galliera. There was no programme, no leader, and all of *The Five* showed their modern designs individually. *The Five* were later joined by Georges Bastard, Le Corbusier, and Pierre Jeanneret, exhibiting until 1929, a decisive year in the history of French modernity, decorative arts, and the SAD.

In the group presentations at the Salons, as with the Urban Art Section of the Salon d'Automne, or in the operations of the 1910–1920s conducive to collective work, it is important to identify the fundaments and premises of the uniting of modern artists in the late twenties.

At the 1928 Salon des Artistes Décorateurs, Djo-Bourgeois, René Herbst, and Charlotte Perriand [20] associated their collections, reiterating the move made in 1924 by Chareau and his friends, without subscribing however to a principle of synthesis. [21]

Djo-Bourgeois was one of the regulars at the joint exhibitions and construction sites with Chareau, Mallet-Stevens and their friends, and adopted Jourdain's principles in his own way, particularly distinguishing himself in the design of small spaces. In the same circle, Herbst, fascinated by *street decor*, inaugurated French research into the use of industrial materials for furniture. As for Charlotte Perriand, she was a newcomer who, after having worked in the vein of contemporary decorative art, became Le Corbusier and Jeanneret's associate for furniture, in late 1927.

This new generation continued the research undertaken by its elders and started thinking about a new way of living.

After steering clear of the Salon des Artistes Décorators for two years, Chareau wanted to return to it under the conditions that his friends and himself enjoyed: as a group exhibition. In the name of around twenty designers, he requested a shared location, which Mallet-Stevens eventually supervised. [22] But the SAD provided a location deemed unsatisfactory by the future exhibitors, who withdrew from the event (most of them even on a permanent basis) before creating their own association: the Union des Artistes Modernes (UAM) [French Union of Modern Artists].

Unlike what is generally affirmed, Chareau's role was essential in the creation of the Union. He was the instigator and director of the project of collective stands at the Salon, along with Herbst and Mallet-Stevens, then one of the main proponents of the refusal to exhibit there, advocating the split with the SAD, and consequently, the creation of a Union. But above all, he was one of the primary stakeholders in the movement that laid the foundations of the new group.

Although a founding member of the Union, Chareau nonetheless remained in the wings, as he was not part of the Committee or an active member, not apparently attending any of the General Meetings in 1929. Chareau showed his work in the first exhibition of the UAM in 1930 as a guest member. This absence and status seem incomprehensible, given the extent to which they contradict Chareau's artistic intentions, his federating personality, and his past work as a rallying agent.

However, a letter in his handwriting reveals the reasons for this abandonment. On 3 May 1929, when the UAM was just settling into its new role, Chareau expressed a "compelling need to take pause and withdraw from all forms of action in order to complete some important work".[23] Conscious of his inability to become fully involved, he preferred "not to belong to any form of collective movement for a short while".[24] His withdrawal was therefore temporary and his decision, far from signifying a desertion, illustrates just the opposite, the strength and seriousness of his commitment: "As you know, I do not do anything by halves, and I could not resign myself to being an easy-going and passive member," he wrote.[25]

In 1931, Chareau returned among the friends that he had never really left[26], assumed his legitimate status as an active member[27] and, logically, joined the new Committee alongside Mallet-Stevens. His commitment was intact. While the association had difficulty finding its purpose, he encouraged his friends to clearly establish their "goal", and did not hesitate to ask the hard questions: was the UAM "a gathering of interests or a gathering of ideas?"[28] Above all, the organiser of the 1924 stand strived to make the Union evolve towards a more collective, militant spirit, after the second exhibition, in favour of a collective presentation[29] much more in line with the spirit of the group of disappointed former members of the SAD. He once again assumed the role of the "audacious mover and shaker" that he never ceased, and will never cease, to be.

—

Notes

[1] Waldemar George, "Les Intérieurs de Pierre Charreau [sic]", L'Amour de l'Art, March 1923, pp. 483–488.
[2] L'Arlequin, June 1923.
[3] Georges Le Fèvre, "À l'Exposition des Arts Décoratifs. Déclarations de Quelques Décorateurs", L'Art Vivant, n° 12, 15 June 1925, p. 28. 27–28.
[4] Henri Clouzot, "Les Ensembles Mobiliers", La Renaissance de l'Art Français et des Industries du Luxe, August 1925, pp. 349–362. Guillaume Janneau, "Introduction à l'Exposition des Arts Décoratifs. Considérations sur l'Esprit moderne", Art et Décoration, May 1925, p. 136.
[5] Raymond Subes, "Introduction", in Henri Clouzot, La Ferronnerie Moderne, Nouvelle Série, Éditions d'Art, Charles Moreau, Paris, undated, unpaginated.
[6] Henri Clouzot, "Le Meuble Français Moderne", op. cit.
[7] Guillaume Janneau, "Introduction à l'Exposition des Arts Décoratifs. Considérations sur l'Esprit Moderne", op. cit.
[8] Eileen Gray exhibited the screen La Nuit, at the Salon des Artistes Décorateurs, see Elise Koering, "Eileen Gray et les Arts Décoratifs: un Autre Regard", fabrica, no 4, December 2010, p. 114–143.
[9] Élisabeth de Gramont, "Les Laques de Miss Eileen Gray", Feuillets d'Art, February 1922.
[10] Ivanhoé Rambosson, "Un Grand Hôtel à Tours", Art et Décoration, February 1928, pp. 33–39; Jean Badovici, "L'art d'Eileen Gray", Wendingen, n° 6, 1924, pp. 12–15; Gaston Varenne, "Quelques ensembles de Pierre Legrain", L'Amour de l'Art, 1924, pp. 401–408.
[11] Gaston Varenne, "L'Esprit Moderne de Pierre Chareau", op. cit.
[12] "He was entirely imbued with the primordial importance of 'the man' in the creation of the artificial setting in which he must live," Bernard Bijvoet in relation to Chareau, cited by René Herbst, in Un Inventeur. L'Architecte Pierre Chareau, Paris, Édition Salon des Arts Ménagers - UAM, 1954, p. 12.
[13] For some, he even constitutes a movement in his own right. Waldemar George, "Les Intérieurs de Pierre Chareau [sic]", L'Amour de l'Art, March 1923, pp. 483–488.
[14] Albert Boeken, "Salon d'Automne 1923", translation. Archives Eileen Gray, V&A Museum, London; Christian Zervos, "Les Tendances Actuelles de l'Art Contemporain. I. Le Mobilier: Hier et Aujourd'hui", La Revue de l'Art, January 1925, pp. 68–75.
[15] In collaboration with Jean Badovici, the villa E 1027, in Roquebrune-Cap-Martin.
[16] Lucien Santini, "Le Salon des Artistes Décorateurs", La Construction Moderne, 27 July 1924, p. 505.
[17] Le Corbusier deemed this ensemble "important and interesting" but remained critical with respect to the overly "decorative" spirit of the designers: "Charming, intelligent chairs, but that are perhaps too 'chatty'. The same goes for the armchairs. If chairs and armchairs upstage Picasso, Léger, Derain, Utrillo, or Lipchitz, chairs and armchairs are insolent." Paul Boulard (Le Corbusier), "Le Salon de l'art décoratif au Grand Palais", L'Esprit Nouveau, n° 24, June 1924, unpaginated.
[18] Glassmaker Louis Barillet, sculptors Laurens and Lipchitz, gold and silversmith Claudius Linossier, etc.
[19] Francis Jourdain, in Bulletin de la Vie Artistique, 1925, pp. 494–495.
[20] With Jean Fouquet, Gérard Sandoz, Raymond Puiforcat, Jean Luce and Les Vins Nicolas.
[21] Their apartment was in fact a juxtaposition of individual stands.
[22] "Due to illness, he gave up the idea of supervising this collection." See Cécile Tajan, 1929. La scission S.A.D.–U.A.M., Mémoire de Maîtrise d'Histoire de l'Art, Université Paris IV Sorbonne, 2005, p. 9.
[23] Pierre Chareau was then engaged in the construction of the Maison de Verre.
[24] Letter from Pierre Chareau, 3 May 1929. Individual file "Pierre Chareau". UAM Archives, Bibliothèque des Arts Décoratifs.
[25] Chareau added: "I continue to support you and reiterate to you my pledge to withdraw from the Société des Artistes Décorateurs, which, like you, I consider to have been seriously negligent. I support you wholeheartedly." Ibid. Furthermore, he accepted the "disbanding" of The Five.
[26] Chareau was present at the meeting of 3 March 1930. Minutes of the General Meetings. UAM Archives, Bibliothèque des Arts Décoratifs.
[27] In December 1930. Ibid.
[28] "He [Chareau] thinks that it is a gathering of ideas, otherwise what would be the point of the split with the Artistes Décorateurs who have superior means to ours." Committee meeting, 2 July 1931. Ibid.
[29] Committee meeting of 2 July, 11 July and 14 October 1931. Ibid.

p. 113

The 1930s: Pierre Chareau and the Union of Modern Artists

JEAN-FRANÇOIS ARCHIERI

During the first exhibition of the Union des Artistes Modernes (UAM)[*1] organised in 1930 at the Pavillon de Marsan, Pierre Chareau presented articles of furniture as a guest: a book-case, a desk with a metal frame, a rug by Jean Burkhalter, and a circular coffee table connected by a hinge to a side cabinet in waxed mahogany. He exhibited a varied array of techniques and finishes, with a highly personalised aesthetic that juxtaposed the homogeneity of the furniture by Le Corbusier, Pierre Jeanneret, and Charlotte Perriand, bearing the hallmarks of the Thonet manufacturer. Following this exhibition, the UAM members unanimously offered to make Chareau an active member.

This event represented the modern trend among decorators, a trend that aimed to provide its contemporaries with new elements to suit their lifestyle and to produce everyday forms (objects, furniture, and architecture) adapted to the technological progress of society. It accentuated the opposition between the partisans of a national tradition championed by "the luxury industry" and the supporters of a modern progressive spirit represented by a production-line industrial configuration. There was a deep divide between two views of French society that marked the early thirties in its period of economic crisis.

From its first event, the UAM was confronted by the participation of Deutscher Werkbund at the Salon des Artistes Décorateurs in June 1930, the avant-garde wing of the German decorator-architects, directed by Walter Gropius, the former Bauhaus director. The contrast between the German and French sections was made clear here: technical skill / refinement, collective / individual. Through this opposition, the critics recognised the French UAM group of contemporary decorators as the most advanced, the most daring at the expo, capable of matching the efforts undertaken by the architects from across the Rhine.

The first orientations of the UAM were revealed in 1929 by the publication of a news bulletin and twenty albums from *L'Art International d'Aujourd'hui* collection by publisher Charles Moreau. Each album consisted of a selection of French and foreign examples, organised by themes with an introduction by each of the UAM members. Chareau was in charge of the preface of album n°7, *Meubles*.

In an even more visible operation by the UAM, Robert Mallet-Stevens directed the interior design of the offices of the newspaper *La Semaine à Paris* in March 1930. He created the façade with his faithful collaborators, Louis Barillet, master glassmaker, and the Martel brothers, sculptors. Each decorator handled the treatment of a complete space: furniture, decoration, and lighting. Also, along with others, Chareau provided designs for the reception area and the newsroom, and Francis Jourdain created the directors' office.

Critics unanimously considered this first demonstration as an exemplary success of applied decorative art and congratulated the authors for their talented designs, imagination, and ability to consider comfort within the framework of modern life.

Concomitant with the creation of the UAM, the International Congresses of Modern Architecture were organised to provide an international event for theoretical debate, beginning with the Congrès de la Sarraz in June 1928. At the national level, André Bloc created *L'Architecture d'Aujourd'hui* magazine in November 1930, an active instrument of representation for the modern movement. Its committee of core contributors consisted of tutelary figures Frantz Jourdain and Auguste Perret, and representatives of the avant-garde from the CIAM and the UAM: Chareau, André Lurçat, Robert Mallet-Stevens, Gabriel Guévrékian, and Francis Jourdain.

During the second UAM exhibition in 1931,[*2] Chareau again presented furniture and the model of a building under construction in Paris for Doctor Jean Dalsace, in association with Bernard Bijvoët, architect, and Louis Dalbet, wrought-iron craftsman. This was the first public unveiling of the Maison de Verre, and other presentations were to follow.[*3] But it was not until the publication of the report in *L'Architecture d'Aujourd'hui* that commentary and critical analysis was made. Opposite the photos of buildings from the Berlin-Siemens Stadt colony (1929) by Walter Gropius, the model emanated all the subtle magic of its elegance and transparency. Other foreign contributions were invited, including those of Willem-Marinus Dudock, and Alberto Sartoris, as well as an evocation of the *Città Nuova* (1913) by Sant'Élia.

Following this exhibition, Chareau was elected to the UAM Committee alongside Jean Carlu, Robert Mallet-Stevens, and Charlotte Alix. He wanted a debate to define directions and called for a collective presentation and the rejection of individual stands.

It was in a context of economic crisis and a noxious political climate that the third exhibition opened in 1932 at the Pavillon de Marsan, under the aegis of the Union Centrale des Arts Décoratifs (UCAD)[*4]. Owing to economic concerns, the principle of solo stands was continued, with the exception of the collective presentation of graphic designers. Chareau exhibited furniture, along with photos of the Beauvallon Clubhouse.

In the graphic design and advertising section that brought together the best specialists of the thirties[*5], the presence of Russian artists and the poster by Jean

Carlu *Pour le Désarmement des Nations* (1932) [For the Disarmament of Nations] gave rise to a slanderous article *L'URSS et l'Industrie Allemande dans nos Regroupements Artistiques* [The USSR and the German Industry in our Artistic Groups] by Thiébault-Sisson and provoked the removal of the poster by the UCAD.

The UAM demanded a right of response, proclaiming the financial independence of the Union and affirming, *"its members are not pursuing any other goal than that of communicating their art"* [6]. It also demanded the reinstatement of the poster by the UCAD, which led to a radical split and rendered any future exhibition at the Pavillon de Marsan impossible.

Besides this incident, the publication in 1932 of Paul Iribe and Gustave Umbdenstock's pleas (*Défense du Luxe. La défense de l'Artisanat*) [In Defence of Luxury: the Defence of Craft] motivated the UAM to respond to the various attacks with a manifesto. Louis Cheronnet, the director of *Art et Décoration* magazine, was the writer.

The fourth exhibition in 1933 [7] devoted considerable space to architecture. However, Chareau presented a collection of veneered furniture (sofa / adjacent book-case, large storage cabinet / book-case, and a large light-coloured rug by Hélène Henry). The critics highlighted a glass and metal table whose upper panel cut lengthwise enabled a floral arrangement to be displayed.

The ultra-modern architectural trends were presented with photographs, plans, and models. Also worthy of note were Robert Mallet-Stevens' Villa Cavrois in Croix, Le Corbusier and Pierre Jeanneret's town-planning project for the city of Algiers, Georges-Henri Pingusson's Hôtel Lattitude 43 in St-Tropez, Paul Nelson's hospital complex in Lille, André Lurçat's École de Villejuif and its furniture, and Alberto Sartoris' Église de Loutier.

At the time of publication of the manifesto *Pour L'Art Moderne, Cadre de la Vie Contemporaine*, [Towards Modern Art: the Framework of Contemporary Life] in July 1934, the UAM held an exhibition on Rue Mallet-Stevens in Paris. On this occasion, Jean Carlu, Georges-Henri Pingusson and André Salomon reaffirmed in their speeches the necessity to simplify forms, to define and satisfy the needs and aspirations of the majority of people, and that only the adaptation of current aesthetic currents to the evolution of society would allow us to overcome this period of recession. The manifesto answered the accusations of the detractors point for point, but remained in a defensive position without managing to produce an unambiguous theoretical summary on the offensive.

Elected to the Committee for the year 1934, Georges-Henri Pingusson initiated meetings between artists and industrialists with the help of *L'Architecture d'Aujourd'hui*, in a complex arrangement that was not entirely successful, but that created the conditions within the Union for potential agreements.

The first alliance came to fruition when Paul Breton, Curator of the Salon des Arts Ménagers, entrusted the organisation of a housing exhibition to *L'Architecture d'Aujourd'hui*, which the UAM became involved in. This new forum finally allowed them to reach a wide audience and to rethink the home, furniture, and functional spaces with a view to industrial production accessible to all. The first exhibition in 1934 [8] presented models and photos of architecture, featuring Chareau, Raymond Fischer, Le Corbusier, and Robert Mallet-Stevens. In 1935 [9], a second exhibition organised by Chareau and René Herbst, entitled *Galerie des Décorateurs*, presented a collection of serial objects at moderate prices. Besides the organisers who participated with metal furniture, Robert Mallet-Stevens (brick chimney), Frantz-Philippe Jourdain and André Louis (fireplace), André Lurçat (kitchen), Pierre Barbe, Jean Ginsberg, Georges-Henri Pingusson and Louis Sognot, all members of the UAM, were also present.

A second agreement was established by way of André Salomon, a lighting engineer, with the Office Central d'Électricité, who invited the Union to participate in its second Salon de la Lumière (1934) organised by Marcel Roche. The experience was repeated for the third Salon de la Lumière in 1935 [10] which took place in the Building de la Compagnie Parisienne de Distribution Electrique. This salon presented the latest research from the close collaboration between the architect, the decorator, and the engineer, over three floors. Robert Mallet-Stevens and André Salomon presented all the artistic disciplines of the UAM. Each creation implemented a particular application of light: stained-glass windows, sculptures, paintings, jewellery, gold and silverwork, Chareau's luminous library, luminous posters by Cassandre and Jean Carlu, and a diorama of Algiers by night by Le Corbusier and Pierre Jeanneret.

René Herbst, the advisor to the Office Technique de l'Utilisation de l'Acier (OTUA), called on the UAM, with the consent of the Office, to promote a new metal component among shipbuilding manufacturers, that offered better heat resistance for producing the cabins of luxury liners in steel. Six projects [11] including four that were fully furnished, produced in collaboration with manufacturers, were presented at the 1934 Salon d'Automne and served as the Union's annual collective exhibition. This "technical" part was completed by more artistic disciplines, including a decorative painting by Fernand Léger.

A partial representation of the projects was shown at the Salon Nautique International de Paris (1935) and as part of the exhibition Invitation au Voyage at the Musée Galliera (1936). The projects were well received by critics and appeared in the eyes of the public as effective solutions for avoiding fires at sea.

The OTUA renewed the collaboration experience in 1936 with school furniture projects presented at the 1937

Salon d'Automne and the Salon des Arts Ménagers.

The preparation for the 1937 International Exposition*12 started in April 1932 with negotiations regarding the participation of major artists' societies (Artistes Décorateurs, Salon d'Automne, and so on). Very quickly, the representatives of the UAM*13 were antagonistic and in the minority: refusing to back the proposed directions, they quit. It was not until early 1935 that a debate was organised within the UAM pertaining to the form that its intervention should take within the framework of this international event. The UAM considered obtaining subsidies for the creation of a pavilion that would be used for annual salons. René Herbst, in charge of general relations with decision-making bodies, led the negotiations in a difficult political climate (demonstrations, strike action, and preparations for legislative elections) in order to obtain loans and resolve technical issues. The arrival to power of the Front Populaire in April 1936 promoted the participation of the UAM, buoyed by shared cultural and social ideas.

In January 1936, Georges-Henri Pingusson was commissioned by his friends, in association with Frantz-Philippe Jourdain and André Louis, to produce the UAM Pavilion on the banks of the Seine, and Jean-Charles Moreux was in charge of the garden.

The goal was to demonstrate and express the group spirit defined in the 1934 manifesto in an exemplary manner, commencing with the design of the building and the presentation of works by all of its members.

Two exhibition principles were retained that established the topography of the spaces and the overall appearance of the building. A collective space of the "bazaar" variety (a collection of quality everyday objects, handcrafted or mass-produced at reasonable prices) suggested by Francis Jourdain, and a gallery of collections (one stand per designer). The treatment of the constructive details of the pavilion revealed the characteristic signs of a new architectural modernity to the public: visible metal structure, construction on piles, access ramps, staircases (including the main staircase by Jean Prouvé in the entrance hall), transparency of façades, and signposts.

The 1937 International Exposition marked the final collective event by the members of the UAM prior to World War II.

The dramatic challenges of the conflict did not entirely dissolve the ties between Chareau and the UAM. After the Liberation of France, during the extraordinary session of the general meeting held on 26 January 1945, Robert Mallet-Stevens, the Chairman, evoked Pierre Chareau and his presence in New York. Gabriel Guévrékian and Jean Carlu passed on his news upon their return from the United States. All of his friends unanimously requested and hoped for his swift return to France. But this return was always deferred.

In Paris in 1949 at the Musée National d'Art Moderne, a formal tribute was paid to Pierre Chareau during the official inauguration of a room that reunited the elements from the study of an embassy presented at the 1925 International Exposition. This work bore witness to his influence on the evolution of the decorative arts. The presentation was due to the valuable support of M. and Mme Dalsace, Hélène Henry, Rose Adler, the Conservation du Musée, and René Herbst.

*"My dear René (Herbst), tell all of those who are helping you how much I thank them from the bottom of my heart, and that, if I don't write more often, it is that frequently, in the hours when I could do so, tiredness overcomes me and deprives me of the powers I am in such dire need of. Once again, thank you, thank you all. Yours, Pierre Chareau."*14

In a final testimony of recognition, after his death, René Herbst, Chairman of the UAM, published a monograph of his work in 1954, based on documentation provided by Mme Chareau: *L'Architecte Pierre Chareau, un Inventeur,* [Pierre Chareau the Architect: an Inventor] prefaced by Francis Jourdain and co-published by the Salon des Arts Ménagers and the Union des Artistes Modernes.

—

Notes

*1 Musée des Arts Décoratifs, Pavillon de Marsan, Paris (11 June – 14 July 1930)

*2 Galerie Georges Petit, Paris (27 May – 18 June 1931)

*3 Second presentation of the model at the Salon d'Automne of the same year, then Galerie Vignon in 1933 and Galerie Cahiers d'Art 1934

*4 Musée des Arts Décoratifs, Pavillon de Marsan (4 February – 7 March 1932, extended until 17 March)

*5 Jean Carlu, Paul Colin, Cassandre (pseudonym of Adolphe Mouron), Charles Loupot, Charles Peignot

*6 cf. *L'Entreprise Française*, n° 1, 25 February 1932, p. 4 – 6 et n° 4, 25 April 1932, p. 9 Letter of reply from the UAM

*7 Galerie La Renaissance, Paris (30 May – 28 June 1933)

*8 Exposition de l'Habitation - 11th Salon des Arts Ménagers, Grand Palais, Paris (1 – 18 February 1934)

*9 2nd Exposition de l'Habitation - 12th Salon des Arts Ménagers, Grand Palais, Paris (31 January – 17 February 1935)

*10 3rd Salon de la Lumière, Building CPDE, 40 Rue du Rocher, Paris (11 October – 3 November 1935)

*11 René Herbst in collaboration with Bres, Calex, Krieg and Zivi; Pierre Barbe and Ronéo; Gascoin and the Atelier de Construction Jean Prouvé, Robert Mallet-Stevens and the Société Flambo. Pierre Chareau and G-H. Pingusson, full-scale models.

*12 Exposition Internationale des Arts et des Techniques dans la Vie Moderne, Paris 1937

*13 Robert Mallet-Stevens, René Herbst and Jean Fouquet

*14 cf. *L'Architecte Pierre Chareau, un Inventeur,* by René Herbst, Édition Salon des Arts Ménagers - Union des Artistes Modernes, Paris 1954, p. 12

Documents from the 1930s

translated by Anna Knight from French to English

---

p. 104

*Perspective Showing
the Services of the Dining Room*

Paul Nelson

A cart suspended on two rails serfives the dining table. It is in the form of a lunette and opens automatically, but as it passes the two doors between the main room and the kitchen, they shut automatically. These swing doors are built in a special way that ensures a perfectly watertight seal and prevents the cooking odours from penetrating into the main room. On its path, the cart passes through the closets of a small service corridor, whose sliding partitions open up towards the main room, the glass washing machine, the dishwasher closet, and it stops at the sink. Besides this transport device, the drawing clearly shows the spatial flow of the house.

THE HOUSE IN RUE ST-GUILLAUME

Our modern era has created a life with new sensibilities and reflexes. But architecture has not yet evolved sufficiently to be able to express it, since it cannot only do so through a detail, a façade, hardware, or the use of certain materials, or formulas such as horizontal or vertical windows. It is disheartening to bear witness to this decorative application of "modernity" transformed into fashions sported by the most pompous of the pompous, and to witness the rise of these so-called "pure" buildings that, like posters, have nothing to do with the products they advertise. Contemporary architecture has better ways to spend its time — perhaps with less sensationalism — but in ways in which the philosophical sensibility of the architect will be able to establish the spiritual and physical blueprint for this new life, and to express this in the plans; and in which technical knowledge of construction will allow these plans to be executed in ways that work effectively. A Parisian doctor allowed Chareau to provide proof of such an approach.

Concentration is the essential characteristic of this new life. Ever since the direct means of the bicycle defined an era, man has strived to concentrate his efforts by mechanical means: from the telephone, telegraph, and automobile (two-dimensional feats) to the airplane, wireless transmission, and television (three-dimensional feats). The home must therefore be a machine that concentrates the sensations of life. Today, man knows space and movement in space in particular. It is no longer a study in planes and cross-sections that will allow the architect to satisfy his requirements, but the fourth dimension — time — intervenes. We must create spaces that can be covered within a limited lapse of time. We must hone the fourth dimension. The house on Rue Saint-Guillaume stirs up this sensation.

First, we must start by limiting the space in order to create it. (Windows, or transparent walls, are basically a direct link with the exterior and destroy the impression of space. They must therefore be used with a great deal of discretion, where a defined function exists). It is now a matter of enhancing the fourth dimension in this space, limited by translucent glass tiles, by contrasting the dynamic with the static. The static in architecture is the structural framework that carries what is (or should be) eternally immobile. The energy expressed by horizontal and vertical distribution is completely independent from this, through fixed and mobile partitions, through restrictive furniture, staircases, etc. Columns are boundary markers that are regularly spaced and irregularly measure the space covered, through the arrangement of functions.

Chareau's house is not immobile: it is not photographic but cinematographic. You have to walk through the spaces to appreciate it — another point of contact with contemporary man.

As you enter this house, first of all you have the strange impression of having been transplanted to another planet. You get used to this, you understand it, and you want to live there, to visit the whole space, to experience it.

It is well built. It is functional. It is not only based on abstract guidelines, it actually works. The walls stand upright; the sliding doors slide; there are no leaks. The air conditioning works. You don't die of either the cold or the heat, apparently. It exists.

This house represents a serious point of departure. Problems are dealt with technically, and have been courageously resolved down to the slightest details. Purely aesthetic research was not the goal; but it is curious to note that, through technical research alone, this house gets ahead of sur-realist [sic] sculpture. Calder and Giacometti could find inspiration in it. The suspended pivoting door in front of the main staircase is an exquisitely beautiful sur-realist sculpture, as are the metal wardrobes. Chareau achieved this without wanting to create "art for art's sake".

"Modern architecture" is dying. It has become romantic and sentimental in ways best expressed in literature or music. Now is the hour of technological architecture, the architecture of a complete production restricted to the requirements of the new way of life, and to true knowledge of construction. Chareau had the intelligence to pace himself: that is why he has made a thing of beauty, which marks a point of departure towards real architecture.

(Paul Nelson "La Maison de la rue Saint-Guillaume", *L'Architecture d'Aujourd'hui*, numeró 9, novembre–décembre, 1933)

---

p. 106

A Visitor's Observations

JULIEN LEPAGE

It is particularly difficult, if not impossible, to give a clear idea of the Maison de Verre in a publication with plans and photos. Two things escape both the lens and the pencil: the space that shifts with each of the visitor's steps, endlessly developing, and the details that bring this space alive. I was also even surprised myself, when I saw the photographs, that I couldn't find in these static black-and-whites the house that feels as though it is living in perpetual transition, an organism articulated by the many patellae of a rigorous system.

They are not just practical details that have been added to the defined form of the house. On the contrary, everything has been designed to accentuate these patellae and even the static functions are translated into a mechanical operation. The main staircase, which ascends from the cloakroom in the main room, is suspended like a ladder, and the architect has taken care to reveal the points of this suspension; suspended wardrobes form dividing elements; the shelf for passing the tea from the office to the lady's bedroom is designed as a half-circle shelf, pivoting in a nook, thus discreetly and effectively marking the communication between two rooms with very different functions. A simple through-shelf may perhaps have rendered the same service; but he wouldn't have accentuated it. The house vibrates with such expressive mechanisms; there are gauzes made of perforated sheet metal, revolving about a light aluminium rod, which hide the toilette areas in the bedrooms; wall elements covered in metal, that slide into double tracks made of hard wood, making all degrees of opening possible between two rooms; glass partitions, light veils, and thick curtains. The beds sliding on their mobile scaffolding, and the little cabin-style staircase with the telescopic suspension, connecting the boudoir and the lady's bedroom, are all precision instruments.

Besides this capricious stairwell, the four staircases in the house were each designed in a special way. We have already spoken of "the monumental staircase" of the main room, whose steps, attached to metal arms, are covered with a plastic rubber mat, a material applied in all of the representative rooms; there is the staircase in steel filigree, which leads to the doctor's day room; the intimate staircase, covered with a parquet flooring in warm tones, which ascends from the office to the bedrooms; and the service staircase in concrete.

Everywhere, we note the same concern to make a function visible, to express even the possibilities of a function, not to simply provide for the owner's real needs, but to arrange things in such a way as to accommodate even his potential needs: to give rise to new desires in him, by satisfying them in advance by way of a refined mechanism, that he, the owner, was not yet aware of. The architect also regrets that "this highly cultivated family do not yet live in accordance with the rhythm of the house". This is a curious indication, a loaded avowal that proves that the house has made itself almost independent, that, as a machine, it imposes its laws on its owner.

The word "machine" suggests something cold and off-putting. In this sense, there is no mechanization in this house. There is nothing threatening about any of the instruments. They are treated with so much lightness, their operation is so well acknowledged, that they are more like organs than instruments. Take the aluminium trellises hiding old furniture in the lady's bedroom: see how they revolve so well on their slender axis; how intricately their meshwork is entwined. It is pleasant to manœuvre these agreeable tools; to follow the architect in his fondness for a thousand-and-one "slave" organs; to be enchanted by doors made of a simple strip of cambered sheet metal with coiled edges, its rhythm enlivening the long gallery in front of the bedrooms. You open them, by pressing on the discreet lock, and discover with delight the gracious rows of shoes, arranged between them and the wooden doors of the wardrobe.

I could infinitely cite such arrangements, all of which radiate the charm of beautiful human tools. But I'm afraid that the reader will presume that this house is a mass of utilitarian details, which is absolutely not the case. On the contrary, the house is a defined composition, whose vital core is its main hall. From there, all of its parts emanate out to their various special destinations: the dining room / office / kitchen wing invisibly occupies all of one side of the room and communicates with it via the dining room; the family wing, which is hidden behind the metal closets, serves as a parapet of the gallery; finally, there is the medical wing, which occupies the greater part of the ground floor and communicates with the hall via the doctor's day room.

By taking the large staircase with no railing, against the glass wall of this room, which becomes more spacious as you ascend, a powerful, almost solemn, impression is hard to avoid. This impression is emphasised in two rather special ways, which the architect made use of to create this space:

The staircase that goes up to the gallery of bedrooms does not stem from the main hall.

The communication between the two floors thus remains hidden; the gallery is in the main room, like the balcony in a theatre, and the room maintains a very different character from that of a "hall".

By night, outdoor lamps light this space through the large glass wall. The large glass surface thus retains its character as a light diffuser.

It is surprising to see how the architect, by using more or less transparent windows in the epidermis of the house's translucent bricks, was able to evoke an intimate, free, liveable character in the bedrooms; an official, calm atmosphere in the patients' waiting room; a precise, scientific character in the surgery; and a gentle, feminine feeling in the boudoir suspended over the garden.

The reader can grasp these possibilities by studying the cut-away views and photographs, and can create an idea of the suggestive character of the main room, whose translucent wall does not contain any transparent glass.

In conclusion, let us note another very curious experience that this original work provides for us. From the structural work right down to the minute details, the house was entirely built by craftsmen, with no input whatsoever from major firms. The architect describes the house as a "model built by craftsman with a view to industrial standardisation". Leaving aside this troubling question of standardisation, we note that there is a very craft-focused spirit throughout. We believe that this spirit is highly important to the architect's work (if only to prepare for the industrial work).

It would appear that this ardent architect-artisan that Pierre Chareau incarnates even, in his quest for perfection, allowed himself to lose sight of the very strict limits that we trace for ourselves. I have already cited the phrase regarding the owner, not living to the rhythm of the house.

In the course of our visit, I noticed that the slave components in this house have become autonomous to the point of conjuring new needs for the inhabitant. But I believe that our main task as architects is not to aim to create new needs, but to rigorously define and simply satisfy (as simply as possible!) existing needs.

After the nervous excitement of a day in the metropolis, we are delighted to note, upon our return, that at least in the home, life has remained free of all complications; that we can eat our meals, just as our great-grand-fathers before us, seated on chairs around a table, and by serving ourselves not through some eating contraption, but with cups, plates, and spoons. If this division of our life is qualified as dualistic: well, we'll just have to accept this dualism. We accept that real life must be endowed with a form, which is our particular role as architects: and that means life as we find it, and in which we ourselves participate. I believe that any other tendency is utopian. Let us not be afraid to say that the era of utopianism in architecture is over.

This does not however render Pierre Chareau's effort any less interesting. An admirable work has been created. A valuable experiment has been undertaken. Furthermore, a problem has been posed: that of the very fundaments of our trade.

(Julien Lepage "Observations en visitant", *L'Architecture d'Aujourd'hui*, numeró 9, novembre–décembre, 1933)

---

p. 109

La Maison de Verre

Pierre Chareau

I have often heard it said: "The home is not an airplane or a liner, or a laboratory — let us accept the religion of the Lares Gods rather than the tyranny of the Machine God."

While the production of the Maison de Verre attempts to resolve various prevailing problems in contemporary life, the solutions are above all human and based on routine usage that recognises them as such.

This house was designed in 1925 and has been occupied since 1931, and thus now allows the meaning of the research undertaken to be more clearly identified.

Architecture is a social art. It is both the pinnacle of all Arts and an expression of the human masses. An architect can only create if he listens and if he understands the voice of thousands of men, if he suffers their suffering, if he struggles alongside them to liberate them. He uses the iron that they forged; he guides them towards the future because he knows what belongs to the past. But he must live only to serve them.

These men ask for order; they ask an action to be well executed, with less pain; they ask to conquer time. Our research must strive to help them.

The translucent façade does not use glass for the sake of glass, but if we examine the plan of this building built on the foundations of an old 17th century hotel (approximately 14 by 14 metres) and if we take into account the normal height of a floor and windows through which light is distributed, we realise that one third of the former residence was deprived of light. An even more conclusive test (and ordeal) came later; at the time it was decided to build the house, it was surrounded by gardens.

When it was barely finished, it was rumoured that the romantic garden running alongside it would be destroyed, and some time after, a 25-metre high wall sealed off the horizon and… could have plunged the façade on the garden side into obscurity forever. But—and here, I must admit that this was a very important affirmation for me—nothing was changed; the light penetrated everywhere as it had before.

Elsewhere, according to the calculations of my associate and friend, J. By Vœt [sic], we were able to recuperate 25 to 30 percent of useless terrain for a town-planning project.

Men ask to be able to isolate themselves, but also to be able to conveniently socialise and move about comfortably. Through spatial arrangements and by using the appropriate techniques now available to us, all of this can be given to them in their homes.

Whether we use translucent façades or not, the problem remains. Houses and town planning are by-products of the times, on a human scale.

All contemporary architectural solutions are created by taking these essential relationships into account.

("La Maison de Verre de Pierre Chareau commentée par lui-même", *Le Point*, Colmar, 1937)

Notices

by Olivier Cinqualbre and Yuki Yoshikawa,
translated by Joe Garden and Anna Knight from French to English.
Each description starts with the indication of the page number where the relative artworks are reproduced.

---

p. 46
Chareau-Lurçat Creations
Reference models: Sofa, 1921 and High-Backed Armchair, 1924–1927
—
A sofa (1921) and a high-backed armchair (1924) are the two iconic pieces that came out of the collaboration between Jean Lurçat and Pierre Chareau. Their relationship grew out of their mutual acquaintance with Jean Dalsace. It was a relationship that occurred early in Chareau's career and was to turn into a long-lasting friendship. The work issuing from their partnership was critically praised and led to Chareau's first publication.[*1]

While in the design of the armchair it is possible to see a mix of diverse influences (medieval proportions, 19th century armrests, Mackintosh for the height of the back), these two pieces of furniture share a refinement in their stylistic characteristics; the contrast between the form and the colourful medium of expression is thus all the more striking.

In properties such as the Bernheim's in Villeflix, the Maison de Verre, or the Dreyfus' apartment, Chareau's furniture (when not a joint creation) stands out from Lurçat's wall paintings or from in front of partitions. Besides this sofa and armchair, wall tapestries would also cover a stool seat, and chair seat and back. At the end of the 1930s, Lurçat would also have the opportunity to create the drawings for the creation of the high-backed armchair.[*2]
—
Notes
[*1] Michel Dufet, "Deux Décorateurs Modernes: Chareau et Lurçat", *Feuilles d'Art*, no. 1, 1929, pp. 39–46.
[*2] Destined in particular for creations carried out in Switzerland by Louis Moret (Louis Moret Foundation archives).

---

p. 48
Lamp with triangular alabaster plates.
Reference model: Floor Lamp called "The Nun", 1923
—
Triangular alabaster plates, overlapping by two or by four, crown the Nun series: lamp, table lamp, and reading lamp.

Created in 1923, this model would be produced in three sizes and the shaft in two materials — metal and wood. The wood versions — generally in Cuban mahogany and in sycamore for the table lamp — show some variation in their dimensions, but apart from the smallest model, all feature the same rolled and folded cone design that was more natural in the metal examples. For these latter versions, further variations also existed, resulting from sculptured designs or from technical procedures. The metal Nun is an example of the synergy between the creative expression of Pierre Chareau and the fabrication in the Dalbet company, as André Dalbet explains: "Some of the work requested by Pierre Chareau required tricks and invention in order to be carried out. This is the case with the lamp known as The Nun, whose conical base is made with one curved sheet of metal. In order to find the correct cutting line that would ensure the upright level position of the cone, I had to hang the base in a tub of water so that the surface of the water would be at the right level for the lamp. The mark indicating where to cut the base was therefore obvious by the water mark on the cone."[*1]

Certain Nuns had lampshades in parchment (table lamp, 1923) or later, in fabric (lamps from the Grand Hôtel de Tours, 1927).

—

Note
[*1] Interview with Mr André Dalbet (Louis Dalbet's son), conducted by Bernard Bauchet, 28 December 1990.

---

p. 49
Lamps with alabaster plates "Quarter-circle screen"
Reference model: Table Lamp, 1923

—

It was the simple and conventional geometric shape of the quarter-circle that started Chareau's research and the subsequent fabrication by Louis Dalbet. The latter forged the supports and mountings, but also determined the size and fitting of the alabaster.[*1]

The simplest use was the model with one element (single fan in front of the light bulb), or with two elements superposed. The next step in the process of creating variations was to combine a pair of plates and join them along one of their sides, forming an angle — a combination that could be said to resemble butterfly wings. This pairing approach resulted in a number of wall-mounted models (single and superposed) and a chandelier (three pairs that fitted in between three single plates — a model presented at the Salon d'Automne in 1923).

Inverted, this pair would also be fitted on a cross bar for a wall lamp and used on two versions of a table lamp. Here, the form of the diffuser allows movement: shifting along the length of the cross-bars, rotation of the electrical parts and rotation of the stand at the base, which was made from a folded triangular piece of metal. This table lamp also had variations: with a lampshade (Salon d'Automne, 1923), with a base made of a vertical tube and a counterweight (including a wooden version for the nursery, 1924) and one with metal reflectors in addition to diffusers.

—

Note
[*1] Louis Dalbet archives, Bibliothèque Kandinsky, MNAM-CCI.

---

p. 50
Lamp with "elytron" "canopy block" alabaster plates
Reference model: Alabaster Plates, 1923

—

Departing from classic styles of lampshades in favour of his lamp creations, Pierre Chareau would use alabaster plates to diffuse the light. All of the lamps created between 1923 and 1932 can be separated into four families determined by the form of these alabaster plates.

Along with the simple geometric shapes of the quarter-circle and the triangle, Pierre Chareau also used the rectangle. A number of these modules were juxtaposed and assembled into a bright row of lights called the "applique ruche" [beehive lamp] (1924). The dimensions varied depending on where they were destined for — made lengthwise, usually straight but sometimes curved. This row of lights was mounted high on the wall and often replaced the mouldings. On the ceiling, they decorate recesses of the same height, giving the impression that they are inlaid. In contrast to these simple uses, Chareau also put together pieces where the plates became a series of light-refracting facets. This was the case for a ceiling lamp made up of eight alabaster plates, and for a wall lamp (the "elytron" model) made with three plates, the direction of the overlapping plates being the difference between two of the elytron models.

In contrast to previous models, where the light diffusion was carried out by plates in complex combinations of simple geometric shapes, the "canopy" model referred more to the mineral aspect of alabaster: the base element is a block that covers the light bulb from where the light is radiated. Unable to be carved, the block is created by assembling plates. Once again, the geometry is rigorous and the shape simple — resembling a triangular prism.

---

p. 52
"Fan" shape
Reference model: Fan-Shaped Low Table, 1923–1924

—

It is not known whether Pierre Chareau took the fan shape

(a shape he would use throughout his career) from one of his furniture creations or from one of his interior layouts to later apply it to one or other pieces. The first time that Chareau used this fan style in his renovations was with the boudoir panels, presented at the Salon d'Automne in 1923.

The table only appeared in apartments a few years later (1924, 1926) — or at least, this is what the period publications indicate. This table includes two, three, or four segments. Each segment is made up of a curved upright part and a triangular tabletop, in decreasing sizes. The segments nest into one another and the joint functions with a metal hinge. It is the metal hinge made by the Dalbet firm, which allows the item to be accurately dated. The "telephone" model is characterized by the replacement of the base by a hollow parallelepiped column designed to store telephone directories. The telephone itself could be found at the top of the piece.

"Pierre Chareau excels at making the most out of entrance-ways. He always manages to section off a corner with a fan door, behind which might be a toilet, a bookshelf, a useful wardrobe. [...] One of his small tables has a number of surfaces, and it is to the nesting tables of our grandmothers what the Charleston is to the Boston.

It would be wonderful to find this table in lots of entrance-ways, with or without a telephone on top, which shortens distances while wearing out nerves."[1]

Chareau would later use the fan principle once again, but with a different material — that of metal — to create the "helix" table.

—

Note
[1] Ernest Tisserand, *L'Art Vivant*, 15 February 1926, p. 148.

---

p. 54
Lanique Apartment
72 Avenue Henri Martin, 1923–1924
—

While the decoration of the dining room was entrusted to Francis Jourdain, Chareau was in charge of the rest of the apartment.[1] This renovation is particularly important in the chronology of Pierre Chareau's work, because on one hand it is one of the first examples of the importance of his collaboration with Louis Dalbet, and on the other it was the opportunity to experiment with layout — the fruits of his research on mobility. Dalbet's forge work was not yet used on the furniture itself, but it was nevertheless present on anything to do with lamps, "beehive" lamps, "flower" ceiling lights or "canopy" wall-mounted lights; or to do with accessories "tripod" flower stands, wall shelves, swivelling small tables fixed to the wall as bedside tables, radiator covers, or curtain rails. In addition, Dalbet's technique was undoubtedly used for the creation of the mobile elements in the small living room. This small living room is truly creative: the way in which the original space has been treated elevates it to the status of an artwork, and a noble one at that, all the while retaining its distributive function. To do this, Chareau mastered the constraints of the curved wall, continuing it around the whole room to form a perfect cylinder.

Joists divide the ceiling into quarters pointing towards the centre, with the sliding panels rotating in a fan shape.[2] In this space, a "handkerchief" game table is the natural fit — a symbol of a well-modulated occupation of space.

—

Notes
[1] For this job, Chareau worked with his friend Jacques Lipschitz, whose various creations, sculptures, and accessories feature in the interior design.
[2] Here he repeats the layout used for a boudoir presented at the Salon d'Automne in 1923.

---

p. 55
Motif: "lyre"
Reference model: Sofa MP 215, Armchair SN 37, circa 1923
—

Around 1923, Pierre Chareau created a number of pieces of seating furniture — stools, a bergère armchair, additional armchairs, a sofa — with bases moulded in the shape of a lyre that, while they may not have constituted a family of furniture, at least represented a generation, the same generation exhibited in the office-library of "A French Embassy" in 1925.

Some of his first armchairs displayed this same motif without moulding, but this moulding would soon come to add a touch of refinement. The office armchair and bergère armchair both have a "gondola" shape, while others have a straight back. This variation carries through to the shape and joint of the armrests. The most commonly used woods were rosewood or walnut, with the body of the chair made of beech. The upholstery was in leather or velvet, or sometimes in patterned fabric designed by Hélène Henry.

One armchair included the novelty of a reclinable back with two positions, featuring a very simple device — behind the chair back, a hinged bar could adjust the position up and down. These pieces of furniture demonstrate a certain lightness and elegance that hadn't been present in Chareau's first armchairs, which had seemed somewhat heavy, as well as some outmoded influences.

---

p. 58
Office-Library
Exposition Internationale des Arts Décoratifs et Industriels Mod-

ernes [International Exposition of Modern Industrial and Decorative Arts] | A French embassy, the pavilion of the Société des Artistes Décorateurs [Society of Artist-Decorators], Paris, 1925 –

—

"A French embassy" — this was the brief given to the Société des Artistes Décorateurs for its participation in the exposition. In architect Charles Plumet's pavilion, after winning a competition, Pierre Chareau was assigned the creation of an "office-library". "From the original smoking room of Francis Jourdain, painted in a lemon-yellow shade and furnished with no other intention than comfort, we entered Pierre Chareau's office-library. It displayed a rare ingenuity, a whimsy that was both unexpected and logical, audacity tempered by a keen sense of the practical."[*1] Accounts and reports were plentiful, and all were complimentary. "Under a white cupola, from where light shines and which can also be ingeniously hidden during the day by a sliding ceiling, the office occupies the centre of the room. To the left and right, book-filled shelves are mounted on sliding rails. This cleverly designed movable layout keeps the office itself separate, and allows space in the two angles for two small, independent rooms containing a writing desk each. The room itself is made with palm wood with alternating grain, used sometimes in small sections, sometimes in large. The walls have no ornamentation and disappear under this palm wood covering. The entrance doors are masked by brocaded silk door hangings, whose discreet brilliance furthers the harmony of the wood, with the rest of the walls being covered in shelving, as are all libraries. This office can be considered one of the most recent successes, as well as one of the most ingenious, in this kind of research. It highlights not only Mr Chareau's qualities as a decorator, but also as an architect."[*2]

The circular space and panels arranged in a fan-shape extended and fuelled the research that Chareau had begun with the boudoir presented at the Salon d'Automne in 1923, and continued with the small living room in the Lanique apartment the following year. A sketch from 1924 shows that Chareau had retained this solution since the beginning of the project.[*3]

If, in contrast to previous jobs, the whole of the space isn't entirely closed, here the "thick" walls of the movable library shelves replace simple vertical panels with real technical prowess. The cupola noted above contains the correct number of panels for it to close completely, functioning therefore as a diaphragm. Louis Dalbet, Hélène Lantier (H. Henry), Jean Lurçat, and Pierre Legrain also collaborated on the project, and a bronze by Jacques Lipschitz was presented. Elements of this layout were put up again at the Marsan Pavilion in 1927, accompanying other furnishings. This ensemble now belongs to the national collection and is permanently exhibited at the Musée des Arts Décoratifs [Museum of Decorative Arts].

—

Notes

[*1] Gaston Varenne, "L'Exposition des Arts Décoratifs. Le Mobilier Français", *Art et Décoration*, July–December 1925, p. 4. The article opens with a drawing of Chareau's layout.
[*2] Gabrielle Rosenthal, "L'Exposition des Arts Décoratifs et Industriels Modernes", *L'Art Vivant*, no. 20, 15 October 1925, p. 17.
[*3] Document kept at the drawings room at the Musée des Arts Décoratifs.

---

p. 60

Day Room

Exposition Internationale des Arts Décoratifs et Industriels Modernes | A French embassy, the pavilion of the Société des Artistes Décorateurs, Paris, 1925

—

Above the smoking room and adjoining Francis Jourdain's fitness room, Pierre Chareau created a day room in a limited space. Contrasting with the sobriety of the smoking room and the spartan rigour of the fitness room, this installation seems full of objects and lively, warm and welcoming.

The pieces of furniture in a light-coloured wood — storage unit, table, and stool (seat covering by Jean Lurçat) — belong to the first generation of furniture. The suspended bed and the layout of the walls are particularly innovative — a result of the collaboration with Louis Dalbet. The suspended bed has a number of variations to the fixtures depending on the desired location and balance: double stirrup brackets such as found here or in the open-air room in the Villa Noailles; four fixing points in the Chareau home, Rue Nollet; or a system combining wall fittings and poles.

With the wall layout, Chareau is inventing. It could be built-in furniture pushed to its limits: the function of the piece of furniture being entirely replaced by that of the wall — if this principle wasn't based on a disassociation, on the autonomy of surfaces. The structure is in wrought iron, includes integrated lighting and allows paintings to be hung as well as upholstery fabrics to be stretched over it. If the association between fabric and paintings had not already been part of Chareau's repertoire, it could be tempting to see this work as a forerunner to the modular and transportable picture rails in modern museums.

---

p. 62

Dining Room in a Colonial Residence, 1925

Exposition Internationale des Arts Décoratifs et Industriels Modernes | Indochina Pavilion, Paris.

154

—

"At the Indochina Pavilion, I am presenting a dining room in golden wood." In a response to a journalist who asked him about his participation in the exposition, Chareau didn't add anything further to this comment, having devoted most of his remarks to his major work, the office-library.*¹ The critic Guillaume Janneau was, however, only interested in the lamp: "these lamps made with alabaster plates — the first fan-shaped, the second with intersecting planes like the petals of an enormous rose."*²

Information about this project has been handed down to us in different forms — drawings (one in colour) and photographs. Differences and similarities between these documents can shed light on Chareau's work. It is not surprising that one of the photographs and the stencil are similar — the stencil was created from the image for use in publications and to reduce the chromatic deficiencies. On the other hand, the differences between the drawings can illustrate the evolution of the project. Chareau played on details to bring purity and lightness to the decor. Lamps hang from the white surface of the ceiling, which appears between the four awnings. In the dining room, a wall tapestry and two of Chana Orloff's motherhood sculptures on steles frame a sideboard. Doors and passages are at the same height and disappear behind curtains held up by a rail that surrounds the whole room. On the floor, geometric patterns required a stencil in order to be fully expressed, perhaps even surpassing reality.

—

Notes
*1 Georges Le Fèvre, *L'Art Vivant*, no. 12, 15 June 1925, p. 28.
*2 Guillaume Janneau, "L'Exposition Internationale des Arts Décoratifs et Industriels Modernes", *Beaux-arts*, no. 12, 15 June 1925, p. 185.

---

p. 64
Madame Ullmann Bedroom
Reference model: Dressing Table and Armoire, 1925–1927

—

Among the twenty or so interior home decorations carried out by Pierre Chareau, a certain type of room design appears naturally. While studies are associated with a male clientele, the bedroom, including that of the couple, is more often feminine. Next to the bed and the bedhead, the iconic piece is the dressing table, along with that indispensable item, the storage cabinet. The dressing table, all the while retaining its usual characteristics (small size, presence of a mirror, drawers, plain tabletop, etc.), frees itself from this tradition. The dressing table that Chareau proposed to his client is sober and somewhat severe. The base is a single, smooth upright plane of the same depth as the piece of furniture itself: only a few insets enliven the surface. For the mirror, classic circle, oval, or square shapes are discarded in favour of a rectangle that runs the whole length of the piece. The only refinement in the dressing table is the contrast between the types of wood that form the tabletop. The centre part in sycamore stands out from the rest of the mahogany table. The storage cabinet repeats the same combination of woods: the exterior is entirely in mahogany and the interior fittings are in sycamore. The rigorous functionality of the item is tempered by the elegance of its tonal contrasts and the care taken in the details, such as the ivory keys. These two refined pieces of furniture introduce, in their own way, the radicality of wood-metal furniture, be it for dressing tables or linen cupboards.

---

p. 66
Reifenberg Mansion
4-6 rue Mallet-Stevens, Paris, 1927

—

The decoration of the first floor of the Reifenberg mansion, built by Robert Mallet-Stevens, was assigned to Pierre Chareau. The living room, dining room, and bedroom all present the pure volumes of a parallelepiped. Chareau was to introduce curves and reliefs. In the living room, he contents himself with creating a hallway, demarcated by a false ceiling and the back of a curved bookshelf. The shape of the room is soberly underlined by a metal row of lights, running the full length of the wall and including two "flower" fittings that provide a rhythmic counterpoint. In the dining room, he continues his intervention on the ceiling: he multiplies the planes and the edges for a geometric composition, integrating the row of lights into the opposing and symmetrical L-shaped casings. In the bedroom, he introduces curved lines to his rectangular layout: the solid cylindrical shape of a cupboard and the supple arc of a curtain rail. While the nature of the curtain partition is to separate and isolate, the overhang of the cupboard marks the border between the two spaces. The shape of the cupboard fits its originality: inside, a mirror, storage fixtures, shelves, drawers, and hangers share sections of a drum that pivots on its own central axis, all enclosed by a cambered sliding door. It prefigures certain closets in the Maison de Verre — the one in the dining room or those in the bathroom, which are more sophisticated in their movement.

---

p. 68
Interior Design of Reception Halls of the Grand Hôtel
Tours, France, 1927

—

This commission was issued by Paul Bernheim. Compared to the decoration of apartments or the presentation of layouts at salons, it represented a change in scale for Pierre Chareau. Not only in terms of its specifications and the considerable dimensions of the designs to produce, but also by the amount of pieces of furniture to deliver. The project was exceptionally well-received by industry media, which gave an account of this space, now destroyed.*1 Firstly, the ability of Chareau to respond to a set of specifications was confirmed. These included technical concerns (the acoustics in the grand reception room and especially in the music room had to be of high quality); organizational concerns (the sequential arrangement of spaces); and decorative concerns (the specific atmospheres of the various functions). Next, Chareau's capacity to master both the art of the overall composition and the details was fully asserted: the impressive design work on the ceilings and underneath the galleries, and the presence of mirrors in the railings of the grand room are two examples. Finally, Chareau once again displayed his skill in choosing, matching, and bringing materials into play. He used wood (marquetry and small bricks of mahogany as wall coverings, sycamore panelling inset with silver metal, and wood floorings with geometric patterns combining various woods), fabrics from Hélène Henry, and metal and glass. In this demonstration of virtuosity, two elements are particularly noteworthy for the way in which they represent Chareau's axes of research at the time: movement and an innovative use of glass. He established a separation between the smoking room and the bar using movable panels in a fan shape — based on the same principle as for the office-library. Mobility was also applied to the floorboards of the grand hall, allowing the stage to be lifted, or used as tiered seating for the audience. It is not the glass ceiling in this grand hall that merits study: the process for creating this was an old one, and it was only the inset mirrors that gave it its character. On the other hand, the use of glass on the walls is more original, to such a degree that different chroniclers gave different descriptions. For some, it was made of opaque glass, for others from ground glass, and for others still, from mirrors without silvering. They described its colour as green, olive green — a colouration given by the walls — and praised the effects: "A bluish-green immensity surrounds us in which imprecise lighting is reflected, similar to that trained on the Seine under the bridges, in the evening. Mr Pierre Chareau is a poet. He has created the ideal atmosphere for a music room. Being careful not to commit the error of introducing paintings or sculptures likely to attract the audience's attention, he has created an undefined atmosphere, especially favourable for listening to music.

The eye can lose itself on the horizon without encountering anything to stop it."*2

—
Notes
*1 Ernest Tisserand, "Une Oeuvre Nouvelle de Pierre Chareau Ensemblier", *L'Art et les Artistes*, no. 83, January 1928, pp. 130–134. Ivanhoé Rambosson, "Un Grand Hôtel à Tours", *Art et Décoration*, February 1928, pp. 33–39. Gaston Varenne, "Un Ensemble de Chareau au Grand Hôtel de Tours", *L'Amour de l'Art*, no. 2, February 1928. P. F., "Un Hôtel Moderne à Tours", *Art et Industrie*, January 1928, p. 46. *Encyclopédie des Métiers d'Art — Décoration Moderne*, tome 1, Paris, Editions Albert Morancé, (undated), contains an important collection of photographs by Thérèse Bonney.
*2 I. Rambosson, op. cit., p. 38 and 39.

---

p. 70

Tubular Furniture for the Hôtel de Tours
Reference model: High Stools, MT 344 and EF 596, 1927

—

Here, it is not a set of multiple variations in form or technique that justifies this kind of collection, but rather the stylistic unity that was sought here for a particular commission. The renovation of reception rooms at the Grand Hôtel de Tours represented both a shift in scale and in specifications compared to previous installations. Here, the arena was public, there were multiple, large spaces, and some of the functions of the rooms were new for Chareau to work with. In regards to the furniture, his response varied depending on the purpose of the rooms. For the banquet hall, he did not create ornate seating, but was satisfied with classic, simple chairs. For the living room, dining room, and hall (all rooms that he had already had the opportunity to create), he used both his older and more recent creations — armchairs and table chairs. Chareau only designed new furniture for the correspondence room and the smoking bar.

In the bar, the furniture consisted of high stools with wooden seats and tubular legs, and "little individual bars", all in wood and with an imposing shape.

While Chareau played with the contrast between office desktops and gaming tables, seats in solid wood and lightness of tubes until a visual imbalance was reached, these same formal tropes place this production on the fringe of modern tubular furniture. The technique used here — parkerised sections, assembled with sleeves and wooden feet — seems backward in today's world of nickel-plated and angled tubes. Perhaps in the progression of his creative work it is possible to identify the figure of a Pierre Chareau who had little concern for conforming to the latest fashions.

---

p. 72

Clubhouse of the Golf Hôtel of Beauvallon
Beauvallon, Var, France, 1927–1929

—

Pierre Chareau was commissioned in 1926 by Émile Bernheim, one of Annie Dalsace's uncles and the developer of the Beauvallon golf course. Construction began in early 1929. With its cubist architecture and smooth white facades, the Clubhouse calls to mind the architecture of the Villa Noailles, built by Robert Mallet-Stevens and also on the Côte d'Azur. Chareau was perfectly familiar with it after having been invited to create his open-air room there, as well as the preceding creations of his Dutch collaborator Bernard Bijvoet. The latter's experience with concrete does not even seem to have been a determining factor: as with the Villa d'Hyères, it was above all a question of aesthetics.

A juxtaposition of different spaces with specific functions made up the building. The main part, containing the bar and meeting room, dominated the whole due to its height. The curve of its facade invited entry, heightening the panoramic view outside all the while. Chareau gave it a false depth, leaving space at ground level for flower tubs and running a casing with a row of lights up the side of the bay windows. The recessed openings accentuated the cramped effect by a pediment that appeared disproportionate. Perhaps it had been devised as a visual reference point in the middle of the vegetation. The cloakrooms, kitchen, and heating room were situated at the back, with simple reinforced concrete cubes, lit up by strips underneath the overhang of the roof-terrace. A covered terrace served as a hub, with the centrally positioned fireplace leading off to all spaces. With its pleasing proportions, it contrasted with the bulk of the bar area. Kenneth Frampton critically analysed the Clubhouse: "From an architectural point of view, the main anomaly of this work is that it looks like an incomplete Cubist construction, which, no matter from which side you approach it, is always unbalanced, as if its creator was somehow embarrassed by the need for an exterior form."[1] At the time, the industry media had a kindly reception for its creator: his sensitivity, respect for the site and the "highly romantic note" contributed by the fireplace were evoked.[2] It was the same for the general public: "Since Chareau's Clubhouse, the golfers and sportsmen who visit Beauvallon are no longer satisfied with the English-style cottage, whose charm only comes from ivy and shade and with which each golf club attempts to coquettishly woo its patrons. So here, as with wherever he goes, Chareau has taught people their needs, attitudes, and gestures, and he serves these."[3]

—

Notes
[1] Marc Vellay, Kenneth Frampton, *Pierre Chareau. Architecte-meublier 1883–1950*, Paris, Éditions du Regard / Via, 1984, p. 238.
[2] *L'Architecture d'Aujourd'hui*, no. 3, 1934, p. 89.
[3] *Tourisme*, p. xviii

—

p. 74
Villa Vent d'Aval
Beauvallon, Var, France, 1927–(?)

—

A mystery surrounds this project. The viewpoint of historians with respect to this villa alternates between silence and disinterest. Until now, this work was considered as a later one in Chareau's French career, even perhaps being carried out after his departure for the United States, thereby clearly escaping his control.[1]

Testimonies and sources have now shed light on this project.

The first testimony is from Dollie Chareau: "In 1927, he built the Clubhouse at Beauvallon (Var), as well as a private home for Mr Edmond Bernheim to whom Pierre Chareau owes his free expression and with whom he achieved his dream of becoming an architect."[2] The second came from a young woman employed in 1928 in the Atelier Pierre Chareau and who remembers having made models not only of the Clubhouse, but also the villas. This information is corroborated by René Cravoisier who notes a work placement with Chareau at this time, in his curriculum vitae and who mentions having worked on these projects. Other sources officially connect the villa and the Clubhouse: a photo album bears both project names on its cover and a local publication announces the beginning of the construction sites for both buildings by the same company, Reynes.[3]

Moreover, the stylistic identity supports the theory of their joint development; conversely, to place the design of the Villa Vent d'Aval ten years later and therefore after the Maison de Verre, would be to introduce an obvious misinterpretation in the evolution of Chareau's work. In effect, the construction of the projects does not seem to have been simultaneous. Similarly, the comparison between the actual building and the photographs of the model reveal significant signs of conformity. There are some differences here and there, but these are in the details. Generally, all of the modifications lessened the quality of the project that the model had presented. Such is the case with the decision not to include the wall that would have given structure to the upper-floor terrace and the removal of the large bay windows.

The building was made up of a main part in an L-shape on two levels, and an orthogonal wing on one level, with a combination of both full and empty spaces. A number of elements characterize this villa: a large terrace upstairs, half-covered and closed in on one side; and on the opposite side, the roof which extends out in a porch, defining a sheltered space on the ground. On the roof, a concrete wall curves around and creates a well of light on the floor below. These features don't always seem to have been fully mastered; this is undoubtedly what gives the Villa Vent d'Aval its slightly awkward style, but also indicates that it played an experimental role.

—

Notes
[1] Marc Vellay dates the plans from 1937–1939. (M. Vellay, *Pierre*

Chareau. Architecte-meublier 1883–1950, Paris-Marseille, Rivages, 1986, p. 62.)
*2 Dollie Chareau, in *L'Architecture d'Aujourd'hui*, no. 31, September 1950, p. vii.
*3 The album is conserved by the Musée des Arts Décoratifs. The information appears in *Les Tablettes de la Côte d'Azur*, 11 January 1929.

p. 76
Technique: Flat Metal
Reference model: Chair MC 763, MC 767, MC 849, 1927

—

In most interior layouts designed by Pierre Chareau, the collaboration with Louis Dalbet is evident from the decorative elements made with wrought iron. This technique is based on the simplicity of the material — thin and flat iron. It was also used for a series of pieces of furniture, deriving from the Clubhouse of Beauvallon commission. The covered terrace was made up of an ensemble of small tables and chairs. The table would resemble an occasional table if its centre leg was not made up of four curved uprights giving it the form of a diabolo. Its top is made of wood. The chairs had a totally flat back, a curved seat, and a base that at ground level had a frame open at the front. One variation was almost identical except that it was foldable — the seat was made up of three elements that fitted together, the frame at the base having the same dimensions as the back. Seen from the side, the movement was like that of a fan and gave the name "fan-shaped folding chair" to this model, which Chareau would use when applying for a patent. The folding chairs were made entirely of metal, while the other rigid model also had a number of variations whereby it was covered (either just the seat, or both seat and back) with leather or fabric. The original has the rustic appearance of a piece of outdoor furniture. Later, particularly for the interior design of the reception areas for La Semaine à Paris newspaper offices, Chareau would provide more sophisticated versions. While the back remained flat, the seat was sometimes curved, and covered with leather or woven wicker. This style was also available as a bench — with or without a back support.

p. 78
"Wood-metal"
Reference model: "Robert Mallet-Stevens" Desk, 1927

—

"Wood-metal" is not so much a technique — which these terms alone would not suffice to define — as it is a period in Chareau's furniture work: his most iconic modern period. The desk Pierre Chareau commissioned Louis Dalbet to create for his interior in Rue Nollet included a tabletop in rosewood surrounded by a strip of wrought iron. On one side, the base was held by a strip of metal in an upside-down T-shape; on the other, the base acted as a cross-bar and held up the tabletop and the upper shelf. Again, it was a question of a simple metal strip, the stability at floor-level being ensured by the curve of its edges as substitute leg ends. A pivoting shelf was built in under the tabletop, which balanced the other edge.

While certain other pieces of furniture had been adjusted to create variations, here, it was rather a combination of different elements. Once the principle of the metal structure was confirmed, the design of the work surface, the location and number of pivoting tablets, the presence of drawers or metal casings, or suspended wooden boxes were available in multiple variations, able to be put together on demand. A choice of wood was also possible, in black-dyed beech, rosewood, and so on, or the treatment of the metal could also be varied, with nickel-plating, or painted black and waxed. Furthermore, the orders were referenced according to clients' commissions — there is therefore a Chareau model, Fleg, Kapferer… One of these would be created for Robert Mallet-Stevens. In total, from 1927 to 1931, approximately twenty-five desks were produced.

The stool, which often accompanied the desk, had a wooden seat and was held up by a metal strip that, at ground level, formed a T-shape. At each end, two fine metal shafts connect to the overhang of the seat.

p. 84
The Maison de Verre — the process of its creation
Rue Saint-Guillaume, Paris, 1927–1931

—

Pierre Chareau's major work and a mythic object in the history of 20th century architecture, the Maison de Verre has aroused a great many analyses and interpretations since it was built. However, due to a lack of sources, the very history of this creation remains highly fragmentary. The lack of archives from the Atelier Pierre Chareau, the lack of documents in the Dalbet archives concerning the construction site on Rue Saint-Guillaume, and the scarcity of testimonies from Chareau's collaborators (at the top of which would be Bernard Bijvoet) explains this state of affairs. For a long time, knowledge about the Maison de Verre came from "field research" and from the reproduction of drawn documents and copies of plans and details in an attempt to compensate for the lack of originals. This is the path that Bernard Bauchet took when he was in charge of the renovation works, providing the most successful restitution to date. The approach was archaeological and retrospective, continually requiring trips back and forth from the site to check the archives (predominantly photographs). This essay will trace the creation of the Maison de Verre through the presentation of some of the available documents and through Pierre Chareau's own comments on his work.

1925: this is date that Pierre Chareau attributed to the "conception" of the House.*1 Without doubt, if not the start of the real design phase, it is at least the beginning of a thought process that is later validated by a statement of ownership belonging to Mr Dalsace, recorded on 25 October 1925.*2 Mr and Mrs Dalsace wished to leave their apartment on boulevard Saint-Germain. They had been given the opportunity to reside in a property belonging to the Bernheim family, situated in the Saint-Germain des Près neighbourhood. They were not able to make use of the whole building from the courtyard to the garden, as the uppermost floor was occupied. They called on Pierre Chareau, their interior decorator and friend, and we can speculate that, at the beginning, they only asked him for a simple renovation. However, Chareau was to engage in a real architectural project, and furthermore, a design of the utmost originality.

The request for a building permit dated 23 November 1927 gives a certain amount of specific information. Firstly, a reading of the plans reveals specifications for living arrangements: on the ground floor there would be service rooms and a dining room; the first floor would be devoted to receiving guests (though it did include a linen room); and on the second floor there would be bedrooms and bathrooms. Secondly, we note that the main principles were already defined: on one hand, a retaining of the levels due to the column structures, and on the other, a reorganization from two levels to three. Moreover, a number of elements such as varying heights, spaces between floors and multiple stairways were indicated, giving the space a rich complexity. Thirdly, the treatment of the facades draws our attention. The facade overlooking the courtyard already had its definitive form with its glass tiles, and the other overlooking the garden had glass panels made up of vertical panes. Chareau explains the moment the idea came to him:

"I had to build between two adjoining walls," he tells us, "and the plans envisaged arrangements relating to the needs and tastes of modern life. There was only one way to obtain as much light as possible: create entirely translucent facades. I started trials in 1927, by using large, thick panes that were frosted on one side. This first test was not at all satisfactory. In any case, and given that the problems with ventilation and heating had been resolved in quite a special way, the idea of removing all windows was adopted — we would only include small openings for security. That is how, in abandoning the idea of large tiles, we began to look for elements that, once brought together, could provide us with unlimited surfaces — but without the gaping holes that the large panes provided. For such a small test, we couldn't dream of studying new materials. Amongst those that existed, I chose Nevada bricks*3 which seemed to respond best to the specific problem."*4

The request for a work permit for "interior transformations" was turned down on 13 December 1927, after a visit by the "voyer" [council] architect,*5 whose refusal was justified as follows:

"[...] Whereas:
1. The submitted plans are incomplete, insufficiently priced and do not allow a full appreciation of the exact nature of the proposed works; and that the below points are lacking: a) the overall plan of the property; b) two copies of the drainage plans; c) plans of the ground and other floors before renovation;
2. The ceiling height of part of the ground floor and part of the first floor would be less than 2.8m (art. 17, decree 1902)."*6

Other than the absent council requirements, the imprecisions identified only confirm the incomplete state of the project: we can thus identify inconsistencies such as the location of the "empty spaces" above the storage room or part of the linen room.

A second project was filed on 11 August 1928 and received authorization on 21 August after being advised by the public works department.*7

There were a number of significant differences with the previous submission. The project itself had evolved: the ground floor was entirely reserved for a medical clinic. If there still seemed to be a hesitation over how the reception space was to be divided (living room on the ground floor and hall / dining room upstairs), the layout of the upper floors became more rational. The stairs were in their final places and some of the partitions had found their raison d'être. The project was more organized than the previous one, due to the improvements given to the service wing (now coming around into the courtyard) and its connection with the main part of the building. The facades had also been modified: the facade overlooking the garden now included glass tiles, and the facade over the courtyard had recessed panels whereas previously it had had a smooth surface. We start to get the idea of the framework, which gives the impression of a work created with modules. At this stage in the project, a number of elements were still uncertain, for example the supporting structure as drawn is reminiscent of a concrete construction. Conduits and chimneys disappeared without any indication being given of the heating system.

The construction period, with photographs documenting this, constitutes a second source of historic documents. We can see the different steps — demolition and the start of the works, the creation of the facades and floorplans. The work site attracted visitors and articles, which do provide some information.

"A House of Glass", read the title in the review *Glaces et Verres*. The "great wall of glass" is described as being "light", "solidly well-built", and "shifting". Although the aesthetic was hailed, it was the technique that called for precisions...

"For the installation, I perfected a method which you will forgive me for not sharing... Here are the first results, but please do not publish any photographs of the whole building yet. You may show, if you must, fragments of the surface obtained by the assembly of glass bricks. The full meaning of the facades will only be completely intelligible once all of the elements have been incorporated — and some of these important ones are still missing."*8

The article ended with the promise of a future article, once the construction site was finished. But there was no follow up, and so, unfortunately, there are no more comments from the creator of the Maison de Verre.

The elements evoked by Chareau correspond undoubtedly to those needed for the finishing touches to the facades, that is, the work done by Louis Dalbet and his workers. Once the glass bricks had been put in place by the firm Dindeleux, specialising in translucent concrete, *9 the major works would be succeeded by the refinement of the iron works. After that, the glass framework for the entrance and the totality of the openings in the rear facade would be completed. Similarly, the layout of the built-in furniture was progressively giving structure to the interior. Along with the photographs of the construction site, the German journal *Wasmuths Monatshefte* published a set of drawings and a view of the scale model that was presented at the Salon d'Automne in 1931.*10 Neither of these two documents present the works in the final state. A series of three drawings (neither dated nor signed, but commonly attributed to Bijvoet because of the "Dutch workmanship" in the graphic style) revealed devices that would never be made: screen partitions and mobile trunks on wheels, suspended by railings. The construction was apparently completed towards the end of 1931 or the beginning of 1932. Responding to René Chavance, Pierre Chareau explained himself in the following way: "I wanted to draw a veil between the occupant and the outside world, like a tent canvas, where all you would have to do is place the table and the bed. This table, this bed, or rather the apartments of a contemporary family, I have placed according to strictly rational conditions, but also with an ease that prevented me from considering any other form of construction."*11

Since then, the Maison de Verre has lived a double life: one with the Dalsace family within its walls, and another at the forefront of the international architecture scene.

Notes

*1 "La Maison de verre de Pierre Chareau commentée par lui-même", *Le Point*, Colmar, 1937, p. 51. Please refer to the full text attached. (p. 109)

*2 This document appears in the "Requests for building permits" file in the series VO [voirie] 11 (archives from the Ville de Paris, 1 Fi 455).

*3 Nevada: a type of brick or "glass brick", industrially produced by the big glassworks company, Saint-Gobain, at the end of the 1920s.

*4 M. D., "Une maison de verre", *Glaces et Verres*, no. 6, June 1930, pp. 19 – 20.

*5 "Voyer" architects were the architects working for the city of Paris, who checked adherence to the regulations and that construction was in accordance with the building permits.

*6 Archives de la Ville de Paris, VO11 3266.

*7 Ibid.

*8 M. D., op. cit.

*9 Translucent concrete is the name given to vertical or horizontal panels and vaults, made of glass bricks moulded in concrete.

*10 Lonia Winternitz, "Glas / das Haus eines Arztes in Paris / Architekt: Pierre Chareau, Paris", *Wasmuths Monatshefte*, Nov – Dec 1931, pp. 497 – 498.

*11 René Chavance, "Applications et techniques nouvelles du verre", *Art et Décoration*, 1932, p. 312.

---

p. 96
The Maison de Verre — the layout plan
—

While Paul Nelson attempts a theoretical analysis of the Maison de Verre in *L'Architecture d'Aujourd'hui*, Julien Lepage (alias Julius Posener) shares some observations from his visit. The fact remains that the Maison de Verre is a difficult place to understand due to its singularity and complexity. It is therefore necessary to describe it, even if this description cannot recount the luxuriousness of the spaces and interior design. Two elements founded the evolution of the Maison de Verre: the fact that a workplace is part of the house (a doctor's clinic), and that while in the previous building there had been two levels, three were now created.

When Pierre Chareau received the commission, he discovered a small traditional mansion in the suburb of Saint-Germain — a residential building on the road front, with several floors and access via a coach gate. The building itself is between the courtyard and the garden. In the courtyard, a small service wing comes around from the left side. Chareau had to create a new space, all the while maintaining the upper levels, one floor in a square shape, and the attic. Once in the courtyard, the Maison de Verre reveals itself. The eye is drawn by the facade of glass tiles. On the ground floor the wall is also made of glass, but in this instance a transparent glass that, in contrast with the surface of the glass tiles, provides a light and fragile foundation. The service wing is also covered with glass tiles, but given its function, also includes windows. The huge wall of glass tiles, with no opening, is without doubt one of the first blind walls in modern architecture. Originally the translucent concrete (a technique using panels of glass tiles) presented a smooth concrete surface. In the early 1950s, the facade was renovated and the metal structure of the panels were left exposed and painted black. At the same time, above the Maison de Verre, the two traditional floors were replaced with two levels — the second slightly set back and featuring a roof-terrace above. The upper living areas were and still are accessed by way of a stairway to the right of the house.

Entrance to the house is through a discreet side entrance. Three doorbells indicate the arrival of visitors: for the doctor, for the staff and for the house. The doctor's clinic is situated on the ground floor, which is organized according to the various routes of foot traffic. Patients head towards the reception where they announce themselves and then go to the waiting room before being invited to enter the doctor's office and the various examining rooms. At the end of their appointment, they return via the reception and retrace their steps. It is in effect a loop with the reception area as the central hub. The doctor accesses the first floor via a private staircase, which is elegant and made of metal. The service staff have their own paths of access to the side of the house, using a masonry staircase covered in black terrazzo. Access to the garden is also from this side. From the ground floor, a third, magnificent, stairway leads the visitors upstairs. Contrary to a classical layout which aligns the entrance way and stairway, this one obliges the visitor to turn towards the courtyard facade. And so the guest goes up, struck by the diffused light from the glass tiles. This metal staircase is in itself a masterpiece. It features encased glass, with reinforced glass to the sides and transparent glass for the doors. In order to indicate a separation from the medical clinic, the exit from the stairs is via two glass doors, whose transparency can be reduced by a folding metal mesh covering. The size of these openings almost turns them into mobile walls, one flat and the other with an impressive curve. The steps of the stairway seem to float: they consist of simple flat surfaces without risers, placed on two metal rails. Once upstairs, visitors must once again turn on their heel to discover the living room.

This floor hosts receptions — both small and large. Large: in the living room that also acts as a projection room for avant-garde films or concerts. Small: for when the mistress of the house invites her friends to the small living room, or for dinners in the dining room (the only set of furniture not designed by Chareau). The latter is connected to the kitchen situated in the service wing by a succession of offices and corridors hidden from view. The master also has a space that he can make more private. Between the living room and the office, a sliding wall offers a wide view as soon as it opens. The living room, even without taking into consideration its possible extensions, is the largest space in the house — due to its floor surface area and its double height. This is the area from where the structure can most clearly be seen. Metal posts are visible throughout all three levels. At the top they hold up the old structure of the building and also the different levels that make up the floors. They are in red and black — red for the paint that covers the riveted steel columns, and black for the slate tiles that cover the sides of the pillars. Their striking presence is slightly diminished by the range of colours of the different materials used: black metal mesh, light beige rubber tiles on the floor, silver grey duralumin surfaces, chests made from orange tree wood, and a luminous bluish tone from the glass tiles, but also all of the different shades of the furniture and partitions, paintings and book spines in the imposing bookcase. As mentioned earlier, this facade is completely blind; there is no opening, no way of seeing out. The question of ventilation then needs to be asked. It is resolved by a mechanical set up: controlled by a hand wheel, a double row of full metal panels opens along the whole height of the volume, directing the desired amount of air. The size of the glass tile facade is obvious from inside, including the presence of metal stiffeners spanning the full height — once again red denotes vertical metal elements. The glass tiles from the 1950s differ to those from the 1930s because of the finer surface grain and its more pronounced shade of blue. The facade overlooking the garden combines glass tiles and transparent panes, and has a green-yellow tint (due to the sulphur contained in the glass reacting over the years). There are no glass tiles in the lady's small living room: windows do overlook the garden, but these are original windows. In the industrial wagon windows, the windowpanes go up and down in standard sills. Here, the search for comfort takes precedence: in winter, a carpet can be placed on the slate tile floor; net curtains and wall coverings hang from railings; a small fireplace is present to warm up the atmosphere more than the temperature. This room contains two spectacular accessories: the first is the striking retractable metal staircase leading to the room on the floor above; the other, quite hidden, is the serving hatch in a corner of the room, for being served tea as if by magic. Works of art are hung on the wall, notably including a relief by Jacques Lipchitz.

Only one staircase (with both the step and riser made from mahogany) leads to the second floor. This is the private floor where the bedrooms are to be found. It is like an immense mezzanine above the empty space of the living room. This floor best illustrates the way in which Pierre Chareau constructs spaces through built-in furniture. This principle can be seen directly from the corridor leading to the bedrooms. In the living room, boxes and shelves provide storage, while in the bedrooms, large closets form the partitions between the rooms. The similar and repetitive alignment of doors spanning the full height of the building give this arrangement its character. The doors are metal, domed for rigidity and painted in black gloss. In the bedrooms, the wall is the same because the cupboards open from both sides: clothes are hung by the service staff in the corridor and removed by the individual from the bedrooms. Each room has its own bathroom, which are integrated in the children's rooms, with an en suite bathroom for the parents. The furniture in the Dalsaces' bedroom is from the apartment on Boulevard Saint-Germain — Chareau's first commission — that he incorporates here in a new environment. The classic style of the furniture contrasts with the mobile wardrobes and the mid-height revolving partitions (all in frosted metal) that give structure to the various spaces in the bathroom. Here, hygiene and storage encouraged Chareau to provide additional inventions and refinements. The bathroom and the three bedrooms are accessible one to the other along the length of the closets, and all access the balcony that runs along the side of the building and overlooks the garden. The view of this little park today does not give an accurate impression of how it would have looked at the time. The vegetation, in particular the trees, has grown vigorously and the remains of the original floorplan has practically disappeared.

The facade overlooking the garden is quite different to that overlooking the courtyard. Openings alternate with glass tile panels to reveal the goings-on behind. The horizontal windows on the ground floor accompany the patients from the waiting room to the doctor's office. The bow window on the first floor belongs to Mrs Dalsace's small living room and is extended by a small glass conservatory. The bedroom floor gives a false impression of being set back, due to the balcony, and aligns windows and doors in regular rows, incorporating them as part of the glass tile gridwork. Large projectors are suspended below the balcony, lighting up indoor spaces through the glass facades at night. In the courtyard, two large metal ladders, detached from the facade, support the projectors. At dusk, the Maison de Verre looks like a magic lantern, and once night falls, lit up from the outside, it remains alive.

(Olivier Cinqualbre and Yûki Yoshikawa)

p. 122

Headquarters of La Semaine à Paris Newspaper
28 Rue d'Assas, Paris, 1930

—

The interior design of the newspaper premises was led by the Union des Artistes Modernes [Union of Modern Artists].

Pierre Chareau was invited to produce the entrance rooms, the hall, a vestibule and the editing office. Two choices illustrate his involvement: on one hand, the unity of the furnishings and decoration obtained by using only metal elements, and on the other, the manipulation of volumes to amplify our perception of space. Shelves, plant holders, rows of lights, movable partitions, but also small shelves, chairs and benches emerged from Louis Dalbet's forge. Chareau again used the idea of the metal chairs originally designed for the Clubhouse of Beauvallon. But the coverings, stuffing and lining of this outdoor furniture would have to become more comfortable. They received little attention from chroniclers, and when they did, reviews were critical: "A few months ago, we criticised some of the chairs that were present there and that had been exhibited at the Salon d'Automne. Certainly they are original, but without any special touch. We will not return to this, but it would be inaccurate not to acknowledge that they are at their best within the whole sophisticated layout at 'La Semaine à Paris'"[*1]. On the other hand, everyone mentioned the panels and the ceiling made with black moleskin, "where, like a bottomless lake, the objects are reflected"[*2].

Depth of surface-mirrors, differentiation of spaces by floor coverings, simulation of inlaid volumes, Chareau played with the smallness of spaces in order to "impress on them a surprisingly large size".[*3]

—

Notes

[*1] Ernest Tisserand, "Les 'Artistes Modernes' à 'La Semaine à Paris'", *L'Art Vivant*, 1 May 1930, no. 129, p. 362.
[*2] P. L., "Les Nouveaux Bureaux de 'La Semaine à Paris'", *L'Art et les Artistes*, no. 106, 1930, p. 244.
[*3] Ernest Tisserand, op. cit.

p. 124

D. Dreyfus Apartment
9 Rue Le Tasse, Paris, 1932

—

In around 1930, the interior design of a very large apartment was assigned to Pierre Chareau. Speaking of him, a critic stated: "Modern decoration does not only consist of choosing the carpet and paint for the walls. It concerns above all the repartition and arrangement of space. You tear down all the walls of the old apartment in order to get one single room that is as big as possible. Then it is a question of recreating the many rooms with their different functions that once existed in this large empty room, without losing the benefit of the vast newly-found space. To achieve this, you can use high screens that serve as movable partitions and glass partitions that isolate more thoroughly, without ruining the lovely effects of a long perspective. And so the role of the decorator concurs with that of the architect."[*1]

A number of layouts would develop this notion of mobility that Chareau was exploring: sliding wall table, sliding door suspended on visible rails, revolving shelves, double rounded doors, in glass, whose rotation was ensured by an upper pivot — a repeat of the system at play in the Maison de Verre. The partitions were, strictly speaking, panels that folded, but the installation drew more on the movable partitions. The rail was suspended by a metal structure — a fine crossbeam. The partition of space was conserved and the focus was on obtaining flexibility and transparency.

"Even though he restricts himself to light colours on bare walls made of stone and metal, Pierre Chareau always manages to avoid soulless austerity."[2]

—

Notes

[1] Pierre Migennes, "Sur Deux Ensembles de P. Chareau", *Art et Décoration*, 1932, p. 130.
[2] Ibid., p. 132.

---

p. 126
M. Fahri Apartment
Avenue Raphaël, Paris, 1932

—

"In these architectural compositions, wardrobes have the same value in substance, relief or colour as a cornice or a column. Iron and glass can surpass their merits as mere construction materials (that is, fixed elements) in order to be used in a piece of furniture (mobile elements) and thus in ways contrary to traditional uses. They therefore become a link between stone (walls) and wood (armchairs and tables)."[1] Revolving shelves in front of radiators and a mobile coffee table on wheels illustrate these remarks.

It is still iron and glass that allow Chareau, according to the author, not to have to retreat in the face of "the biggest audacities": "there isn't, believe me, anything more adventurous than, as he did in M. F...'s living room, erecting in the middle of the room a glass door attached to the wall at only one side, the other side remaining unattached. When the need arises, it can be extended by a screen that separates the room in two. The remarkable result justifies the audacity."[2] In fact, it is a glass partition that can be covered by curtains. On the other hand, the partition doesn't totally determine a space — its overhead railing is suspended by three fine ceiling mounts and brings its movement in space to an end. The interplay of curves and counter-curves, the rivalry in its transparency, the contrast between solid and movable elements, and static glass elements gives a strange feeling to the space — one that is appropriate to its use: a dining room right in the middle of a living room.

—

Notes

[1] Pierre Migennes, "Sur Deux Ensembles de P. Chareau", *Art et Décoration*, 1932, p. 30.
[2] P. Migennes, op. cit., p. 131 and 132.

---

p. 127
Technique: "Modern Tube"
Reference model: Hat Stand, 1932

—

Apart from a few disparate pieces developed later on and sometimes belonging to minor types of furniture, it must be acknowledged that Pierre Chareau did little to contribute to the "revolution" of the use of the tube. When the foreign masters, Marcel Breuer or Ludwig Mies van der Rohe, and when his colleagues, Eileen Gray, René Herbst, Jean Burkhalter, Le Corbusier, Jeanneret, and Perriand developed the use of the steel tube, Chareau remained strangely reserved. Since he was close to Louis Dalbet, perhaps Chareau was unable to find in him a partner capable of liberating himself from an existing way of doing things so as to better respond to the imperatives of new techniques.

The "hat stand developed for the Maison de Verre" is representative of the last creative period of Pierre Chareau and accompanied the completion of the new interior of the Dalsace couple. That this hat stand has found its place in the Maison de Verre stems from the commission clearly responding to a standard need, but especially from the fact that its aesthetic and the technicality of its production were directly derived from the building site of the house. The work has not been assigned to this place; it is, among others and at a modest scale, like an incarnation. The hat stand was thought of as a piece of furniture, autonomous and mobile. The base was made from flat metal, in an oval shape borne by four wheels. The tubular structure was a rectangular parallelepiped with rounded angles. Attached to this frame, the hat stand and the coat pegs were also made from tubes. The base and structure were painted black, the shelf was in raw duralumin: the functional element stands out owing to the matt silver colour of its support.

---

p. 128
Villa Tjinta Manis
Bazainville, Yvelines, France, 1937

—

On a parcel of land bought in 1935, Pierre Chareau built a country house for the dancer Djemel Anick, who belonged to his circle of friends.

Because of its modest size, it could be thought that this work was hushed up, or even rejected by its creator, however it was mentioned by Dollie Chareau in her brief speech at *L'Architecture d'Aujourd'hui* in the period following the death of her husband, and it appeared in the posthumous work coordinated by René Herbst.[1] Completed in around 1937, the house did not enjoy any photographic coverage — contrary to all of his other furniture and architectural productions — nor was it the subject of any publication.

Whether it be the structure (wooden pole-beams), the general organization (a classic layout of pieces of furniture according to the floors) or the roofing (a simple design), nothing indicated Chareau's involvement. Only a few details catch our attention: the use of Heraclitus panels on the facade, the bolted assembly of the doors and windows (these overhang the walls slightly and open towards the exterior). These few elements didn't affect the traditional and rustic appearance of the building, clearly built with a shoestring budget in mind.

Moreover, the project shows a clear influence described in testimonies: traditional architecture from Valais that Chareau had seen not long before, on one of his visits to Switzerland.[*2] Hence the wooden structure, masonry base, and access to the upper level can be understood in this light.

—

Notes

[*1] Dollie Chareau, in *L'Architecture d'Aujourd'hui*, no. 31, September 1950, p. vii, and *Un Inventeur, l'Architecte Pierre Chareau*, collection edited under the direction of René Herbst, Paris, Editions du Salon des Arts Ménagers, Union des Artistes Modernes, 1954.

[*2] According to the testimony of Louis Moret, recorded by Christian Leprette.

---

p. 129

Small Objects

Reference model: Fruit Display Stand, circa 1930; Paper Organizer, circa 1930; Fire screen, circa 1924; Fireplace accessories shovel and tongs for logs, circa 1924

—

Around 1924, Pierre Chareau opened a shop at 3 Rue de Cherche-Midi: La Boutique. This is where he met with his clients, showing them pieces of furniture and large photo albums containing all his creations. He also had some small utilitarian and decorative objects for sale there. To accompany the fireplaces that he designed, Chareau had fireplace tools made by the Dalbet workshop — grills, fire screens, andirons, tongs and shovels. Once again, Chareau's inventiveness was supported by Dalbet's savoir-faire. The designs are refined, with modern lines.

In La Boutique, Chareau hosted art exhibitions organized by Jeanne Bucher, before she opened her own gallery in the adjacent building. La Boutique was suitable for the sale of small objects: different kinds of mirrors, window boxes and plant holders, standing ash trays — all made of wrought iron. In the mid-1930s, other sophisticated creations appeared: an office accessory, made of a simple strip of gloss metal, the folds of which held sheets of paper, envelopes and business cards, and an inkpot (now missing). More original, a plate to present fruit on, destined to adorn a console table or a dining table, is more like a domestic jewel than a banal object. Pairs of cherries or bunches of grapes sat on a fine metal shaft and were reflected in the mirror on the base of each support.

In a small way, the provision of these small objects, such as cushions made by Dollie Chareau, came to make up for the lack of real commissions during the years of economic crisis.

---

p. 132

Home and Studio of Robert Motherwell

East Hampton, New York State, USA, 1947

—

"The house was really something out of the ordinary. The floor, nearly one metre above ground level, faces directly south during the winter solstice. The south facade was nearly entirely made with small panes of glass overlapping like weatherboards. Chareau had observed this construction process in a neighbouring factory and the effect pleased him enormously. Thanks to the large glass surface area on the south wall, the heating bills were minimal — around $12 a month, if I remember correctly. The floor was concrete, which wasn't very pleasant in winter, but we didn't have enough money to put down parquet or tiles. To build the house, we had to cut down a number of pine trees, whose trunks were still stuck in the ground. One day, I had the idea that by cutting the trunks into circles a few centimetres thick, then joining them with mastic, I could obtain an interesting object, but also a surface that would be nice to walk on. No sooner said than done!"[*1]: Robert Motherwell stated, while still a young painter.

For anyone who looks at an image of the house or studio, it is strange to notice that the principle element of these constructions (prefabricated military barracks, which is where this unusual and memorable form comes from) is not at all obvious. When the house-studio was created in 1950, the text, unsigned, included unedited information given by the architect. Chareau begins the description by justifying the use of common industrial elements as follows: "The Quonset Hut, a shelter for the American army at war, offered the following possibilities: a) at the end of a campaign, they became stock to be sold off cheaply; b) the curved joist of the frame is remarkable — made of folded iron, its shape allows nails to be fixed inside and out; c) the exterior envelope is made of corrugated iron placed across the frame, or the interior insulating wall as requested; d) the diameter of a Quonset Hut is about 6m. It is sold in sections of approximately 3.6m that can be joined up."[*2]

In these lines, we recognise a whole generation's fascination with an industrial, standardized product can be found. The appropriation of this structure by the architect began with its dimensions: an 18-metre-long nave for the house and another at 10.8m for the studio. This was followed by the digging in of the building into the ground (−1.2 metres) and the placing of the structure of the Quonset Hut on a light foundation. These two operations allowed the creation of an upper floor and finally, the opening of a south-facing bay for a glass conservatory (10.8 m × 3.6 m high). In order to successfully transform the hut into a house, the above steps also required the installation of beams and the creation of a joinery structure below the main structure along the whole bay. Chareau was quick to make the most of what he had, transforming what was repetitive into rhythm, playing with asymmetry within a perfect solid form.

—

Notes

[1] Extract from a written testimony, recorded by Christian Leprette, 5 August 1984. With the kind permission of the Dedalus Foundation, New York, and Christian Leprette.
[2] "Maison d'Été pour un Peintre à Long Island, Pierre Chareau, Architecte", *L'Architecture d'Aujourd'hui*, no. 30, July 1950, p. 51.

---

p. 133
"One-room" House
East Hampton, New York State, USA, 1947

—

The erection of this "gazebo" on land that Robert Motherwell had granted him, represented part of the amount due by the painter for the building of his house and studio. Motherwell described his financial difficulties and the communication problems they had to overcome (a reciprocal lack of understanding of each other's language), but also the fact that he considered himself a satisfied customer.[1]

This building, as basic as it is, carries a dual symbolism: it was the only habitation that Chareau was to design for his own use, and though incomplete, it was his final residence.

The facades were built with concrete block masonry and terracotta for the large joins, but the layout sketches visible on the insides of the walls indicate an attempt to manage without a coating. The numerous bays were for glazed window-doors, which had the distinctive feature of having been fitted to bare walls and opening outwards — their base overhanging slightly to avoid any leaks. In a space with no partitions or bearing walls, the centre was occupied by a utilities block with chimney and boiler, toilet and shower, and a small kitchen. Areas separated by simple bamboo curtains or movable panels flowed out from this central point.

Minimalism and brutalism: the "one-room" house came from the same urges that would lead Le Corbusier to build his "Cabanon" [summer cabin] in Cap-Martin a few years later.

—

Note

[1] Extract from a written testimony, recorded by Christian Leprette, 5 August 1984.

---

p. 134
La Colline
Spring Valley, New York State, USA, 1950

—

This modest building is the last work of Pierre Chareau, his final attempt at a professional job during his American exile. Saved from oblivion by the testimonies of his clients, musician Germaine Monteux and writer Nancy Laughlin, La Colline only features in the Chareau historiography through mute photographs.[1]

The brief, a "country retreat", and the use of wood as the construction material, immediately create a link with Djemel Anick's house. But this was the land of shingles and sash windows. Furthermore, the detailed elements of the brief — i.e. good acoustics for the piano room and the requirement for separated workspaces — makes the architectural solution more understandable. The acoustic quality was obtained by a ceiling cupola over a pentagonal room. This space, the focal point of the project, determined the rest, forcing Chareau not to shy away from a number of rooms containing an angle. It is undoubtedly this originality that gives the plans a touch of modernity, even for the early 1950s.

However, a certain awkwardness has to be acknowledged in the arrangement of space, which is reminiscent of the difficulties Chareau had encountered with his first building, the Clubhouse of Beauvallon. Inside, Chareau is back in his comfort zone, particularly in the use of partition walls: shelves inset at full depth; benches, radiators, and lighting integrated into the perimeter; and soundproof closets.

—

Note

[1] "Une Maison Française aux Etats-Unis", *Art et Décoration*, no. 27, 1952, p. 24 and 25; the Maison de Verre archives.

略 歴

1883	ピエール・ポール・コンスタン・シャローは8月4日、フランス、ボルドーで生まれる。
1900	パリの国立美術学校の建築学科の入学試験を受けるも不合格となる。
1903	イギリスの家具会社ワリング・アンド・ギローのパリ支店に就職し、1914年まで働く。
1904	英国人ルイザ・ダイト（愛称ドリー）と結婚する。
1914	第一次世界大戦に出征し、1919年に帰国する。
1919	サロン・ドートンヌに初めて出品する。
1919	パリのサン＝ジェルマン大通りのダルザス氏のアパルトマンの内装を手がける。
1921	サロン・ドートンヌの会員となる。
1922	芸術家装飾家サロン（SAD）に初めて出品する。
1924	シェルシュ＝ミディ通り3番に「ラ・ブティック」を開店する。
1924	SADの会員となる。
1924	マルセル・レルビエ監督の映画「人でなしの女」、主人公の歌姫のアパルトマンのセットを担当する。
1925	パリ現代産業装飾芸術国際博覧会に参加、SADが主催する「フランスの大使の館」をテーマとするパヴィリオンで「書架のある執務室」と「体操室の休憩室」を、インドシナ・パヴィリオンで「コロニアルスタイルの住まいの食堂」を発表する。
1925	レジオン・ドヌール勲章のシュヴァリエを受章。
1927	トゥール市のグラン・オテルの大ホール、ロビー等のインテリア・デザインを手がける。
1927	パリのマレ＝ステヴァンス通りのレファンベール邸のインテリア・デザインを手がける。
1928	スイスのラ・サラ城の近代建築国際会議（CIAM）に創設メンバーとして参画。
1929	ヴァール県ボーヴァロンのホテルのゴルフ場のクラブハウスが竣工。
1929	『今日の国際芸術』20巻シリーズのうちの第7巻『家具』を担当、刊行。
1930	近代芸術家連合（UAM）の会員となる。
1930	UAMの展覧会に初めて出品する。
1930	『ラルシテクチュール・ドージュルデュイ［今日の建築］』誌の編集委員会に加わる。
1930	ラ・スメース・ア・パリ新聞本社のエントランスホールのインテリア・デザインを手がける。
1931	ダルザス医師の邸宅「ガラスの家」、サン＝ギヨーム通りに竣工。
1932	L.T.T.社（フェザントリー通り）の社屋のインテリア・デザインを手がける。
1932	ドレフュス家のアパルトマンのインテリア・デザインを手がける。
1932	ファーリ家のアパルトマンのインテリア・デザインを手がける。
1934	鉄利用のための技術局（OTUA）のコンペ「鉄を活用した客船の客室デザイン」に応募。
1935	ブリュッセル万博のフランス館の建築部門責任者に就任。
1936	OTUAのコンペ「学校用家具」に応募。
1937	「ヴィラ・ティンタ・マニス」（舞踏家ジェメル・アニク別荘）の竣工。
1937	パリ万博でUAMのパヴィリオンで「レセプションセンター」を、新時代館パヴィリオンで公園のプロジェクトを出品する。
1938	レジオン・ドヌール勲章のオフィシエ章を受章する。
1938	国立美術館の作品購入委員会に参画。
1938	OTUAのコンペ「鉄筋構造のビル建設」に応募。
1940	第2回の「海外のフランス」サロン展に「植民地の兵士のための家」を出品する。
1941	渡米。
1941	「永遠のフランス」キャンペーンに参加。
1947	ロバート・マザウェルの住居兼アトリエがニューヨーク州イースト・ハンプトンに竣工。
1950	「ラ・コリーヌ」（ジェルメース・モントゥーとナンシー・ローリン邸）がニューヨーク州スプリング・ヴァレーに竣工。
1950	ニューヨーク州イースト・ハンプトンで逝去、行年67歳。

Biography

1883	birth of Pierre Paul Constant Chareau in Bordeaux, France
1900	failed the entrance examination to the Ecole Nationale Supérieure des Beaux-Arts, Paris, architecture section
1903	employed in the Parisian branch of Warring & Gillow, English furniture and decoration company, until 1914
1904	married to Louise Dyte (known as Dolly), an Englishwoman
1914	drafted during World War I, until 1919
1919	first participation in the Salon d'Automne
1919	interior design of the Dalsace apartment, Boulevard Saint-Germain, Paris
1921	becomes a member of the Salon d'Automne
1922	first participation at the Salon des Artistes Décorateurs
1924	opening of "La Boutique", 3 Rue du Cherche-Midi, Paris
1924	becomes a member of the Salon des Artistes Décorateurs
1924	decor of the apartment of La Cantatrice in the film L'Inhumaine [The Inhuman Woman] by Marcel L'Herbier
1924	interior design of the Lanique apartment, Avenue Henri-Martin, Paris
1925	participation at the Exposition internationale des Arts Décoratifs et Industriels Modernes. Pavilion of the Société des Artistes Décorateurs (SAD) "Une Ambassade française": Office-library and day room; Indochina Pavilion: dining room in a colonial residence
1925	is made a Knight of the Legion d'Honneur
1927	interior design of the reception rooms of the Grand Hôtel de Tours
1927	interior design of the Reifenberg mansion, Rue Mallet-Stevens, Paris
1928	founding member, in La Sarraz (Switzerland) of the Congrès Internationaux d'Architecture Moderne (CIAM) [International Congresses of Modern Architecture]
1929	completion of the Clubhouse of the Golf Hôtel de Beauvallon, Beauvallon
1929	publication of "Meubles", volume 7 of L'Art International d'Aujourd'hui
1930	member of the Union des Artistes Modernes (UAM)
1930	first participation at an exhibition of the UAM
1930	member of the patronage committee of L'Architecture d'Aujourd'hui
1930	interior design of the reception hall of La Semaine à Paris, Rue d'Assas, Paris
1931	completion of the home of Doctor Dalsace (Maison de Verre), Rue Saint-Guillaume, Paris
1932	interior design of the offices of the L.T.T. company, Rue de la Faisanderie, Paris
1932	interior design of the Dreyfus apartment, Rue Le Tasse, Paris
1932	interior design of the Fahri apartment, Avenue Raphaël, Paris
1934	participation in the OTUA competition "Cabin of a luxury liner in steel"
1935	in charge of the architecture section of the French pavilion at the Exposition Internationale de Bruxelles
1936	participation in the OTUA competition "School furniture"
1937	completion of the "Tjinta Manis" villa, Bazainville
1937	participates in the Exposition Internationale des Arts et Techniques de Paris. Pavilion of the UAM: the "Reception Centre"; Pavillon des Temps Nouveaux: a park project
1937	is made an Officer of the Légion d'Honneur
1938	member of the State acquisitions commission at salons
1938	participation in the OTUA competition "Construction of a steel building"
1940	exhibits a "Colonial soldier's home" at the 2nd Salon de la France d'Outre-Mer
1941	departure for the United States of America
1941	member of "France for Ever"
1947	completion of the home-studio of Robert Motherwell, East Hampton, New York
1950	completion of La Colline, Spring Valley, U.S.A.
1950	Pierre Chareau dies in East Hampton, New York

参考文献（出版年順）

Selected Bibliography in Chronological Order

定期刊行物　Articles

———

Dufet M.: «Deux décorateurs modernes, Chareau et Lurçat», *Feuillets d'art*, n° 1, 1921, pp. 39–46.

«Pierre Chareau», *Mobilier et Décoration d'intérieur*, n° 1, November–December 1922, p. 27.

«Réalisations et projets. Boudoir par Chareau», *Les Arts de la maison*, Autumn–Winter 1923, pp. 45–50.

Varenne G.: «L'esprit moderne de Pierre Chareau», *Art et Décoration*, May 1923, pp. 129–138.

Gauthier M.: «Art décoratif. Pierre Chareau», *L'Art et les artistes*, n° 46, pp. 281–286.

«Boutique par Pierre Chareau», *Mobilier et décoration d'intérieur*, December 1924, p. 19.

Pierre Chareau: «Chambre de jeune homme, 1924», *Les Arts de la maison*, Autumn–Winter 1924.

Edmond Fleg: «Nos décorateurs, Pierre Chareau», *Les Arts de la maison*, Winter 1924.

Documents d'architecture. Art français contemporain, presented by Jean Badovici, Albert Morancé, Paris 1925, pl. 5, 12, 24, 31 and 38.

L'Art décoratif français 1918–1925, Albert Lévy, Paris 1925, p. 84

Janneau G.: *Formes nouvelles et progammes nouveaux*, Paris 1925.

«Enquête», *L'Amour de l'art*, n° 12, December 1925, pp. 489–493.

Zervos Ch.: «Architecture intérieure. Enquêtes», *Cahiers d'art*, January 1926, p. 14.

Rémon G.: «Nos artistes décorateurs, Pierre Chareau», *Mobilier et Décoration*, n° 3, February 1926, pp. 48–58.

Les Arts de la maison, Summer 1926, pl. xxi–xxx.

Chavance R.: «Chez un cinéaste» (Marcel L'herbier), *Art et décoration*, July–December 1927, pp. 43–48.

Chavance R.: «Quelques exemples d'installations modernes de Mallet-Stevens», *Mobilier et Décoration*, August 1927, p. 36.

Sezille L. P.: *Devantures et boutiques*, A. Lévy, Paris 1927, pl. 14 and 28.

Georges W.: *Intérieurs et ameublements modernes*, E. Moreau, Paris 1927, pl. 19–23.

Tisserand E.: «Une oeuvre nouvelle de Pierre Chareau ensemblier», *L'Art et les artistes*, n° 83, January. 1928, pp. 130–134.

P. F.: «Un hôtel moderne à Tours», *Art et Industrie*, January 1928, p. 46.

Rambosson I.: «Un grand hôtel à Tours», *Art et Décoration*, February 1928, pp. 33–39.

Varenne G.: «Un ensemble de Chareau au Grand Hôtel de Tours», *L'Amour de l'art*, n° 2, February 1928, pp. 59–62.

Henriot G.: «Pierre Chareau», *Mobilier et Décoration*, n° 12, November. 1928, pp. 215–230.

Rambosson I.: «Pierre Chareau à Tours», *La revue de l'art ancien et moderne*, June–December 1928, pp. 135–138.

Chareau P.: «Meubles», *L'Art international d'aujourd'hui*, n° 7, 1929.

Répertoire du goût moderne, vol n° 5, A. Lévy, Paris 1929.

«Appartement de M. G. décoré par Pierre Chareau», *Art et Industrie*, n° 11, November 1929, pp. 13–16.

Hôtels de voyageurs, vol. 2, Éditions Charles Moreau, Paris ca 1930, pl. 19–22.

Encyclopédie des métiers d'art — Décoration moderne, t. i, Éditions Albert Morancé, Paris undated.

«Aménagement des bureaux de La Semaine à Paris», *Encyclopédie des métiers d'art — Décoration moderne*, t. ii, Éditions Albert Morancé, Paris undated, pl. 57–59.

Tisserand E.: «Les "artistes modernes" à La Semaine à Paris», *L'Art vivant*, n° 129, May 1930, p. 362–367.

P. L.: «Les nouveaux bureaux de La Semaine à Paris», *L'Art et les artistes*, n° 106, 1930, pp. 243–244.

M. D.: «Une maison de verre», *Glaces et Verres*, n° 17, June 1930, pp. 19–20.

Rémon G.: «Au Pavillon de Marsan. La première exposition de l'Union des Artistes Modernes», *Mobilier et décoration*, July 1930, pp. 1–13.

Tisserand E.: « L'exposition de l'Union des Artistes Modernes », *L'Art vivant*, August 1930, pp. 628–631.

« Deuxième exposition de l'Union des Artistes Modernes », *Mobilier et décoration*, July–December 1931, pp. 27–29.

Winternitz L.: « Glas, das Haus eines Arztes in Paris », *Wasmuths Monatshefte*, November–December 1931, pp. 497–498.

Gallotti, J.: « La IIIème exposition de l'Union des Artistes Modernes », *Art et décoration*, January 1932, pp. 97–102.

Pascal G.: « Au Pavillon de Marchan. L'Union des Artistes Modernes », *Beaux-arts*, 25 February 1932, p. 11.

Zahar M.: « A l'exposition de L'Union des Artistes Modernes », *Art et Industrie*, n°3, March 1932, pp. 17–20.

Duiker J.: « Het huis van Dr Dalsace in te rue St-Guillaume te Parijs », *De 8 en Opbouw*, n°18, September 1932, pp. 155–164.

Migennes P.: « Sur deux ensembles de P. Chareau », *Art et Décoration*, 1932, pp. 129–140.

Chavance R.: « Bureaux industriels par Pierre Chareau », *Art et Décoration*, 1933, pp. 123–128.

Brunon Guardin G.: « A l'Union des Artistes Modernes », *Beaux-Arts*, n°23, 9 June 1933.

Dossier de L'Architecture d'aujourd'hui, n° 9, November–December 1933.

« Un hôtel particulier à Paris » par Pierre Vago.

« La maison de la rue St-Guillaume » par Paul Nelson.

« Observations en visitant » par Julien Lepage (pseudoname of Julius Posener), pp. 5–15.

Nouveaux intérieurs français, Paris : C. Moreau, 1933, pl. 14 et 15.

Coignat R.: « La maison de verre de Pierre Chareau », *Arts et Décoration*, February 1934, pp. 49–56.

« Club de golf à Beauvallon », *L'Architecture d'aujourd'hui*, n° 3, 1934, p. 89.

« A house of glass in Paris », unsigned, *The Architect & Building News*, 13 April 1934, pp. 40–43.

« Visite de la Maison de Verre », unsigned, *Lux*, November 1934, pp. 142–143.

« Maison en acier et verre », unsigned, *Acier*, 1934, pp. 64–67.

« En vue de l'exposition de 1937. Le concours des musées d'Art moderne », article by A. Bloc, *L'Architecture d'aujourd'hui*, n° 10, December 1934–January 1935, pp. 12–25.

Chareau P.: « La création artistique et l'imitation commerciale », *L'Architecture d'aujourd'hui*, n° 9, September 1935, pp. 68–69.

« A l'exposition de Bruxelles (section française) », *L'Architecture d'aujourd'hui*, n°10, October 1935, p. 60.

« La "Maison de verre" de Pierre Chareau commentée par lui-même », *Le Point*, May 1937, pp. 51–52.

Cheronnet L.: « Cabinet de travail et du salon de réception de l'administrateur du Collège de France », *Art et Décoration*, April 1938, pp. 113–120.

« Nouveaux procédés de construction d'immeubles », *L'Architecture d'aujourd'hui*, n° 2, February 1939, p. 63.

« Robert motherwell's quonset house », *Harper's Bazaar*, June 1948, pp. 86 et 87.

« Maison d'été pour un peintre à Long Island, Pierre Chareau, architecte », *L'Architecture d'aujourd'hui*, n° 30, July 1950, p. 51

Dollie Chareau, L'*Architecture d'aujourd'hui*, n° 31, September 1950, pp. vii.

« Une maison française aux États-Unis », *Art et Décoration*, n° 27, 1952, p. 24–25.

Tallet M.: « The Maison de Verre revisited » *Architecture and Building*, May 1960, pp. 192–195.

Roth A.: « "Maison de verre", 31 rue Saint-Guillaume, Paris 1931–32 » *Werk*, n° 2, February 1965, pp. 52–56.

Frampton K.: « Maison de verre » *Arena*, April 1966, pp. 257–262.

Rogers R.: « Parigi 1930. La "casa di vetro" di Pierre Chareau: una rivoluzione che non continua », *Domus*, n° 443, October 1966, pp. 8–20.

Frampton K.: « Maison de verre », *Perspecta*, n° 12, 1969, pp. 77–126.

Frampton K.: « La Maison de verre de Pierre Chareau et Bernard Bijvoet » *Architecture, Mouvement et Continuité*, n° 46, December 1978, pp. 27–43.

« Un projet inédit de Pierre Chareau », *Architecture, mouvement, continuité*, n° 51, March 1980, pp. 49–54.

Vellay M.: « Agli estremi del mattone Nevada », *Rassegna*, n° 24, 1985, pp. 6–17.

作品集　Works

Un inventeur, l'architecte Pierre Chareau, collected under the direction of René Herbst, Paris : éditions du Salon des arts ménagers, Union des artistes modernes, 1954.

二川幸夫 企画・撮影，フェルナンド・モンテス 文：『ダルザス邸（ガラスの家）』GAグローバル・アーキテクチュア No. 46, A. D. A. EDITA Tokyo Co., Ltd. *La Maison de Verre*, photographs by Y. Futagawa, text by F. Montes, Global Architecture, n° 46, 1977.

Vellay M., Frampton K.: *Pierre Chareau. Architecte-meublier 1883–1950*, Éditions du Regard / Via, Paris 1984.

Vellay M.: *Pierre Chareau. Architecte meublier*, Paris : Éditions Rivages, 1986.

二川幸夫 企画・撮影，ベルナール・ボシェ，マルク・ヴェレ文：『ガラスの家：ダルザス邸』A. D. A. EDITA Tokyo Co., Ltd. (Bauchet B. et Vellay M., *La Maison de verre*, with photographs by Y. Futagawa, A.D.A. EDITA, Tokyo 1988.)

Taylor B. B.: *Pierre Chareau, architect and designer*, Taschen, 1993.

Pierre Chareau : architecte, un art intérieur, under the direction of O. Cinqualbre, published on the occasion of the exhibition at Centre de création industrielle, 3 November 1993 through 17 January 1994, Centre Georges Pompidou, Paris 1993.

Cinqualbre O.: *Pierre Chareau: la Maison de verre 1928–1933. Un objet singulier*, Jean-Michel Place, Paris 2001.

Vellay D.: *La Maison de verre : le chef-d'oeuvre de Pierre Chareau*, avec les photographies de F. Halard, Actes Sud, Arles 2007.

二川幸夫 企画・撮影，二川由夫 文：『ガラスの家（ダルザス邸）』世界現代住宅全集13, A. D. A EDITA Tokyo Co.,Ltd. («La Maison de Verre» photographs by Yukio Futagawa, text by Yoshio Futagawa, Residential Masterpieces, n° 13, A.D.A. EDITA, Tokyo 2012)

出品資料リスト
List of Works

凡例 Notes：

展覧会コーナー名

出品資料番号［カタログ掲載頁］ 分類
Catalogue number
（plate number）
［page of the colour plate］

作品資料名
制作者、撮影者、出版元
制作年
技法・素材
サイズ（cm）
資料・写真所蔵先

Title
Author
materials / techniques
Collection
所蔵先目録番号
Inventory number in the
collection it belongs

・サイズは高さ×幅、あるいは
　高さ×幅×奥行で示した
・オリジナルプリントと記した以外の
　写真は、オリジナルの写真から
　あらたにプリントを起こして展示した
・出品資料番号は本カタログで
　各資料に付した番号と一致する。
　ただし番号に＊を付した資料は本書に
　図版の掲載がない参考資料である
・各コーナー名は展覧会に固有のものである
・資料の分類は以下の略称で記した。
　写真：写｜図面：図｜模型：模｜
　映像：映｜立体資料：立｜平面資料：平｜

序

001［p.16］ 写
ピエール・シャローの肖像
撮影：ロール・アルバン＝ギヨ
（本名ロール・アルバン）
1925年／フレッソンプリント・台紙
22.4×16.5、台紙付き32.7×24
ポンピドゥー・センター、パリ国立近代美術館

*Portrait of Pierre Chareau
photographed by Laure Albin Guillot
(pseudonym of Laure Albin)
Fresson print mounted on cardboard
Centre Pompidou - MNAM
AM 1988-671*

002＊ 写
ピエール・シャロー、
ノレ通りの自邸にて
1925-1927年
モノクロプリント

*Pierre Chareau, in his home
in Rue Nollet
Monochrome print*

003［p.34］ 平
ピエール・シャローの名刺
制作年不詳
印刷した紙、裏に書き込みあり
10×14.4
ポンピドゥー・センター、パリ国立近代美術館、
カンディンスキー図書館

*Pierre Chareau's business card
Printed paper, inscription on backside
Centre Pompidou - MNAM -
Bibliothèque Kandinsky
BK Fds Dalbet B 1*

第一世代の家具

004［p.32］ 図
家具各種 スケッチ
ピエール・シャロー
制作年不詳
印刷した紙、グラファイトによる書き込み
38×57.5
ポンピドゥー・センター、パリ国立近代美術館

*Furniture collection
Pierre Chareau
Print with annotations in graphite pencil
Centre Pompidou - MNAM
AM 1997-2-212
Don de la Fondation Louis Moret en 1997*

005［p.39］ 図
肘掛け椅子のスケッチ
ピエール・シャロー
制作年不詳
インクとグラファイト・
台紙に貼ったトレーシングペーパー
18.5×17.5
ポンピドゥー・センター、パリ国立近代美術館

*Armchair
Pierre Chareau
Chinese ink and graphite
on tracing paper mounted on cardboard
Centre Pompidou - MNAM
AM 1997-2-168
Don de la Fondation Louis Moret en 1997*

006［p.23］ 図
リクライニング式の椅子
平面図、立面図、詳細図、透視図
ピエール・シャロー
1923年
グラファイト・トレーシングペーパー
34×46.5
ポンピドゥー・センター、パリ国立近代美術館

*Armchair with reclining back
Pierre Chareau
Graphite on tracing paper
Centre Pompidou - MNAM
AM 1997-2-196
Don de la Fondation Louis Moret en 1997*

007［p.23］ 図
木製スツール 立面図、平面図、透視図
ピエール・シャロー
制作年不詳
グラファイト・トレーシングペーパー
33×43.5
ポンピドゥー・センター、パリ国立近代美術館

*Wooden stool／Pierre Chareau
Graphite on tracing paper
Centre Pompidou - MNAM
AM 1997-2-219
Don de la Fondation Louis Moret en 1997*

ref.001［p.18］ 平
玄関ホール ダルザス家の
アパルトマン、サン＝ジェルマン大通り
『フランスのインテリア』誌より、pl.5、
1925年、ジャン・バドヴィッチ編集、
アルベール・モランセ出版、パリ

*Entrance hall of the Dalsace apartment
on Boulevard Saint-Germain.
Coloured photograph from
INTERIEURS FRANÇAIS, published
by Albert Morancé, Paris*

170

008 [p.19] 写
飾り棚
ピエール・シャロー　撮影者不詳
撮影年不詳
セピア調ゼラチン・シルバープリント
（オリジナルプリント）
15.5×11.6
ポンピドゥー・センター、パリ国立近代美術館、
カンディンスキー図書館

Bookcase
unknown photographer
Sepia toned gelatin silver print
Centre Pompidou - MNAM -
Bibliothèque Kandinsky
BK Fds Pierre Chareau CHA 03

009 [p.19] 写
伸長式のテーブル
ピエール・シャロー
撮影：アンリ・ガルニエ
撮影年不詳
セピア調ゼラチン・シルバープリント
（オリジナルプリント）
16.2×11.4
ポンピドゥー・センター、パリ国立近代美術館、
カンディンスキー図書館

Expansion Table
photographed by Henri Garnier
Sepia toned gelatin silver print
Centre Pompidou - MNAM -
Bibliothèque Kandinsky
BK Fds Pierre Chareau CHA 04

010* 写
肘掛け椅子
ピエール・シャロー
撮影：アンリ・ガルニエ
1920年
セピア調ゼラチン・シルバープリント
（オリジナルプリント）
16.8×12
ポンピドゥー・センター、パリ国立近代美術館、
カンディンスキー図書館

Armchair
photographed by Henri Garnier
Sepia toned gelatin silver print
Centre Pompidou - MNAM -
Bibliothèque Kandinsky
BK Fds Pierre Chareau CHA 19

011* 写
肘掛け椅子
ピエール・シャロー　撮影者不詳
撮影年不詳
セピア調ゼラチン・シルバープリント
（オリジナルプリント）
17×10.7
ポンピドゥー・センター、パリ国立近代美術館、
カンディンスキー図書館

Armchair
unknown photographer
Sepia toned gelatin silver print
Centre Pompidou - MNAM -
Bibliothèque Kandinsky
BK Fds Pierre Chareau CHA 21

012* 写
クルミ材を用いた書棚
ピエール・シャロー　撮影者不詳
1921年
セピア調ゼラチン・シルバープリント
（オリジナルプリント）
13.3×21.2
ポンピドゥー・センター、パリ国立近代美術館、
カンディンスキー図書館

Walnut bookcase
unknown photographer
Sepia toned gelatin silver print
Centre Pompidou - MNAM -
Bibliothèque Kandinsky
BK Fds Pierre Chareau CHA 68

013* 写
肘掛け椅子
ピエール・シャロー　撮影：Photo REP
1922年
セピア調ゼラチン・シルバープリント
（オリジナルプリント）
13.9×18.4
ポンピドゥー・センター、パリ国立近代美術館、
カンディンスキー図書館

Armchair
photographed by Photo REP
Sepia toned gelatin silver print
Centre Pompidou - MNAM -
Bibliothèque Kandinsky
BK Fds Pierre Chareau CHA 98

014* 写
肘掛け椅子
ピエール・シャロー　撮影者不詳
1924年
ゼラチン・シルバープリント
（オリジナルプリント）
14.8×11.4
ポンピドゥー・センター、パリ国立近代美術館、
カンディンスキー図書館

Armchair
unknown photographer
Gelatin silver print
Centre Pompidou - MNAM -
Bibliothèque Kandinsky
BK Fds Pierre Chareau CHA 80

015* 写
肘掛け椅子
ピエール・シャロー　撮影者不詳
撮影年不詳
セピア調ゼラチン・シルバープリント
（オリジナルプリント）
19.2×20.2
ポンピドゥー・センター、パリ国立近代美術館、
カンディンスキー図書館

Armchair
unknown photographer
Sepia toned gelatin silver print
Centre Pompidou - MNAM -
Bibliothèque Kandinsky
BK Fds Pierre Chareau CHA 93

シャローとリュルサの協働作品

016 [p.47] 図
アンティーク調ソファー
平面図、立面図　1：20
ピエール・シャロー
黒チョーク・トレーシングペーパー
28×23.5
ポンピドゥー・センター、パリ国立近代美術館

Corbeille sofa／Pierre Chareau
Black chalk on tracing paper
Centre Pompidou - MNAM
AM 1997-2-187
Don de la Fondation Louis Moret en 1997

017 [p.47] 図
タピストリー下図／ジャン・リュルサ
グラファイト、墨・ヴェラム
38.5×42　縮尺不明
ポンピドゥー・センター、パリ国立近代美術館

Tapestry design／Jean Lurçat
Graphite and Indian ink on vellum
Centre Pompidou - MNAM
AM 1997-2-218
Don de la Fondation Louis Moret en 1997

018 [p.45] 図
ハイバックの肘掛け椅子
透視図、立面図
ピエール・シャロー
1924-1927年
グラファイト・トレーシングペーパー
38×25　縮尺不明
ポンピドゥー・センター、パリ国立近代美術館

High-backed armchair
Pierre Chareau
Graphite on tracing paper

Centre Pompidou - MNAM
AM 1997-2-223
Don de la Fondation Louis Moret en 1997

019 [p.45] 写
炉辺椅子
ピエール・シャロー　撮影者不詳
1930年
ゼラチン・シルバープリント
(オリジナルプリント)
19×14.7
ポンピドゥー・センター、パリ国立近代美術館、カンディンスキー図書館

Fireside chair
Pierre Chareau
unknown photographer
Gelatin silver print
Centre Pompidou - MNAM - Bibliothèque Kandinsky
BK Fds Pierre Chareau CHA 22

020 [p.36] 写
化粧台、スツールと炉辺椅子
ピエール・シャロー　撮影者不詳
撮影年不詳
ゼラチン・シルバープリント
(オリジナルプリント)
17×23
ポンピドゥー・センター、パリ国立近代美術館、カンディンスキー図書館

Dressing table and stool with fireside chair
Pierre Chareau
unknown photographer
Gelatin silver print
Centre Pompidou - MNAM - Bibliothèque Kandinsky
BK Fds Pierre Chareau CHA 62

021 [p.47] 写
柳製の家具のある子供部屋、第15回装飾家芸術家サロン（SAD）出品作
ピエール・シャロー　撮影者不詳
1923年
ゼラチン・シルバープリント
(オリジナルプリント)
11.7×16.6
ポンピドゥー・センター、パリ国立近代美術館、カンディンスキー図書館

Willow furnitures in a children's room. Exhibition at XV SALON DES ARCHI-TECTES DÉCORATEURS, 1923.
Pierre Chareau
unknown photographer
Gelatin silver print
Centre Pompidou - MNAM - Bibliothèque Kandinsky
BK Fds Pierre Chareau CHA 72

022 [p.46] 平
ミシェル・デュフェ著、ピエール・シャローとジャン・リュルサによる挿図「二人の近代的装飾家、シャローとリュルサ」、『現代文学美術選集　フイエ・ダール』誌1921年10–11月、no.10 より、ルシアン・フォーゲル出版、パリ
1921年／印刷物
24.9×19.7
ポンピドゥー・センター、パリ国立近代美術館、カンディンスキー図書館

FEUILLETS D'ART, no. 10, October–November issue 1921. Publication on literature and contemporary art, published by Lucien Vogel.
illustration by Pierre Chareau and Jean Lurçat et al.
Publication
Centre Pompidou - MNAM - Bibliothèque Kandinsky
BK RP 150

023* 写
歌姫クレールのアパルトマン
映画『人でなしの女』
（マルセル・レルビエ監督）より
美術装飾：ピエール・シャロー
映画製作・監督：マルセル・レルビエ
1924年／モノクロプリント

Set for the apartment of the diva from the film "L'inhumaine" directed by Marcel L'Herbier.
Pierre Chareau
Monochrome print

金物職人ダルベとの出会い

024 [p.43] 立
暖炉用品　スコップと薪挟み
ピエール・シャロー
1924年頃／金属／高さ 50
ポンピドゥー・センター、パリ国立近代美術館

Fireplace accessories, shovel and fire tongs
Pierre Chareau
Metal
Centre Pompidou - MNAM
AM 2008-1-142
Don de Aline et Pierre Vellay en 2006

025 [p.42] 立
暖炉のスクリーン／ピエール・シャロー
1924年頃
アーチ形金属の骨組み、リベット鋲
40×54×40
ポンピドゥー・センター、パリ国立近代美術館

Firescreen／Pierre Chareau
Structure in metal, painted and riveted
Centre Pompidou - MNAM
AM 2008-1-139
Don de Aline et Pierre Vellay en 2006

026 [p.42] 写
肘掛け椅子と暖炉用品の空間展示
1926年のSAD会場にて
ピエール・シャロー
1926年／モノクロプリント

Armchair and fireplace exhibited at Salon des artistes décorateurs, 1926
Pierre Chareau
Monochrome print

027 [p.42] 図
植木鉢入れ　透視図
ピエール・シャロー
黒チョーク・トレーシングペーパー
8.5×7　縮尺不明
ポンピドゥー・センター、パリ国立近代美術館

Wrought-iron plant holder
Pierre Chareau
Black chalk on tracing paper
Centre Pompidou - MNAM
AM 1997-2-164
Don de la Fondation Louis Moret en 1997

028 [p.20] 写
工房でハンマーを振り上げる鍛冶職人
撮影者不詳
ゼラチン・シルバープリント
(オリジナルプリント)
24×18
ポンピドゥー・センター、パリ国立近代美術館、カンディンスキー図書館

Three metalwork craftsmen at the studio
unknown photographer
Gelatin silver print
Centre Pompidou - MNAM - Bibliothèque Kandinsky
BK Fds Dalbet B4

029 [p.21] 写
製図台に向かう金物職人ルイ・ダルベ
撮影者不詳
ゼラチン・シルバープリント
(オリジナルプリント)
9×6.4
ポンピドゥー・センター、パリ国立近代美術館、カンディンスキー図書館

Metalwork craftman Louis Dalbet at his desk

unknown photographer
Gelatin silver print
Centre Pompidou - MNAM - Bibliothèque Kandinsky
BK Fds Dalbet B 4

030 [p.20] 平
シャローからダルベに宛てた手紙、
1926年1月5日付、パリ発信
ピエール・シャロー
紙にタイプ／27.1×21.3
ポンピドゥー・センター、パリ国立近代美術館、
カンディンスキー図書館

Letter by Pierre Chareau addressed to Louis Dalbet, dated January 5th 1926, from Paris.
Pierre Chareau
Typed paper
Centre Pompidou - MNAM - Bibliothèque Kandinsky
BK Fds Dalbet B 1

031 [p.20] 平
シャローの秘書からダルベに宛てた
手紙、1925年5月13日付、パリ発信
紙にタイプ／27.1×21.3
ポンピドゥー・センター、パリ国立近代美術館、
カンディンスキー図書館

Letter by Pierre Chareau'secretary addressed to Louis Dalbet, dated May 13th 1925, from Paris.
Pierre Chareau
Typed paper
Centre Pompidou - MNAM - Bibliothèque Kandinsky
BK Fds Dalbet B 1

032 [p.21] 平
シャローからダルベに宛てた注文書
ピエール・シャロー
専用紙に書き込みと捺印
8.3×12.2 – 10.5×15.3
ポンピドゥー・センター、パリ国立近代美術館、
カンディンスキー図書館

Order forms from Chareau to Dalbet
Pierre Chareau
Annotation and impression of the boutique on coupons
Centre Pompidou - MNAM - Bibliothèque Kandinsky
BK Fds Dalbet B 2

033* 平
金物職人ルイ・ダルベの
レターヘッドのモチーフ
薄葉紙に印刷／13.7×11.3
ポンピドゥー・センター、パリ国立近代美術館、

カンディンスキー図書館

Illustration for Louis Dalbet's letterhead
Imprint on tissue
Centre Pompidou - MNAM - Bibliothèque Kandinsky
BK Fds Dalbet B 1

034* 平
金物職人ルイ・ダルベの商標
薄葉紙に印刷／20.2×27.5
ポンピドゥー・センター、パリ国立近代美術館、
カンディンスキー図書館

Louis Dalbet's trademark
Imprint on tissue
Centre Pompidou - MNAM - Bibliothèque Kandinsky
BK Fds Dalbet B 1

前衛芸術家との交流から

035 [p.48] 立
フロアスタンド《修道女》
ピエール・シャロー
1923年／アラバスター、鉄／高さ 172
東京国立近代美術館

Floor lamp called "The Nun"
Pierre Chareau
Alabaster and Iron
The National Museum of Modern Art, Tokyo
ID 0024

036 [p.48] 立
壺（フロアスタンド《修道女》と
同じ形状による）
ピエール・シャロー
1923年頃／アラバスター／70.5×38×40
ポンピドゥー・センター、パリ国立近代美術館

A large vase which evokes the form of the floor lamp called "The Nun"
Pierre Chareau
Alabaster
Centre Pompidou - MNAM
AM 2008-1-133
Don de Aline et Pierre Vellay en 2006

037 [p.27] 平
シャルロット菓子のある静物画
パブロ・ピカソ
1924年／油彩・布／54×65
ポンピドゥー・センター、パリ国立近代美術館

Still life with charlotte
Pablo Picasso
Oil on canvas
Centre Pompidou - MNAM

AM 3291 P
Legs de M. Maurice Meunier en 1995

038 [p.29] 立
横たわる女／ジャック・リプシッツ
1921年／ワニス・石膏／33×47.4×16.5
ポンピドゥー・センター、パリ国立近代美術館

Reclining female
Jacques Lipchitz
Patina on plaster
Centre Pompidou - MNAM
AM 1976-833
Don de la Jacques et Yulla Lipchitz Foundation en 1976

アラバスター製の照明器具

039 [p.49] 立
テーブルランプ／ピエール・シャロー
1923年／鍛造鉄、銅、アラバスター
30×30×35
ポンピドゥー・センター、パリ国立近代美術館

Table lamp / Pierre Chareau
Wrought-iron, copper and alabaster
Centre Pompidou - MNAM
AM 1995-1-47
Don de Strafor en 1995

040 [p.50] 立
照明器具のシェードのために
切り出したアラバスターのプレート
ピエール・シャロー
1923年頃／アラバスター
17×7×0.5　円直径30、四分円半径16
ポンピドゥー・センター、パリ国立近代美術館

Alabaster plates cut for various lighting sources
Pierre Chareau
Alabaster
Centre Pompidou - MNAM
AM 2008-1-130
Don de Aline et Pierre Vellay en 2006

041 [p.51] 立
照明器具のために「庇ブロック」の形に
切り出したアラバスターのプレート
ピエール・シャロー
1923年頃／アラバスター／11.5×17×14
ポンピドゥー・センター、パリ国立近代美術館

Alabaster plates cut for lamps
Pierre Chareau
Alabaster
Centre Pompidou - MNAM

AM 2008-1-131
Don de Aline et Pierre Vellay en 2006

042 [p.51] 立
照明器具のためにL字形に
切り出したアラバスターのプレート
ピエール・シャロー
1923年頃／アラバスター／28×12×7
ポンピドゥー・センター、パリ国立近代美術館

Alabaster plate to diffuse light sources
Pierre Chareau
Alabaster
Centre Pompidou - MNAM
AM 2008-1-132
Don de Aline et Pierre Vellay en 2006

043 [p.51] 写
「庇ブロック」モデルの照明器具が
とりつけられたサロン
ロベール・ダルザスのアパルトマン
ピエール・シャロー
1926年／モノクロプリント

*The lounge of the
Robert Dalsace's apartment*
Pierre Chareau
Monochrome print

近代的な生活のための家具

044 [p.53] 図
扇状テーブル
平面図、立面図、アクソメ図　1:10
ピエール・シャロー
1923年／黒チョーク・トレーシングペーパー
40×23
ポンピドゥー・センター、パリ国立近代美術館

Fan-shaped low table／Pierre Chareau
Black chalk on tracing paper
Centre Pompidou - MNAM
AM 1997-2-179
Don de la Fondation Louis Moret en 1997

045 [p.26] 写
シャロー自邸のサロン、ノレ通り
1927年頃／モノクロプリント

*The interior of
Pierre Chareau's own apartment*
Monochrome print

046 [p.52] 写
電話機用の扇状ローテーブル
ピエール・シャロー　撮影者不詳
ゼラチン・シルバープリント
（オリジナルプリント）

17.9×24.2
ポンピドゥー・センター、パリ国立近代美術館、
カンディンスキー図書館

*Low table in the shape of a fan
with a shelf attached*
unknown photographer
Gelatin silver print
Centre Pompidou - MNAM -
Bibliothèque Kandinsky
BK Fds Pierre Chareau CHA 58

047 [p.52] 立
書斎机、椅子
ピエール・シャロー
ブラジル産紫檀、布
70.0×176.0×69.0（机）
77.0×70.5×59.5（椅子）
東京国立近代美術館

Desk and armchair ensemble
Pierre Chareau
Brazilian rosewood, fabric
The National Museum of Modern Art, Tokyo
ID 0025

048 [p.54] 写
小サロン　ラニック家のアパルトマン
『住宅芸術』誌より、春夏号、1926年、
アルベール・モランセ出版、パリ
モノクロプリント

*The small living room at the Lanique
apartment. Photograph from LES ARTS
DE LA MAISON, spring-summer issue,
1926, Paris, published
by Albert Morancé, plate 25.*
Monochrome print

ref.002 [p.54] 写
ブリッジゲームのためのテーブル、
通称「ハンカチ」（閉じたところ）
ピエール・シャロー
撮影：アトリエ・シャロー
モノクロプリント／16.1×22.9
ポンピドゥー・センター、パリ国立近代美術館、
カンディンスキー図書館

Folding game table
photograph by Atelier Pierre Chareau
Monochrome print
Centre Pompidou - MNAM -
Bibliothèque Kandinsky
BK Fds Pierre Chareau CHA 13

ref.003 [p.54] 写
ブリッジゲームのためのテーブル、
通称「ハンカチ」（開いたところ）
ピエール・シャロー
撮影：アトリエ・シャロー

モノクロプリント／16.4×22.5
ポンピドゥー・センター、パリ国立近代美術館、
カンディンスキー図書館

Folding game table
photographed by Atelier Pierre Chareau
Monochrome print
Centre Pompidou - MNAM -
Bibliothèque Kandinsky
BK Fds Pierre Chareau CHA 14

049 [p.29] 立
静物／ジャック・リプシッツ
1918–1929年／着彩した石
35.1×45.2×6.5
ポンピドゥー・センター、パリ国立近代美術館

Still life／Jacques Lipchitz
Polychrome on stone
Centre Pompidou - MNAM
AM 1976-826
Don de la Jacques et Yulla Lipchitz
Foundation en 1976

ref.004 [p.37] 平
『住宅芸術』誌（現代装飾を代表する
傑作選集）、1923年–1926年（1924年
冬号）、アルベール・モランセ出版
印刷物／27×22.5
ポンピドゥー・センター、パリ国立近代美術館、
カンディンスキー図書館

*LES ARTS DE LA MAISON. A selection
of the most expressive contemporary
decoration works, winter issue 1924.
Published by Albert Morancé.*
publication
Centre Pompidou - MNAM -
Bibliothèque Kandinsky
BK RP 1161

050 [p.55] 立
肘掛け椅子《SN37》
ピエール・シャロー
1923年頃／布、木／73×74.5×66.5
ポンピドゥー・センター、パリ国立近代美術館

Armchair model SN37
Pierre Chareau
Fabric and wood
Centre Pompidou - MNAM
AM 2008-1-103

ref.005 [p.56] 立
長椅子《MP215》
ピエール・シャロー
1923年頃／布、木
参考、椅子サイズ73×130×65
ポンピドゥー・センター、パリ国立近代美術館

Couch model MP215 made of

174

wood and covered with beige
Ottoman tapestry.
Pierre Chareau
Fabric and wood
Centre Pompidou - MNAM
AM 2008-1-104

051 [p.56] 図

長椅子と肘掛け椅子
平面図、立面図、透視図
ピエール・シャロー
1923年頃／鉛筆・トレーシングペーパー
32×50 縮尺不明
ポンピドゥー・センター、パリ国立近代美術館

Armchair and sofa／Pierre Chareau
Pencil on tracing paper
Centre Pompidou - MNAM
AM 1997-2-190

052 [p.56] 図

光沢仕上げの梨材とキルティング・
サテンを用いた肘掛け椅子と長椅子
平面図、立面図
ピエール・シャロー
グラファイト・トレーシングペーパー
28×36.5
ポンピドゥー・センター、パリ国立近代美術館

Armchair and sofa covered with
pear-tree wood and piqued satin.
Pierre Chareau
Graphite on tracing paper
Centre Pompidou - MNAM
AM 1997-2-197
Don de la Fondation Louis Moret en 1997

1925年アール・デコ博

053 [p.59] 写

フランスの大使のための
書架のある執務室
ピエール・シャロー
撮影：フォトグラフ・リラストリュシオン
1925年
ゼラチン・シルバープリント
（オリジナルプリント）
21.4×16
ポンピドゥー・センター、パリ国立近代美術館、
カンディンスキー図書館

Office-library of "A French Embassy"
Pierre Chareau
photographed by L'Illustration
Gelatin silver print
Centre Pompidou - MNAM -
Bibliothèque Kandinsky
BK Fds Pierre Chareau CHA 41

054 [p.57] 平

カタログ『フランスの大使の館
芸術家装飾家サロン』より、パリ現代
産業装飾芸術国際博覧会、1925年、
シャルル・モロー出版、パリ
1925年／印刷物／32.4×25
ポンピドゥー・センター、パリ国立近代美術館、
カンディンスキー図書館

Office-library of "A French Embassy",
EXPOSITION INTERNATIONALE
DES ARTS DÉCORATIFS ET
INDUSTRIELS MODERNES
(International Exposition of Modern
Industrial and Decorative Arts), 1925,
Paris, published by Charles Moreau.
publication
Centre Pompidou - MNAM -
Bibliothèque Kandinsky
BK RLQ 637

055 [p.61] 図

吊りベッド　透視図
ピエール・シャロー
1925年頃／青インク・トレーシングペーパー
23×29
ポンピドゥー・センター、パリ国立近代美術館

Suspended bed／Pierre Chareau
Blue ink on tracing paper
Centre Pompidou - MNAM
AM 1997-2-154
Don de la Fondation Louis Moret en 1997

056 [p.60] 写

体操室と休憩室、カタログ
『フランスの大使の館：SAD』より、
パリ現代産業装飾芸術国際博覧会、
1925年、シャルル・モロー出版、パリ
撮影：フォトグラフィ・ド・レプ
モノクロプリント
ポンピドゥー・センター、パリ国立近代美術館、
カンディンスキー図書館

Fitness room and a day room of
"A French Embassy", EXPOSITION
INTERNATIONALE DES ARTS
DÉCORATIFS ET INDUSTRIELS
MODERNES 1925. Photograph
from Art et Décoration, 1925.
Photographed by REP
Monochrome print
Centre Pompidou - MNAM -
Bibliothèque Kandinsky

057 [p.62] 写

コロニアルスタイルの住まいの食堂、
インドシナ・パヴィリオン、SAD、
パリ現代産業装飾芸術国際博覧会、
1925年、『アール・エ・デコラシオン』誌

ピエール・シャロー
撮影：フォトグラフィ・ド・レプ
モノクロプリント

Dining Room in a Colonial Residence
at the Indochina Pavilion, Exposition
Internationale des Arts Décoratifs
et Industriels Modernes 1925.
Photographed by REP,
Monochrome print

058 [p.62] 写

食堂椅子
ピエール・シャロー
撮影：アトリエ・ピエール・シャロー
ゼラチン・シルバープリント
（オリジナルプリント）
15.8×21.7
ポンピドゥー・センター、パリ国立近代美術館、
カンディンスキー図書館

Diningroom chair
Pierre Chareau
photographed by Atelier Pierre Chareau
Gelatin silver print
Centre Pompidou - MNAM -
Bibliothèque Kandinsky
BK Fds Pierre Chareau CHA 96

ref.006 [p.39] 写

六角形の肘掛け椅子
ピエール・シャロー
撮影：フォトグラフ・リラストリュシオン
撮影年不詳
ゼラチン・シルバープリント
（オリジナルプリント）
20.1×15.2
ポンピドゥー・センター、パリ国立近代美術館、
カンディンスキー図書館

Armchair in a Hexagonal Form
Pierre Chareau
photographed by L'Illustration
Gelatin silver print
Centre Pompidou - MNAM -
Bibliothèque Kandinsky
BK Fds Pierre Chareau CHA 92

新しい時代の女性のインテリア

059 [p.63] 立

化粧台／ピエール・シャロー
1925-1927年／マホガニー、カエデ
65×80×40
ポンピドゥー・センター、パリ国立近代美術館

Dressing table／Pierre Chareau
Mahogany and sycomore
Centre Pompidou - MNAM

AM 1999-1-140 (1)
Legs de Mme Julia Ullmann en 1998

060 [p.65] 立
化粧台のスツール／ピエール・シャロー
1925–1927年／布、木／40×50×38
ポンピドゥー・センター、パリ国立近代美術館

Stool for a dressing table
Pierre Chareau
Fabric and wood
Centre Pompidou - MNAM
AM 1999-1-140 (2)
Legs de Mme Julia Ullmann en 1998

061 [p.64] 写
化粧台とスツール
ピエール・シャロー、
撮影：テレーズ・ボニー
ゼラチン・シルバープリント
（オリジナルプリント）
20×15.6
ポンピドゥー・センター、パリ国立近代美術館、
カンディンスキー図書館

Dressing table and stool
Pierre Chareau
Photographed by Thérèse Bonney
Gelatin silver print
Centre Pompidou - MNAM -
Bibliothèque Kandinsky
BK Fds Pierre Chareau CHA 60

062 [p.64] 図
化粧台　透視図／ピエール・シャロー
グラファイト・台紙に貼った
トレーシングペーパー
19×21.5　縮尺不明
ポンピドゥー・センター、パリ国立近代美術館

Dressing table / Pierre Chareau
Graphite on tracing paper
mounted on cardboard
Centre Pompidou - MNAM
AM 1997-2-166

063 [p.64] 図
テーブル　透視図／ピエール・シャロー
1925年／黒チョークとグラファイト・厚紙
32.5×43.5
ポンピドゥー・センター、パリ国立近代美術館

Table / Pierre Chareau
Black chalk and graphite on cartridge paper
Centre Pompidou - MNAM
AM 1997-2-176
Don de la Fondation Louis Moret en 1997

ref.007 [p.64] 写
収納家具（外装にマホガニー材、
内装にカエデ材を用いている）
ピエール・シャロー
1925–1927年／カラープリント
参考、家具サイズ130×110×50
ポンピドゥー・センター、パリ国立近代美術館、
カンディンスキー図書館

*Wardrobe made of
mahogany and sycamore*
Pierre Chareau
Colour print
Centre Pompidou - MNAM -
Bibliothèque Kandinsky
AM 1999-1-141

064 [p.66] 写
食堂　レファンベール邸
ピエール・シャロー
撮影：ジョルジュ・ティリエ
撮影年不詳
ゼラチン・シルバープリント
（オリジナルプリント）
16.8×23
ポンピドゥー・センター、パリ国立近代美術館、
カンディンスキー図書館

Reifenberg mansion
Pierre Chareau
photographed by Georges Thiriet
Gelatin silver print
Centre Pompidou - MNAM -
Bibliothèque Kandinsky
BK Fds Pierre Chareau CHA 85

065 [p.67] 平
寝室　レファンベール邸
『室内装飾』誌（『今日の国際芸術』第6巻）、
フランシス・ジュールダン制作、おそらく
1929年、シャルル・モロー出版、パリ
印刷物／32.4×25
ポンピドゥー・センター、パリ国立近代美術館、
カンディンスキー図書館

*INTÉRIEURS (Interiors), presented
by Francis Jourdain, c.1929, Paris,
published by Charles Moreau.*
publication
Centre Pompidou - MNAM -
Bibliothèque Kandinsky
BK Fds Jean Prouvé L 6

グラン・オテル・ド・トゥール

066 [p.70] 図
グラン・オテル・ド・トゥールのための
スツール　立面図、詳細図
ピエール・シャロー
1927年／鉛筆・トレーシングペーパー
9.5×25　縮尺不明
ポンピドゥー・センター、パリ国立近代美術館

Stools for the Grand Hôtel de Tours
Pierre Chareau
Pencil on tracing paper
Centre Pompidou - MNAM
AM 1997-2-224
Don de la Fondation Louis Moret en 1997

067 [p.70] 立
ハイ・スツール《MT344》
ピエール・シャロー
1927年／塗装した鉄、木／90×42×35
ポンピドゥー・センター、パリ国立近代美術館

High Stool model MT344
Pierre Chareau
Painted metal and wood
Centre Pompidou - MNAM
AM 2008-1-108

068 [p.70] 立
スツール《EF596》
ピエール・シャロー
1927年／塗装した鉄、木／70×41×35
ポンピドゥー・センター、パリ国立近代美術館

High Stool model EF596
Pierre Chareau
Painted metal and wood
Centre Pompidou - MNAM
AM 2008-1-109

069 [p.70] 写
グラン・オテル・ド・トゥールのバー
兼スモーキングラウンジの空間再現、
1927年のサロン・ドートンヌにて
モノクロプリント

*Exhibition of the smoking room and
the bar of the Grand Hôtel de Tours
at the Salon d'Automne, 1927.*
Monochrome print
Private collection

070 [p.69] 平
『旅行者のホテル』誌、
第2巻より、おそらく1930年、
シャルル・モロー出版、パリ
印刷物／32.5×25
ポンピドゥー・センター、パリ国立近代美術館、
カンディンスキー図書館

*HÔTELS DE VOYAGEURS (Travellers'
Hotels), vol. 2, c.1930, Paris,
published by Charles Moreau.*

176

publication
Centre Pompidou - MNAM -
Bibliothèque Kandinsky
BK RLQ 2712

「木と金属」の時期

071 [p.78] 立

「ロベール・マレ＝ステヴァンス」
モデルの机
ピエール・シャロー
1927年／ニッケル、塗装した木
103×162×66、93×222、
腰掛け椅子 36×50×30
ポンピドゥー・センター、パリ国立近代美術館

Desk Model "Robert Mallet-Stevens"
Pierre Chareau
Nickel and laquered wood
Centre Pompidou - MNAM
AM 2004-1-20

072 [p.79] 図

衣装整理箱 立面図、透視図
ピエール・シャロー
1927年
グラファイト・トレーシングペーパー
39×17、縮尺不明
ポンピドゥー・センター、パリ国立近代美術館

Linen cupboard / Pierre Chareau
Graphite on tracing paper
Centre Pompidou - MNAM
AM 1997-2-182
Don de la Fondation Louis Moret en 1997

073 [p.79] 図

「木と金属」の時期の机
平面図、立面図、透視図
ピエール・シャロー
1927年
グラファイト・トレーシングペーパー
19×47、縮尺不明
ポンピドゥー・センター、パリ国立近代美術館

Desk from the "Wood-metal" period
Pierre Chareau
Graphite on tracing paper
Centre Pompidou - MNAM
AM 1997-2-213
Don de la Fondation Louis Moret en 1997

074 [p.79] 図

「木と金属」の時期の机
平面図、立面図、透視図
ピエール・シャロー
1927年
グラファイト、青インク・トレーシングペーパー
32.5×65.5、縮尺 1：10
ポンピドゥー・センター、パリ国立近代美術館

Desk from the "Wood-metal" period
Pierre Chareau
Graphite and blue ink on tracing paper
Centre Pompidou - MNAM
AM 1997-2-214
Don de la Fondation Louis Moret en 1997

075 [p.78] 図

「木と金属」の時期の机 平面図、立面図
ピエール・シャロー
1927年
グラファイト、赤鉛筆・オニオンスキンペーパー
23.5×28、縮尺不明
ポンピドゥー・センター、パリ国立近代美術館

Desk from the "Wood-metal" period
Pierre Chareau
Graphite, red pencil on onion skin paper
Centre Pompidou - MNAM
AM 1997-2-216
Don de la Fondation Louis Moret en 1997

076 [p.78] 図

「木と金属」の時期の机
平面図、立面図 1：20
ピエール・シャロー
1927年
鉛筆、色鉛筆・オニオンスキンペーパー
17×19、縮尺 1：20
ポンピドゥー・センター、パリ国立近代美術館

Desk from the "Wood-metal" period
Pierre Chareau
Pencil and colour pencil on onion skin paper
Centre Pompidou - MNAM
AM 1997-2-217
Don de la Fondation Louis Moret en 1997

077 [p.110, 114] 平

『家具』（『今日の国際芸術』第7巻）、
ピエール・シャロー編、おそらく
1929年、シャルル・モロー出版、パリ
印刷物／32.4×25
ポンピドゥー・センター、パリ国立近代美術館、
カンディンスキー図書館

Meubles (Furnitures), presented
by Pierre Chareau, c.1929,
Paris, published by Charles Moreau.
Publication
Centre Pompidou - MNAM -
Bibliothèque Kandinsky
AK Fds Jean Prouvé L 7

078 [p.80] 写

「木と金属」の時期の机
ピエール・シャロー、
撮影：ジョルジュ・ティリエ
ゼラチン・シルバープリント
（オリジナルプリント）
15.5×22.9
ポンピドゥー・センター、パリ国立近代美術館、
カンディンスキー図書館

Desk from the "Wood-metal" period
Pierre Chareau
photographed by Georges Thiriet
Gelatin silver print
Centre Pompidou - MNAM -
Bibliothèque Kandinsky
BK Fds Pierre Chareau CHA 63

079 [p.41] 立

書架机／ピエール・シャロー
木、鉄／98×128×69.0
東京国立近代美術館

Table with a bookshelf
Pierre Chareau
Wood and iron
The National Museum of Modern Art, Tokyo
ID 0026

080* 写

ボールキャスター付きテーブル
ピエール・シャロー、撮影者不詳
ゼラチン・シルバープリント
（オリジナルプリント）
21.2×16.3
ポンピドゥー・センター、パリ国立近代美術館、
カンディンスキー図書館

Table
Pierre Chareau
unknown photographer
Gelatin silver print
Centre Pompidou - MNAM -
Bibliothèque Kandinsky
BK Fds Pierre Chareau CHA 74

081 [p.80] 写

カエデ材の天板と鉄材を用いた
ティーテーブル
ピエール・シャロー、撮影者不詳
撮影年不詳
ゼラチン・シルバープリント
（オリジナルプリント）
16×22.5
ポンピドゥー・センター、パリ国立近代美術館、
カンディンスキー図書館

Tea table made of
wrought-iron and mahogany

Pierre Chareau
unknown photographer
Gelatin silver print
Centre Pompidou - MNAM -
Bibliothèque Kandinsky
BK Fds Pierre Chareau CHA 77

082 [p.40] 写
テーブル付き長椅子
ピエール・シャロー、撮影者不詳
撮影年不詳
ゼラチン・シルバープリント
（オリジナルプリント）
14.5×22
ポンピドゥー・センター、パリ国立近代美術館、
カンディンスキー図書館

Sofa with a table
Pierre Chareau
unknown photographer
Gelatin silver print
Centre Pompidou - MNAM -
Bibliothèque Kandinsky
BK Fds Pierre Chareau CHA 94

モダン・インテリアの展開

083 [p.119] 図
サロン　透視図／ピエール・シャロー
木炭・トレーシングペーパー／38.5×53
ポンピドゥー・センター、パリ国立近代美術館

Lounge／Pierre Chareau
Charcoal on tracing paper
Centre Pompidou - MNAM
AM 1997-2-158
Don de la Fondation Louis Moret en 1997

084 [p.119] 図
子供部屋　透視図／ピエール・シャロー
グアッシュ、グラファイト・強化紙
21.5×28.5
ポンピドゥー・センター、パリ国立近代美術館

Children's room／Pierre Chareau
Gouache and graphite on cartridge paper
Centre Pompidou - MNAM
AM 1997-2-159
Don de la Fondation Louis Moret en 1997

085 [p.119] 図
サロン　透視図／ピエール・シャロー
グアッシュ、グラファイト・強化紙
32×39.5
ポンピドゥー・センター、パリ国立近代美術館

Lounge／Pierre Chareau
Gouache and graphite on cartridge paper
Centre Pompidou - MNAM
AM 1997-2-160
Don de la Fondation Louis Moret en 1997

086 [p.119] 図
サロン　透視図／ピエール・シャロー
グアッシュ・強化紙／32.5×45
ポンピドゥー・センター、パリ国立近代美術館

Lounge／Pierre Chareau
Gouache on cartridge paper
Centre Pompidou - MNAM
AM 1997-2-161
Don de la Fondation Louis Moret en 1997

087 [p.119] 図
サロン　透視図／ピエール・シャロー
グアッシュ・強化紙／30.5×42
ポンピドゥー・センター、パリ国立近代美術館

Lounge／Pierre Chareau
Gouache on cartridge paper
Centre Pompidou - MNAM
AM 1997-2-162
Don de la Fondation Louis Moret en 1997

088 [p.122] 写
ラ・スメーヌ・ア・パリ新聞本社、
ダサ通り『商店の外観と内装』誌より、
シャルル・モロー出版、パリ
撮影年不詳／モノクロプリント

Headquarters of La Semaine à Paris
Newspaper, rue d'Assas, facade
designed by Robert Mallet-Stevens
and windows by Louis Barillet. Photograph from Nouvelles Devantures
et Aménagements de magasins
(New Shop Windows and Interiors),
Paris, published by Charles Moreau.
Monochrome print

089 [p.123] 写
編集室廊下　ラ・スメーヌ・ア・パリ
新聞本社『アール・エ・デコラシオン』誌、
1930年、シャルル・モロー出版、パリ
1930年／モノクロプリント

Interior of the offcie of La Semaine
à Paris, rue d'Assast. Photograph
from Art et Décoration, January—June
issue, 1930, Paris, published
by Charles Moreau.
Monochrome print

090 [p.118] 模
アパルトマンの改装　模型　1:10
ピエール・シャロー
塗装したアクリル樹脂、石膏、化粧板
127×65×37
ポンピドゥー・センター、パリ国立近代美術館

Interior design of an apartment
Pierre Chareau
Painted acrylic, plaster and wood panel
Centre Pompidou - MNAM
Doc (33)
Don de M. Francis Lamond

091 [p.124] 写
可動式のついたてのある
ドレフュス夫妻のアパルトマン内装
ピエール・シャロー
撮影：アトリエ・シャロー
ゼラチン・シルバープリント
（オリジナルプリント）
17.1×23.3
ポンピドゥー・センター、パリ国立近代美術館、
カンディンスキー図書館

Dreyfus apartment
with partitions and folding panels
Pierre Chareauu／photographed by
Atelier Pierre Chareau
Gelatin silver print
Centre Pompidou - MNAM -
Bibliothèque Kandinsky
BK Fds Pierre Chareau CHA 33

092 [p.125] 写
可動式のついたてのある
ドレフュス夫妻のアパルトマン内装
ピエール・シャロー
撮影：アトリエ・シャロー
ゼラチン・シルバープリント
（オリジナルプリント）
23.3×16.6
ポンピドゥー・センター、パリ国立近代美術館、
カンディンスキー図書館

Apartment with partitions
and folding Panels
Pierre Chareau／photographed by
Atelier Pierre Chareau
Gelatin silver print
Centre Pompidou - MNAM -
Bibliothèque Kandinsky
BK Fds Pierre Chareau CHA 56

093 [p.24] 平
『現代趣味目録』1928–1929年、
アルベール・レヴィ出版、パリ
印刷物／32.5×25
ポンピドゥー・センター、パリ国立近代美術館、
カンディンスキー図書館

Répertoire du goût moderne
(Repertoire of Modern Taste), 1928–
1929, Paris, published by Albert Lévy.
publication

Centre Pompidou - MNAM - Bibliothèque Kandinsky
BK RLQ 7423 vol. 5

094 [p.126] 写
応接間と食堂（中央）、ファーリ家のアパルトマン、ラファエル大通り
ピエール・シャロー、撮影者不詳
撮影年不詳
ゼラチン・シルバープリント（オリジナルプリント）
17.1×22.9
ポンピドゥー・センター、パリ国立近代美術館、カンディンスキー図書館

Dining room of Mr. Fahri's Apartment
Pierre Chareau
unknown photographer
Gelatin silver print
Centre Pompidou - MNAM - Bibliothèque Kandinsky
BK Fds Pierre Chareau CHA 35

金属平面を用いた家具

095 [p.76] 立
折りたたみ椅子《MC763》
ピエール・シャロー
1927年／塗装した金属／75×80×36
ポンピドゥー・センター、パリ国立近代美術館

Folding chair model MC763
Pierre Chareau
Painted metal
Centre Pompidou - MNAM
AM 2008-1-105

096 [p.77] 立
椅子《MC767》（固定式モデル）
ピエール・シャロー
1927年／塗装した金属、合金、籐
80×57×35.5
ポンピドゥー・センター、パリ国立近代美術館

Chair model MC767 (rigid model)
Pierre Chareau
Painted metal, alloy and rotin
Centre Pompidou - MNAM
AM 2008-1-106

097 [p.77] 立
椅子《EZ849》（固定式モデル）
ピエール・シャロー
1927年／塗装した金属、籐／79.5×51×35
ポンピドゥー・センター、パリ国立近代美術館

Chair model MC849 (rigid model)
Pierre Chareau
Painted metal and rotin
Centre Pompidou - MNAM
AM 2008-1-107

098 [p.77] 立
鍛鉄製腰掛け／ピエール・シャロー
1927年／革、鉄・鍛造／81×114
東京国立近代美術館

Bench with seatback／Pierre Chareau
Wrought-iron and leather
The National Museum of Modern Art, Tokyo
ID 0022

099 [p.76] 写
畳んだ状態の折りたたみ式椅子《MC763》
ピエール・シャロー
モノクロプリント
ポンピドゥー・センター、パリ国立近代美術館、カンディンスキー図書館

Folded chair／Pierre Chareau
Monochrome print
Centre Pompidou - MNAM - Bibliothèque Kandinsky

100 [p.76] 写
イギリスでの特許登録書類「扇形構造の折りたたみ椅子」
ピエール・シャロー
1927年／モノクロプリント
フランス国立産業所有物研究所

Fan-shaped folding chair, application for the patent in UK
Pierre Chareau
Monochrome print
Institut national de la propriété industriel

南フランスの建築作品

101 [p.73] 模
ボーヴァロンのホテルのゴルフ場クラブ・ハウス模型　1：100
ピエール・シャロー
プラスチック
8.5×14.5×10
ポンピドゥー・センター、パリ国立近代美術館

Model of the clubhouse of the Golf Hôtel of Beauvallon
Pierre Chareau
Plastic
Centre Pompidou - MNAM
Doc (26)

102 [p.73] 写
ボーヴァロンのホテルのゴルフ場クラブ・ハウス　『ラルシテクチュール・ドージュルデュイ』no.3より、1934年4月、アンドレ・ブロック編集、パリ
モノクロプリント

Facade of the clubhouse of the Golf Hôtel of Beauvallon. Photograph from L'ARCHITECTURE D'AUJOURD'HUI (Architecture Today), chief editor: André Bloc, April issue 1934, Paris
Monochrome print

103 [p.73] 写
ボーヴァロンのホテルのゴルフ場クラブ・ハウス　屋根付きテラス『ラルシテクチュール・ドージュルデュイ』no.3より、1934年4月、アンドレ・ブロック編集、パリ
モノクロプリント

Facade of the clubhouse of the Golf Hôtel of Beauvallon. Photograph from L'architecture d'aujourd'hui (Architecture Today), chief editor: André Bloc, April issue 1934, Paris
Monochrome print

104 [p.75] 模
ヴィラ・ヴァン・ダヴァル模型　1：100
ピエール・シャロー
塗装したアクリル樹脂
28.1×24.1×8
ポンピドゥー・センター、パリ国立近代美術館

Model of the Villa Vent d'Aval, Beauvallon
Pierre Chareau
Painted acrylic
Centre Pompidou - MNAM
Doc (21)

105 [p.71] 写
ヴィラ・ヴァン・ダヴァル　南側ファサード
ピエール・シャロー
撮影：ジャック・ルピケ
1993年／カラープリント

Southern facade of the Villa Vent d'Aval
Pierre Chareau
Photographed by Jacques Repiquet
Colour print

106 [p.75] 写
ヴィラ・ヴァン・ダヴァル　西側ファサード
ピエール・シャロー、

撮影:ジャック・ルピケ
1993年／カラープリント

Western facade of the Villa Vent d'Aval
Pierre Chareau
Photographed byJacques Repiquet
Colour print

ガラスの家——
装飾・家具・建築の統合

107 [p.96] 模
ガラスの家 模型 1:100
ピエール・シャロー、
模型制作:シルヴァン・ル・スタム
2006年／人造大理石
建築・文化財・都市 フランス国立博物館

Model of the Maison de Verre
Pierre Chareau,
model by Sylvain Le Stum
Corian
Cité d'architecture et du patrimoine /
Musée des monuments français
MAQ.00269

108 [p.85] 映
医師のロベール・ダルザスが所有する
サン＝ギョーム通りの邸宅。
通りからの入口を入ったところの
中庭に面した玄関のファサード
ピエール・シャロー、
撮影:ジョルジュ・ティリエ
モノクロプリント
ポンピドゥー・センター、パリ国立近代美術館、
カンディンスキー図書館

Property of Doctor Dalsace at rue
Sainte-Guillaume, Paris. Facade of
the townhouse facing the courtyard.
Pierre Chareau,
photographed by Georges Thiriet
Monochrome print for slide show
Centre Pompidou - MNAM -
Bibliothèque Kandinsky

109 [p.85] 映
鉄骨を建てている 建設中のガラスの家
ピエール・シャロー、
撮影:ジョルジュ・ティリエ
モノクロプリント
ポンピドゥー・センター、パリ国立近代美術館、
カンディンスキー図書館

The Maison de Verre under construction
seen from the side of the garden.
A metal structure is inserted.
Pierre Chareau,
photographed by Georges Thiriet
Monochrome print for slide show
Centre Pompidou - MNAM -
Bibliothèque Kandinsky

110 [p.109] 映
3階の庭園側ファサードを内側から見る
建設中のガラスの家
ピエール・シャロー、
撮影:ジョルジュ・ティリエ
モノクロプリント
ポンピドゥー・センター、パリ国立近代美術館、
カンディンスキー図書館

Facade facing the garden on the third
floor at the end of the construction.
Pierre Chareau,
photographed by Georges Thiriet
Monochrome print for slide show
Centre Pompidou - MNAM -
Bibliothèque Kandinsky

111 [p.88] 映
竣工間近のガラスの家
2階サロン 1931年
ピエール・シャロー、
撮影:ジョルジュ・ティリエ
モノクロプリント
ポンピドゥー・センター、パリ国立近代美術館、
カンディンスキー図書館

Salon on the second floor
at the end of the construction.
Pierre Chareau,
photographed by Georges Thiriet
Monochrome print for slide show
Centre Pompidou - MNAM -
Bibliothèque Kandinsky

112 [p.108] 映
2階小サロン(夫人用の居間)
上階の寝室と行き来するための
収納可能な鉄骨の階段が見える
ピエール・シャロー、
撮影:ジョルジュ・ティリエ
モノクロプリント
ポンピドゥー・センター、パリ国立近代美術館、
カンディンスキー図書館

Small living room on the second floor,
at the end of construction
Pierre Chareau,
photographed by Georges Thiriet
Monochrome print for slide show
Centre Pompidou - MNAM -
Bibliothèque Kandinsky

113 [p.106] 映
1階診察室側から待合室を見る
ピエール・シャロー、
撮影:ジョルジュ・ティリエ
モノクロプリント
ポンピドゥー・センター、パリ国立近代美術館、
カンディンスキー図書館

Corridor between the secretary's
office and the facade facing
the garden on the ground floor
Pierre Chareau,
photographed by Georges Thiriet
Monochrome print for slide show
Centre Pompidou - MNAM -
Bibliothèque Kandinsky

114 [p.104] 映
3階の家事室からサロンを見下ろす
ピエール・シャロー、
撮影:ジョルジュ・ティリエ
モノクロプリント
ポンピドゥー・センター、パリ国立近代美術館、
カンディンスキー図書館

Salon seen from the third floor
Pierre Chareau,
photographed by Georges Thiriet
Monochrome print for slide show
Centre Pompidou - MNAM -
Bibliothèque Kandinsky

115 [p.108] 映
3階主寝室浴室の収納棚とついたて
ピエール・シャロー、
撮影:ジョルジュ・ティリエ
モノクロプリント
ポンピドゥー・センター、パリ国立近代美術館、
カンディンスキー図書館

Cupboards and partition of
the main bathroom the third floor
Pierre Chareau,
photographed by Georges Thiriet
Monochrome print for slide show
Centre Pompidou - MNAM -
Bibliothèque Kandinsky

116* 映
2階食堂横の可動壁のなかに
収められた収納棚
ピエール・シャロー、
撮影:ジョルジュ・ティリエ
モノクロプリント
ポンピドゥー・センター、パリ国立近代美術館、
カンディンスキー図書館

Cupboards at the back of
the dining room on the second floor
Pierre Chareau,
photographed by Georges Thiriet
Monochrome print for slide show
Centre Pompidou - MNAM -
Bibliothèque Kandinsky

117 [p.105] 映
2階サロンと大階段を見下ろす
ピエール・シャロー、
撮影:ジョルジュ・ティリエ
モノクロプリント
ポンピドゥー・センター、パリ国立近代美術館、
カンディンスキー図書館

View of the second floor and
the main staircase
Pierre Chareau,
photographed by Georges Thiriet
Monochrome print for slide show
Centre Pompidou - MNAM -
Bibliothèque Kandinsky

118* 映
2階台所
ピエール・シャロー、撮影者不詳
モノクロプリント
ポンピドゥー・センター、パリ国立近代美術館、
カンディンスキー図書館

Kitchen on the second floor
Pierre Chareau,
unknown photographer
Monochrome print for slide show
Centre Pompidou - MNAM -
Bibliothèque Kandinsky

119* 映
2階台所
ピエール・シャロー、撮影者不詳
モノクロプリント
ポンピドゥー・センター、パリ国立近代美術館、
カンディンスキー図書館

Kitchen on the second floor
Pierre Chareau,
unknown photographer
Monochrome print for slide show
Centre Pompidou - MNAM -
Bibliothèque Kandinsky

120* 映
2階のサロンの上に
張り出している3階の廊下
ピエール・シャロー、撮影者不詳
モノクロプリント
ポンピドゥー・センター、パリ国立近代美術館、
カンディンスキー図書館

The gallery on the third floor
overlooking on the Lounge
Pierre Chareau,
unknown photographer
Monochrome print for slide show
Centre Pompidou - MNAM -
Bibliothèque Kandinsky

121* 映
1階の主階段の上がり口
ピエール・シャロー、
撮影:ジョルジュ・ティリエ
モノクロプリント
ポンピドゥー・センター、パリ国立近代美術館、
カンディンスキー図書館

The foot of the main staircase
on the ground floor
Pierre Chareau,
photographed by Georges Thiriet
Monochrome print for slide show
Centre Pompidou - MNAM -
Bibliothèque Kandinsky

122* 映
2階食堂横の収納棚。
奥に小サロンへの配膳口が見える
ピエール・シャロー、撮影者不詳
モノクロプリント
ポンピドゥー・センター、パリ国立近代美術館、
カンディンスキー図書館

Cupboard adjoining
the dining room on the second floor
Pierre Chareau,
unknown photographer
Monochrome print for slide show
Centre Pompidou - MNAM -
Bibliothèque Kandinsky

123* 映
3階主寝室浴室。
収納棚とついたてが見える
ピエール・シャロー、撮影者不詳
モノクロプリント
ポンピドゥー・センター、パリ国立近代美術館、
カンディンスキー図書館

Linen cupboard and partitions
in the main bathroom on the third floor
Pierre Chareau,
unknown photographer
Monochrome print for slide show
Centre Pompidou - MNAM -
Bibliothèque Kandinsky

124 [p.88] 映
3階廊下の書棚が仕上がったところ
ピエール・シャロー、
撮影:ジョルジュ・ティリエ
モノクロプリント
ポンピドゥー・センター、パリ国立近代美術館、
カンディンスキー図書館

The gallery on the third floor
Pierre Chareau,
photographed by Georges Thiriet
Monochrome print for slide show
Centre Pompidou - MNAM -
Bibliothèque Kandinsky

125 [p.104] 映
2階サロン
3階廊下の整理棚の背面が見える
ピエール・シャロー、
撮影:ジョルジュ・ティリエ
モノクロプリント
ポンピドゥー・センター、パリ国立近代美術館、
カンディンスキー図書館

Lounge on the second floor
Pierre Chareau,
photographed by Georges Thiriet
Monochrome print for slide show
Centre Pompidou - MNAM -
Bibliothèque Kandinsky

126 [p.109] 映
1階庭園側のファサード
竣工時のガラスの家
ピエール・シャロー、
撮影:ジョルジュ・ティリエ
モノクロプリント
ポンピドゥー・センター、パリ国立近代美術館、
カンディンスキー図書館

Facade facing the garden
in the final stages of construction
Pierre Chareau,
photographed by Georges Thiriet
Monochrome print for slide show
Centre Pompidou - MNAM -
Bibliothèque Kandinsky

127 [p.25] 写
ガラスの家
ピエール・シャロー、撮影者不詳
1932年
アルバムに貼り付けたゼラチン・
シルバープリント(オリジナルプリント)
21×28.7
ポンピドゥー・センター、パリ国立近代美術館、
カンディンスキー図書館

Exterior of the Maison de Verre
Pierre Chareau,
unknown photographer
Gelatin silver print
pasted on an album
Centre Pompidou - MNAM -
Bibliothèque Kandinsky
BK Fds Salomon B1 (27)

128 [p.103] 写
電気設備盤
ピエール・シャロー、撮影者不詳

1932年
アルバムに貼り付けたゼラチン・シルバープリント（オリジナルプリント）
29×21
ポンピドゥー・センター、パリ国立近代美術館、カンディンスキー図書館

Fusebox in the Maison de Verre
Pierre Chareau,
unknown photographer
Gelatin silver print
pasted on an album
Centre Pompidou - MNAM - Bibliothèque Kandinsky
BK Fds Salomon B5 (152)

129［p.103］写
統合されたスイッチとコンセントパネル
ピエール・シャロー、撮影者不詳
1932年
アルバムに貼り付けたゼラチン・シルバープリント（オリジナルプリント）
28.7×21
ポンピドゥー・センター、パリ国立近代美術館、カンディンスキー図書館

Electrical switches and outlet integrated on a single panel
Pierre Chareau,
unknown photographer
Gelatin silver print
pasted on an album
Centre Pompidou - MNAM - Bibliothèque Kandinsky
BK Fds Salomon B5 (153)

130［p.103］写
電話が取りつけられたスイッチパネル
ピエール・シャロー、撮影者不詳
1932年
アルバムに貼り付けたゼラチン・シルバープリント（オリジナルプリント）
28.7×21
ポンピドゥー・センター、パリ国立近代美術館、カンディンスキー図書館

Telephone installed on the electrical panel
Pierre Chareau,
unknown photographer
Gelatin silver print
pasted on an album
Centre Pompidou - MNAM - Bibliothèque Kandinsky
BK Fds Salomon B5 (157)

131［p.112］写
1階庭側の出入口
ピエール・シャロー、
撮影：ジョルジュ・ティリエ
1932年

ゼラチン・シルバープリント（オリジナルプリント）
23.2×16.4
ポンピドゥー・センター、パリ国立近代美術館、カンディンスキー図書館

Garden view
Pierre Chareau,
photographed by Georges Thiriet
Gelatin silver print
Centre Pompidou - MNAM - Bibliothèque Kandinsky
BK Fds Pierre Chareau CHA 02

132［p.87］写
ガラスの家　第1案の建築許可申請図面
通りからの入口を入ったところの中庭に面した玄関側立面図　1:50
アトリエ・ピエール・シャロー
1927年／モノクロプリント
パリ市公文書館

Preliminary project for the Maison de Verre submitted to the Parisian Building Authorities. Facade of the townhouse facing the courtyard.
Atelier Pierre Chareau
Monochrome print
Archives of the Ville de Paris
2 Fi 640

133［p.87］写
ガラスの家　第1案の建築許可申請図面
1階庭側立面図　1:50
アトリエ・ピエール・シャロー
1927年／モノクロプリント
パリ市公文書館

Preliminary project for the Maison de Verre submitted to the Parisian Building Authorities. Facade of the townhouse facing the garden.
Atelier Pierre Chareau
Monochrome print
Archives of the Ville de Paris
2 Fi 641

134［p.87］写
ガラスの家　第1案の建築許可申請図面
1階平面図　1:50
アトリエ・ピエール・シャロー
1927年／モノクロプリント
パリ市公文書館

Preliminary project for the Maison de Verre submitted to the Parisian Building Authorities. First floor plan.
Atelier Pierre Chareau
Monochrome print
Archives of the Ville de Paris
2 Fi 637

135［p.87］写
ガラスの家　第1案の建築許可申請図面
2階平面図　1:50
アトリエ・ピエール・シャロー
1927年／モノクロプリント
パリ市公文書館

Preliminary project for the Maison de Verre submitted to the Parisian Building Authorities. Second floor plan.
Atelier Pierre Chareau
Monochrome print
Archives of the Ville de Paris
2 Fi 638

136［p.87］写
ガラスの家　第1案の建築許可申請図面
3階平面図　1:50
アトリエ・ピエール・シャロー
1927年／モノクロプリント
パリ市公文書館

Preliminary project for the Maison de Verre submitted to the Parisian Building Authorities. Third floor plan.
Atelier Pierre Chareau
Monochrome print
Archives of the Ville de Paris
2 Fi 639

137［p.89］写
ガラスの家　第2案の建築許可申請図面
通りからの入口を入ったところの中庭に面した玄関側立面図　1:50
アトリエ・ピエール・シャロー
1928年／モノクロプリント
パリ市公文書館

Second preliminary project for the Maison de Verre submitted to the Parisian Building Authorities. Facade of the townhouse facing the courtyard.
Atelier Pierre Chareau
Monochrome print
Archives of the Ville de Paris
2 Fi 648

138［p.89］写
ガラスの家　第2案の建築許可申請図
庭園側の立面図　1:50
アトリエ・ピエール・シャロー
1928年／モノクロプリント
パリ市公文書館

Second preliminary project for the Maison de Verre submitted to the Parisian Building Authorities. Facade of the townhouse facing the garden.
Atelier Pierre Chareau
Monochrome print

Archives of the Ville de Paris
2 Fi 649

139[p.89] 写
ガラスの家　第2案の建築許可申請図
1階平面図　1:50
アトリエ・ピエール・シャロー
1928年／モノクロプリント
パリ市公文書館

Second preliminary project for the
Maison de Verre submitted to the
Parisian Building Authorities.
First floor plan.
Atelier Pierre Chareau
Monochrome print
Archives of the Ville de Paris
2 Fi 645

140[p.89] 写
ガラスの家　第2案の建築許可申請図
2階平面図　1:50
アトリエ・ピエール・シャロー
1928年／モノクロプリント
パリ市公文書館

Second preliminary project for the
Maison de Verre submitted to the
Parisian Building Authorities.
Second floor plan above ground floor.
Atelier Pierre Chareau
Monochrome print
Archives of the Ville de Paris
2 Fi 646

141[p.89] 写
ガラスの家　第2案の建築許可申請図
3階平面図　1:50
アトリエ・ピエール・シャロー
1928年／モノクロプリント
パリ市公文書館

Second preliminary project for the
Maison de Verre submitted to the
Parisian Building Authorities.
Third floor plan.
Atelier Pierre Chareau
Monochrome print
Archives of the Ville de Paris
2 Fi 647

142[p.90] 写
ガラスの家　実測図　配置図　1:100
ピエール・シャロー、
実測図製作：ベルナール・ボシェ
1985年／モノクロプリント
ベルナルド・ボシェ・アルシテクト

Survey map, site plan
Pierre Chareau,
survey map by Bernard Bauchet
Monochrome print
B. BAUCHET Architecte

143[p.91] 写
ガラスの家　実測図
1階平面図　1:100
ピエール・シャロー、
実測図製作：ベルナール・ボシェ
1985年／モノクロプリント
ベルナルド・ボシェ・アルシテクト

Survey map, first floor
Pierre Chareau,
survey map by Bernard Bauchet
Monochrome print
B. BAUCHET Architecte

144[p.92] 写
ガラスの家　実測図
2階平面図　1:100
ピエール・シャロー、
実測図製作：ベルナール・ボシェ
1985年／モノクロプリント
ベルナルド・ボシェ・アルシテクト

Survey map, second floor
Pierre Chareau,
survey map by Bernard Bauchet
Monochrome print
B. BAUCHET Architecte

145[p.93] 写
ガラスの家　実測図
3階平面図　1:100
ピエール・シャロー、
実測図製作：ベルナール・ボシェ
1985年／モノクロプリント
ベルナルド・ボシェ・アルシテクト

Survey map, third floor
Pierre Chareau,
survey map by Bernard Bauchet
Monochrome print
B. BAUCHET Architecte

146[p.2] 映
門を入ったところの
中庭に面した玄関側ファサード
撮影：ジョルジュ・メゲルディトシアン
1993年／カラープリント
ポンピドゥー・センター、パリ国立近代美術館

Facade facing the courtyard
Photographed
by Georges Meguerditchian
Colour print for slideshow
Centre Pompidou - MNAM

147[p.94] 映
玄関側ファサード、右側に
上部アパルトマンへの出入口
撮影：ジョルジュ・メゲルディトシアン
1993年／カラープリント
ポンピドゥー・センター、パリ国立近代美術館

Facade facing the courtyard
Photographed
by Georges Meguerditchian
Colour print for slideshow
Centre Pompidou - MNAM

148* 映
玄関側ファサード、
投光器とはしごが見える
撮影：ジョルジュ・メゲルディトシアン
1993年／カラープリント
ポンピドゥー・センター、パリ国立近代美術館

Facade facing the courtyard
Photographed
by Georges Meguerditchian
Colour print for slideshow
Centre Pompidou - MNAM

149* 映
玄関側ファサード、エントランス
撮影：ジョルジュ・メゲルディトシアン
1993年／カラープリント
ポンピドゥー・センター、パリ国立近代美術館

Entrance at the facade
facing the courtyard
Photographed
by Georges Meguerditchian
Colour print for slideshow
Centre Pompidou - MNAM

150* 映
玄関側ファサード、
正面にサービス棟が見える
撮影：ジョルジュ・メゲルディトシアン
1993年／カラープリント
ポンピドゥー・センター、パリ国立近代美術館

Facade facing the courtyard, looking
through the kitchen / utility wing
Photographed
by Georges Meguerditchian
Colour print for slideshow
Centre Pompidou - MNAM

151[p.103] 映
エントランス
撮影：ジョルジュ・メゲルディトシアン
1993年／カラープリント
ポンピドゥー・センター、パリ国立近代美術館

Entrance

Photographed
by Georges Meguerditchian
Colour print for slideshow
Centre Pompidou - MNAM

152[p.100] 映
パンチングメタルとガラスの扉の
向こうに大階段が見える
撮影：ジョルジュ・メゲルディトシアン
1993年／カラープリント
ポンピドゥー・センター、パリ国立近代美術館

Door made of transparent glass and
perforated metal screen in front of
the main staircase
Photographed
by Georges Meguerditchian
Colour print for slideshow
Centre Pompidou - MNAM

153* 映
ガラス扉越しの大階段
撮影：ジョルジュ・メゲルディトシアン
1993年／カラープリント
ポンピドゥー・センター、パリ国立近代美術館

Door composed of transparent glass
in front of the main staircase
Photographed
by Georges Meguerditchian
Colour print for slideshow
Centre Pompidou - MNAM

154[p.101] 映
大階段をサロンへ上がる
撮影：ジョルジュ・メゲルディトシアン
1993年／カラープリント
ポンピドゥー・センター、パリ国立近代美術館

Main staircase
Photographed
by Georges Meguerditchian
Colour print for slideshow
Centre Pompidou - MNAM

155* 映
大階段を上がりきったサロン入口
撮影：ジョルジュ・メゲルディトシアン
1993年／カラープリント
ポンピドゥー・センター、パリ国立近代美術館

Top of the main staircase
Photographed
by Georges Meguerditchian
Colour print for slideshow
Centre Pompidou - MNAM

156[p.7, 97] 映
2階サロン、右に中庭側ファサードを
見る。換気ガラリは閉まった状態
撮影：ジョルジュ・メゲルディトシアン
1993年／カラープリント
ポンピドゥー・センター、パリ国立近代美術館

Lounge on the first floor,
facade on the right, flaps of
the opening ventilators are shut.
Photographed
by Georges Meguerditchian
Colour print for slideshow
Centre Pompidou - MNAM

157* 映
2階サロン、右に中庭側ファサードを
見る。換気ガラリは開いた状態
撮影：ジョルジュ・メゲルディトシアン
1993年／カラープリント
ポンピドゥー・センター、パリ国立近代美術館

Lounge on the first floor,
facade on the right, flaps of
the opening ventilators are shut.
Photographed
by Georges Meguerditchian
Colour print for slideshow
Centre Pompidou - MNAM

158* 映
2階サロン、中庭側ファサードを見る。
換気ガラリは閉まった状態
撮影：ジョルジュ・メゲルディトシアン
1993年／カラープリント
ポンピドゥー・センター、パリ国立近代美術館

Lounge on the first floor, flaps of
the opening ventilators are shut.
Photographed
by Georges Meguerditchian
Colour print for slideshow
Centre Pompidou - MNAM

159[p.97] 映
2階サロン
撮影：ジョルジュ・メゲルディトシアン
1993年／カラープリント
ポンピドゥー・センター、パリ国立近代美術館

Second floor lounge.
Photographed
by Georges Meguerditchian
Colour print for slideshow
Centre Pompidou - MNAM

160* 映
2階サロン
撮影：ジョルジュ・メゲルディトシアン
1993年／カラープリント
ポンピドゥー・センター、パリ国立近代美術館

View towards the dining room
from the lounge on the second floor.
Photographed
by Georges Meguerditchian
Colour print for slideshow
Centre Pompidou - MNAM

161* 映
2階サロン、右奥に食堂が見える
撮影：ジョルジュ・メゲルディトシアン
1993年／カラープリント
ポンピドゥー・センター、パリ国立近代美術館

Second floor lounge
Photographed
by Georges Meguerditchian
Colour print for slideshow
Centre Pompidou - MNAM

162* 映
2階サロン
撮影：ジョルジュ・メゲルディトシアン
1993年／カラープリント
ポンピドゥー・センター、パリ国立近代美術館

Second floor lounge
Photographed
by Georges Meguerditchian
Colour print for slideshow
Centre Pompidou - MNAM

163* 映
2階サロン、正面の書斎と
間仕切られた状態
撮影：ジョルジュ・メゲルディトシアン
1993年／カラープリント
ポンピドゥー・センター、パリ国立近代美術館

Second floor lounge with
the sliding doors to the doctor's
private study closed.
Photographed
by Georges Meguerditchian
Colour print for slideshow
Centre Pompidou - MNAM

164[p.100] 映
2階サロン、正面の書斎との
間の仕切りが開放された状態
撮影：ジョルジュ・メゲルディトシアン
1993年／カラープリント
ポンピドゥー・センター、パリ国立近代美術館

Second floor lounge with
the sliding doors to the doctor's
private study open.
Photographed
by Georges Meguerditchian
Colour print for slideshow
Centre Pompidou - MNAM

165 [p. 102]　映
2階書斎
撮影：ジョルジュ・メゲルディトシアン
1993年／カラープリント
ポンピドゥー・センター、パリ国立近代美術館

Private study on the second floor
Photographed
by Georges Meguerditchian
Colour print for slideshow
Centre Pompidou - MNAM

166 [p. 98]　映
2階食堂
撮影：ジョルジュ・メゲルディトシアン
1993年／カラープリント
ポンピドゥー・センター、パリ国立近代美術館

Dining Room on the Second floor
Photographed
by Georges Meguerditchian
Colour print for slideshow
Centre Pompidou - MNAM

167* 　映
2階食堂よりサロンを見る
撮影：ジョルジュ・メゲルディトシアン
1993年／カラープリント
ポンピドゥー・センター、パリ国立近代美術館

Perspective from the dining room
to the lounge
Photographed
by Georges Meguerditchian
Colour print for slideshow
Centre Pompidou - MNAM

168 [p. 98]　映
2階小サロン（夫人居間）、
上階の寝室と行き来するための
収納可能な鉄骨の階段が見える
撮影：ジョルジュ・メゲルディトシアン
1993年／カラープリント
ポンピドゥー・センター、パリ国立近代美術館

Small lounge on the second floor
Photographed
by Georges Meguerditchian
Colour print for slideshow
Centre Pompidou - MNAM

169* 　映
2階小サロン（夫人居間）、
上階の寝室と行き来するための
収納可能な鉄骨の階段が見える
撮影：ジョルジュ・メゲルディトシアン
1993年／カラープリント
ポンピドゥー・センター、パリ国立近代美術館

Small lounge on the second floor
Photographed
by Georges Meguerditchian
Colour print for slideshow
Centre Pompidou - MNAM

170* 　映
2階小サロン（夫人居間）の
庭に面した温室
撮影：ジョルジュ・メゲルディトシアン
1993年／カラープリント
ポンピドゥー・センター、パリ国立近代美術館

Green-house at the small lounge
on the second floor
Photographed
by Georges Meguerditchian
Colour print for slideshow
Centre Pompidou - MNAM

171 [p. 103]　映
3階主寝室
撮影：ジョルジュ・メゲルディトシアン
1993年／カラープリント
ポンピドゥー・センター、パリ国立近代美術館

Third floor master bedroom
Photographed
by Georges Meguerditchian
Colour print for slideshow
Centre Pompidou - MNAM

172 [p. 103]　映
3階主寝室浴室
撮影：ジョルジュ・メゲルディトシアン
1993年／カラープリント
ポンピドゥー・センター、パリ国立近代美術館

Third floor master bathroom
Photographed
by Georges Meguerditchian
Colour print for slideshow
Centre Pompidou - MNAM

173 [p. 103]　映
3階子供部屋、左手の金属製仕切りの
中には洗面スペースが隠されている
撮影：ジョルジュ・メゲルディトシアン
1993年／カラープリント
ポンピドゥー・センター、パリ国立近代美術館

Third floor bedroom
Photographed
by Georges Meguerditchian
Colour print for slideshow
Centre Pompidou - MNAM

174* 　映
3階子供部屋、左手の金属製仕切りは
開放され、洗面スペースが見える
撮影：ジョルジュ・メゲルディトシアン
1993年／カラープリント
ポンピドゥー・センター、パリ国立近代美術館

Third floor bedroom. Screened area
on the left side is open and shows
the washing space
Photographed
by Georges Meguerditchian
Colour print for slideshow
Centre Pompidou - MNAM

175* 　映
夜の庭側ファサード
撮影：ジョルジュ・メゲルディトシアン
1993年／カラープリント
ポンピドゥー・センター、パリ国立近代美術館

Facade facing the garden
during evening
Photographed
by Georges Meguerditchian
Colour print for slideshow
Centre Pompidou - MNAM

176 [p. 4]　映
夜の玄関側ファサード
撮影：ジョルジュ・メゲルディトシアン
1993年／カラープリント
ポンピドゥー・センター、パリ国立近代美術館

Facade facing the courtyard
during evening
Photographed
by Georges Meguerditchian
Colour print for slideshow
Centre Pompidou - MNAM

177 [p. 103]　映
庭側のファサード
撮影：ジョルジュ・メゲルディトシアン
1993年／カラープリント
ポンピドゥー・センター、パリ国立近代美術館

Facade facing the garden
Photographed
by Georges Meguerditchian
Colour print for slideshow
Centre Pompidou - MNAM

ref. 008 [p. 82]　写
ガラスブロック「ネヴァダ204A」
撮影：ジョルジュ・メゲルディトシアン
1993年／カラープリント
ポンピドゥー・センター、パリ国立近代美術館

Glass brick, Nevada 204A
Photographed
by Georges Meguerditchian
Colour print for slideshow
Centre Pompidou - MNAM

178* 平

アンリ・マルタン「あるガラスの家」、
『BIP』179–181頁、1934年12月
1934年／印刷物／30×24
ポンピドゥー・センター、パリ国立近代美術館、
カンディンスキー図書館

Une Maison de Verre, article by
B. Henri Martin in BIP December issue,
1934, pages 179–181.
publication
Centre Pompidou - MNAM -
Bibliothèque Kandinsky
BK Fds Salomon B1 (s.n°)

179* 平

ルネ・ド・ラロミギュイエール
「ガラスの壁」、『芸術と医学』、医師
フランソワ・ドバ編集、1933年5月
1933年／印刷物／31.2×24.2
ポンピドゥー・センター、パリ国立近代美術館、
カンディンスキー図書館

Murs de Verre, article by René de
Laromiguière in ART ET MÉDECINE
(Art and Medicine) / directed by
Doctor François Debat, May 1933
publication
Centre Pompidou - MNAM -
Bibliothèque Kandinsky
BK RP 652

180* 平

ピエール・シャロー「ガラスの家に
ついて」、芸術文学雑誌『ル・ポワン』、
1937年第2号（隔月発行）
1937年／印刷物
ポンピドゥー・センター、パリ国立近代美術館、
カンディンスキー図書館

LE POINT, Art and Literature Magazine,
second issue, 1937.
publication
Centre Pompidou - MNAM -
Bibliothèque Kandinsky
BK Fds Cahiers d'art P 5

181 [p.121] 平

ピエール・ヴァゴ「パリのある個人邸」、
ポール・ネルソン「サン・ギヨーム
通りの住宅」、ジュリアン・ルパージュ
「訪問観察記」が掲載された
『ラルシテクチュール・ドージュルデュイ

『今日の建築』』no. 9、1933年11–12月号、
アンドレ・ブロック編集、パリ
1933年／印刷物／32×25.2
ポンピドゥー・センター、パリ国立近代美術館、
カンディンスキー図書館

L'ARCHITECTURE D'AUJOURD'HUI
(Architec-ture Today), Chief editor:
André Bloc, November to December
issue, 1933, Paris. This issue carries
essays on Maison de Verre,
written by Pierre Vago, Paul Nelson
and Julien Lepage.
publication
Centre Pompidou - MNAM -
Bibliothèque Kandinsky
BK RP 666 and BK RP 1155

182 [p.83] 立

ガラスブロック「ネヴァダ204A」
サン＝ゴバン株式会社
1937年／ガラス／20×20×3.7
ポンピドゥー・センター、パリ国立近代美術館

Glass brick, Nevada 204A
SAINT-GOBAIN
glass brick
Centre Pompidou - MNAM
AM 2007-1-147
Don deM. Laurent Moos en 2007

モダンな室内を装飾する生活用具

183 [p.127] 立

ガラスの家のコート掛け
ピエール・シャロー
1931年頃／ジェラルミン、塗装した鉄
210×89.5×30、キャスター直径 53
ポンピドゥー・センター、パリ国立近代美術館

Hat stand from the Maison de Verre
Pierre Chareau
Duralumin and painted metal
Centre Pompidou - MNAM
AM 2008-1-110

184 [p.129] 図

デザートテーブル　透視図
ピエール・シャロー
1932年／水彩、墨・厚紙／14.5×18
ポンピドゥー・センター、パリ国立近代美術館

Dessert table
Pierre Chareau
Water color and indian ink on cartridge paper
Centre Pompidou - MNAM
AM 1997-2-231
Don de la Fondation Louis Moret en 1997

185 [p.129] 立

フルーツ皿（果物掛け）
ピエール・シャロー
1930年／金属、鏡／17.5×7.5×10
ポンピドゥー・センター、パリ国立近代美術館

Fruit display stand / Pierre Chareau
Metal and mirror
Centre Pompidou - MNAM
AM 2008-1-134
Don de Aline et Pierre Vellay en 2006

186 [p.129] 立

手紙用具入れ／ピエール・シャロー
1930年頃／塗装したステンレス
17×10×18
ポンピドゥー・センター、パリ国立近代美術館

Paper organizer / Pierre Chareau
Painted stainless steel
Centre Pompidou - MNAM
AM 2008-1-136
Don de Aline et Pierre Vellay en 2006

187 [p.116] 立

織物見本／エレーヌ・アンリ
（ピエール・シャローによる下図に基づく）
1925年頃／手織り、化学繊維と絹の混紡
15×15
ポンピドゥー・センター、パリ国立近代美術館

Sample of textile, based on Pierre
Chareau's pipe motif drawing
Hélène Henry, based on
the drawing by Pierre Chareau
handwoven artificial fibre and silk
Centre Pompidou - MNAM
DOCDE 2014 -2
Don anonyme, 1991

188 [p.116] 立

織物見本／エレーヌ・アンリ
1925年頃／手織り、化学繊維
15×15
ポンピドゥー・センター、パリ国立近代美術館

Sample of textile / Hélène Henry
handwoven artificial fibre
Centre Pompidou - MNAM
DOCDE 2014 -1
Don anonyme, 1991

189 [p.22] 平

シェルシュ＝ミディ通り「ラ・
ブティック」正面、『商店の
ショウウィンドー』より、1927年、
L. P. セズィーユによる序論と監修、
アルベール・レヴィ出版

Study of the facade for "La Boutique" at Rue de Cherche-Midi, Paris. Devantures de boutiques (Show Windows of Stores), directed and introduced by L. P. Sézille, 1927, published by Albert Lévy, Paris

190 [p.130] 平
パリ市内のショウウィンドーの計画、
『ブティックと商店』より、
1929年頃、ルネ＝エルブスト監修、
シャルル・モロー出版、パリ
印刷物／32.4×25

Study of the facade of a shop in Paris. Boutiques et magasins (L'art international d'aujourd'hui, 8), presented by René-Herbst, c. 1929, published by Charles Moreau, Paris
Publication
Centre Pompidou - MNAM -
Bibliothèque Kandinsky
BK Fds Jean Prouvé L 8

苦難の時代、
そして新天地を求めて

ref. 009 [p.117] 写
1935年のパリ万国博覧会
における写真展示板
ピエール・シャロー、
撮影：L. V. グレゴリウス
モノクロプリント／23.3×16.6
ポンピドゥー・センター、パリ国立近代美術館、
カンディンスキー図書館

Presentation system for photographs realized for Exposition Universelle, 1935, Paris.
Monochrome print
Centre Pompidou - MNAM -
Bibliothèque Kandinsky
BK Fds Pierre Chareau CHA 57

191 [p.128] 模
ヴィラ・ティンタ・マニス（舞踊家
ジェメル・アニク別荘）　模型　1:100
ピエール・シャロー
塗装した樹脂／28×24×7
ポンピドゥー・センター、パリ国立近代美術館

Model for the Villa Tjinta Manis, country house for Djemel Anick
Pierre Chareau
Painted acrylic
Centre Pompidou - MNAM
Doc (31)

192 [p.128] 写
ヴィラ・ティンタ・マニス
（舞踊家ジェメル・アニク別荘）
ピエール・シャロー
モノクロプリント
ポンピドゥー・センター、パリ国立近代美術館、
カンディンスキー図書館

Villa Tjinta Manis, country house for Djemel Anick
Pierre Chareau
Monochrome print
Centre Pompidou - MNAM -
Bibliothèque Kandinsky

193 [p.132] 模
ロバート・マザウエルの
住居兼アトリエ　模型　1:100
ピエール・シャロー
塗装した樹脂／10×20.5×7
ポンピドゥー・センター、パリ国立近代美術館

Model for home and studio of Robert Motherwell
Pierre Chareau
Painted acrylic
Centre Pompidou - MNAM
Doc (32)

194 [p.132] 写
ロバート・マザウエルの住居兼アトリエ
『ラルシテクチュール・ドージュルデュイ
［今日の建築］』no. 30、1950年7月号
より、アンドレ・ブロック編集、パリ
撮影：ロニー・ジャック
モノクロプリント
ポンピドゥー・センター、パリ国立近代美術館、
カンディンスキー図書館

Home and Studio of Robert Motherwell. Photograph from L'ARCHITECTURE D'AUJOURD'HUI (Architecture Today), Chief editor: André Bloc, No. 30, July 1950, Paris
photographed by Ronny Jacques
Monochrome print

195 [p.131] 写
ロバート・マザウエルの住居兼アトリエ
『ラルシテクチュール・ドージュルデュイ
［今日の建築］』no. 30号、1950年7月号
より、アンドレ・ブロック編集、パリ
撮影：ロニー・ジャック
モノクロプリント
ポンピドゥー・センター、パリ国立近代美術館、
カンディンスキー図書館

Home and Studio of Robert Motherwell. Photograph from L'ARCHITECTURE D'AUJOURD'HUI (Architecture Today), Chief editor: André Bloc, No. 30, July 1950, Paris
photographed by Ronny Jacques
Monochrome print

196 [p.133] 写
「ワンルーム」の家（シャロー自邸）
アクソメ図
ピエール・シャロー
モノクロプリント

"One-room" house, Pierre Chareau's home at East Hampton.
Pierre Chareau
Monochrome print

197 [p.134] 模
ラ・コリーヌ（ジェルメーヌ・モントゥー
とナンシー・ローリン邸）　模型　1:100
ピエール・シャロー
塗装した樹脂／18×18.1×7
ポンピドゥー・センター、パリ国立近代美術館

Model of La Colline, home and studio of Germaine Monteux and Nancy Laughlin.
Pierre Chareau
Painted acrylic
Centre Pompidou - MNAM
DOCAR 2012-033

198 [p.134] 写
ラ・コリーヌ（ジェルメーヌ・
モントゥーとナンシー・ローリン邸）
ピエール・シャロー
モノクロプリント

Rear facade, La Colline, Spring Valley.
Pierre Chareau
Monochrome print

Photo credits

© Cité de l'architecture et du patrimoine – Hervé Ternisien
Cat. no. 107

© Jacques Repiquet
Cat. nos. 105, 106

© B. BAUCHET Architecte
Cat. nos. 142–145

© Archives de Paris
Cat. nos. 132–141

© Centre Pompidou - MNAM-CCI, Dist. RMN-Grand Palais – Image Centre Pompidou, MNAM-CCI - distributed by AMF
Cat. no. 044

© Centre Pompidou - MNAM-CCI, Dist. RMN-Grand Palais - Philippe Migeat - distributed by AMF
Cat. nos. 001, 034, 037, 038, 049, 055

© Centre Pompidou - MNAM-CCI, Dist. RMN-Grand Palais - Bertrand Prévost - distributed by AMF
Cat. nos. 024, 025, 036, 050, 067, 068, 095–097, 183, 185, 186, ref. 005

© Centre Pompidou - MNAM-CCI, Dist. RMN-Grand Palais - Georges Meguerditchian - distributed by AMF
Cat. nos. 004–007, 016–018, 027, 039–042, 051, 052, 059, 060, 062, 063, 066, 072–076, 083–085, 182, ref. 007

© Centre Pompidou - MNAM-Bibliothèque Kandinsky - Georges Meguerditchian
Cat. nos. 146–177, ref. 008

© Centre Pompidou - MNAM-Bibliothèque Kandinsky - Georges Meguerditchian ; Philippe Migeat ; Valérie Leconte ; Bruno Descout
Cat. nos. 002, 003, 008–015, 019–023, 026, 028–033, 043, 045, 046, 048, 053, 054, 056–058, 061, 064–065, 069, 070, 077, 078, 080–082, 088–094, 099–104, 108–131, 178–181, 187–197, 198, ref. 001–004, ref. 006, ref. 009

© Centre Pompidou - MNAM-CCI, Dist. RMN-Grand Palais - Droits réservés - distributed by AMF
Cat. nos. 071, 086, 087, 184

写真提供：東京国立近代美術館
Cat. nos. 035, 047, 079, 098

Copyrights

© 2014-Succession Pablo Picasso-SPDA (JAPAN)
Cat. no. 037

© The Estate of Jacques Lipchitz, coutesy Marlborough Gallery, New York
Cat. nos. 038, 049

While every effort has been made to trace copyright holders,
the publisher would be pleased to hear from any whom it has not been possible to locate.

執筆者・翻訳者一覧

オリヴィエ・サンカルブル
Olivier Cinqualbre

建築家、建築史家。フランス設備省および文化省で研究員（専門分野：現代労働空間の建築、産業遺産）を務めた後、ポンピドゥー・センター、パリ国立近代美術館の学芸員に就任。建築コレクション部門の責任者として、数々の展覧会を手がけ、カタログや建築関連の出版物を監修する。主な展覧会に、「トニー・ガルニエ」（1990）、「ピエール・シャロー」（1993）、「エスプリ・ラショナリスト」（1994）、「自由なフォルム」（1996）、「レンゾ・ピアノ」（2000）、「アダルベルト・リベラ」（2001）、「ロベール・マレ＝ステヴァンス」（2005）、「リチャード・ロジャース」（2007）など。
「建築家ピエール・シャローとガラスの家」展（パナソニック汐留ミュージアム）を監修。
ジャン・プルーヴェの研究家としても知られる。DVD『世界の建築鑑賞』シリーズ（フィルム・ディシ／アルテ制作）の研究顧問。

ジャン＝フランソワ・アルキエリ
Jean-Francois Archieri

エンジニア、都市工学者。フランス国立工芸院（CNAM）で建築工業技術を専攻し、ジャン・プルーヴェから博士論文の指導を受ける。また、パリ国立高等美術学校（ENSBA）のトニー・ガルニエ工房で都市工学を学ぶ。ジョルジュ＝アンリ・パンギュソン建築事務所で活動した後、国立高等デザイン大学（ENSCI-Les Ateliers）で教育・研究者になる。
近代芸術家連合（UAM）に関する研究の一環として数々の図録制作や展覧会に参加。具体的には、「1929–1958年における近代芸術家連合」（パリ装飾芸術美術館）、「建設者ジャン・プルーヴェ、ロベール＝マレ・ステヴァンス、アイリーン・グレイ」（ポンピドゥー・センター）、「ルイ・バリエ」（ルーベ工芸美術館ラ・ピシーヌ）、「ジャック・ル・シュヴァリエ」（パリのスクワール・ド・ヴェルジェンヌ15番）など。
主な著作は、『1957–1970年におけるプルーヴェのCNAM講義録』、『ガラス制作の巨匠ルイ・バリエのアトリエ』、『モダンな光明としてのジャック・ル・シュヴァリエ 1896–1987』、『AVモノグラフ149（2011）：ジャン・プルーヴェ 1901–1984』所収論文、及び2012年ナンシー開催「ジャン・プルーヴェ展」図録がある。

エリーズ・クーリング
Elise Koering

建築史博士。2010年に受理された学位論文は「1920年代におけるアイリーン・グレイとシャルロット・ペリアン、及びル・コルビュジエのインテリア問題」。
2011–2012年、ポンピドゥー・センターにおいて、アイリーン・グレイの作品展及び図録のために研究・執筆を担当。とりわけ第二次世界大戦前の建築、家具、国際現代インテリア、及び装飾芸術の各分野におけるモデルニテ（近代性）の諸問題を中心テーマとする研究に専念し、現在はル・コルビュジエのインテリアにかかわる研究を手がけている（同研究はル・コルビュジエ財団の若手研究者奨学金の対象となる）。
主な歴史研究著作としては、ル・コルビュジエの「ヴィラ・ル・ラック」に関する論文、アイリーン・グレイの「ヴィラE1027」に関する論文（アイリーン・グレイと装飾芸術）、及び女性建築家たちの歴史と作品に関する論文（女性クリエイター辞典）がある。

千代章一郎
Shoichiro Sendai

建築論。広島大学大学院工学研究院社会環境空間部門准教授。1968年京都府生まれ。京都大学大学院工学研究科博士後期課程修了。博士（工学）。主著『ル・コルビュジエの宗教建築と「建築的景観」の生成』（単著、中央公論美術出版）、『技術と身体』（共著、ミネルヴァ書房）、『都市の風土学』（共著、ミネルヴァ書房）『感性のフィールド』（共編、東信堂）、Vocabulaire de la spatialité japonaise（共著、CNRS Éditions）ほか。

阿部順子
Junko Abe-Kudo

椙山女学園大学生活科学部生活環境デザイン学科准教授。1970年東京都生まれ。フランス国立建築学校パリ＝ラ・セーヌ校留学（1997–98年）、東京都立大学大学院工学研究科建築学専攻博士課程修了。博士（工学）。Vocabulaire de la spatialité japonaise（共著、CNRS Éditions）ほか、Robert Mallet-Stevens に関する論文およびフランスの団地更新に関する論文等多数。

Pierre Chareau —
architecte de la Maison de verre,
un modern au temps de l'Art déco

Centre national d'art et de culture
Georges Pompidou

Alain Seban
Président

Denis Berthomier
Directeur général

Bernard Blistène
Directeur du Musée national d'art moderne
– Centre création industrielle

Jacques Boissonnas
Président de la Société des Amis
du Musée national d'art moderne

Musée national d'art moderne
– Centre création industrielle

Brigitte Léal
Directrice-adjointe en charge des collections

Frédéric Migayrou
Directeur-adjoint en charge de l'architecture,
du design et de la création industrielle

Ariane Coulondre
Chef du service des collections

Véronique Sorano-Stedman
Chef du service de la restauration des œuvres

Didier Schulmann
Chef du service de la Bibliothèque Kandinsky

Direction de la production :

Stéphane Guerreiro
Directeur

Directeur de la communication
et des partenariats :

Benoît Parayre
Directeur

Alexandre Colliex
Délégué au développement international

Exposition

Commissariat :

Olivier Cinqualbre
Conservateur en chef du service architecture,
MNAM-CCI, Centre Pompidou

Rieko Omura
Conservateur au Panasonic Shiodome Museum

Assistés de Yûki Yoshikawa
Chargée d'études, service architecture,
MNAM-CCI, Centre Pompidou

Coordination :

Thomas Ballouhey
Chargé d'études, service design,
MNAM-CCI, Centre Pompidou

Régie des œuvres :

Emilie Choffel
Régisseuse, direction de la production,
MNAM-CCI, Centre Pompidou

Gestion d'affaires :

Takashi Sumi,
Akiko Terao,
Kyoko Adachi
The Tokyo Shimbun

Scenographie :

Manuel Tardits / mikan

Création de l'affiche :

Kanta Desroches
Kanta Desroches Creative Agency

Catalogue

Edition :

Olivier Cinqualbre
Rieko Omura
Yûki Yoshikawa

Auteurs :

Olivier Cinqualbre
Elise Koering
Jean-François Archieri

Superviseur de la traduction :

Shoichiro Sendai
Institute of Engineering,
Hiroshima University

Traduction :

Junko Abe-Kudo
Sugiyama Jogakuen University

Takahisa Ogawa

Anna Knight

Joe Garden

Zal Heiwa Sethna

Correction d'épreuves :

Nobuyasu Tamiya

Graphisme :

Sho Watanabe

Coordination et production :

Masaru Kawashima,
Nami Watanabe
Kajima Institute Publishing, Co.,Ltd.

Impression, Publication :

Kajima Institute Publishing, Co.,Ltd.

展覧会

監修:

オリヴィエ・サンカルブル
(ポンピドゥー・センター、
パリ国立近代美術館 主任学芸員)

監修補佐:

吉川由紀
(ポンピドゥー・センター、
パリ国立近代美術館 研究員)

コーディネーション:

トマ・バルエ
(ポンピドゥー・センター、パリ国立近代美術館)

作品管理:

エミリ・ショフェル
(ポンピドゥー・センター、パリ国立近代美術館)

学芸担当:

大村理恵子
(パナソニック 汐留ミュージアム 学芸員)

展覧会事務局:

鷲見卓、寺尾晶子、安達恭子(東京新聞)

輸送:

ヤマトロジスティクス

展示デザイン:

マニュエル・タルディッツ／みかんぐみ

展示制作・施工:

アカシオ

告知物デザイン:

カンタ・デロッシュ

図録

編集:

オリヴィエ・サンカルブル

大村理恵子

吉川由紀

執筆:

オリヴィエ・サンカルブル

エリーズ・クーリング

ジャン＝フランソワ・アルキエリ

監修・監訳:

千代章一郎(広島大学大学院准教授)

仏文和訳:

阿部順子(椙山女学園大学准教授)

小川隆久(オガワ・アソシエイツ)

仏文英訳:

アンナ・ナイト

ジョー・ガーデン

和文英訳:

ザール平和セスナ(ソリコンサルタンツ)

校閲:

田宮宣保

デザイン:

渡邉翔

制作:

川嶋勝、渡辺奈美(鹿島出版会)

建築家ピエール・シャローとガラスの家
2014年8月10日　第1刷発行

編 者
ポンピドゥー・センター、パリ国立近代美術館
パナソニック 汐留ミュージアム

発行者
坪内文生

発行所
鹿島出版会
〒104-0028　東京都中央区八重洲2-5-14
電話 03-6202-5200
振替 00160-2-180883

印 刷
三美印刷

製 本
牧製本

© Centre Pompidou, Panasonic Shiodome Museum
2014, Printed in Japan
ISBN 978-4-306-04612-2 C0070

落丁・乱丁本はお取り替えいたします。
本書の無断複製（コピー）は著作権法上での例外を除き禁じられています。
また、代行業者等に依頼してスキャンやデジタル化することは、
たとえ個人や家庭内の利用を目的とする場合でも著作権法違反です。

本書の内容に関するご意見・ご感想は下記までお寄せ下さい。
URL: http://www.kajima-publishing.co.jp/
e-mail: info@kajima-publishing.co.jp